MANUAL BOOKKEEPING

Institute of Certified Bookkeepers

Level II

ICB LEVEL II: **MANUAL BOOKKEEPING**

British Library Cataloguing-in-Publication Data

A catalogue record for this book is available from the British Library.

Published by:

Kaplan Publishing UK
Unit 2 The Business Centre
Molly Millars Lane
Wokingham
RG41 2QZ

ISBN 978-0-85732-778-9

© Kaplan Financial Limited, 2012

Printed and bound in Great Britain.

The text in this material and any others made available by any Kaplan Group company does not amount to advice on a particular matter and should not be taken as such. No reliance should be placed on the content as the basis for any investment or other decision or in connection with any advice given to third parties. Please consult your appropriate professional adviser as necessary. Kaplan Publishing Limited and all other Kaplan group companies expressly disclaim all liability to any person in respect of any losses or other claims, whether direct, indirect, incidental, consequential or otherwise arising in relation to the use of such materials.

All rights reserved. No part of this publication may be reproduced, stored in a retrieval system, or transmitted, in any form or by any means, electronic, mechanical, photocopying, recording or otherwise, without the prior written permission of Kaplan Publishing.

KAPLAN PUBLISHING

ICB LEVEL II: MANUAL BOOKKEEPING

CONTENTS

Introduction — v

Syllabus — vii

Study skills — xi

STUDY TEXT AND WORKBOOK

Chapter		Study text	Workbook Activities Answers
1	Double entry bookkeeping	1	345
2	Accounting for sales – summary	35	351
3	Accounting for purchases – summary	65	355
4	Ledger balances and control accounts	97	357
5	Accounting for VAT	145	362
6	Petty cash	187	367
7	Bank reconciliations	213	368
8	Accruals and prepayments	243	373
9	Depreciation	265	377
10	Preparation of final accounts for a sole trader	289	384
11	Suspense accounts and errors	329	389

Index — I.1

KAPLAN PUBLISHING

CONTENTS

INTRODUCTION

HOW TO USE THESE MATERIALS

These Kaplan Publishing learning materials have been carefully designed to make your learning experience as easy as possible and to give you the best chance of success in your ICB assessments.

They contain a number of features to help you in the study process.

The sections on the Syllabus and Study Skills should be read before you commence your studies.

They are designed to familiarise you with the nature and content of the assessment and to give you tips on how best to approach your studies.

STUDY TEXT

This study text has been specially prepared for the ICB qualification.

It is written in a practical and interactive style:

- key terms and concepts are clearly defined
- all topics are illustrated with practical examples with clearly worked solutions
- frequent activities throughout the chapters ensure that what you have learnt is regularly reinforced
- 'pitfalls' and 'examination tips' help you avoid commonly made mistakes and help you focus on what is required to perform well in your examination.
- practice workbook activities can be completed at the end of each chapter.

ICB LEVEL II: **MANUAL BOOKKEEPING**

WORKBOOK

The workbook comprises:

Practice activities at the end of each chapter with solutions at the end of the text, to reinforce the work covered in each chapter.

The questions are divided into their relevant chapters and students may either attempt these questions as they work through the textbook, or leave some or all of these until they have completed the textbook as a final revision of what they have studied.

ICONS

The study chapters include the following icons throughout.

They are designed to assist you in your studies by identifying key definitions and the points at which you can test yourself on the knowledge gained.

 Definition

These sections explain important areas of Knowledge which must be understood and reproduced in an assessment

 Example

The illustrative examples can be used to help develop an understanding of topics before attempting the activity exercises

 Activity

These are exercises which give the opportunity to assess your understanding of all the assessment areas.

ICB LEVEL II: **MANUAL BOOKKEEPING**

SYLLABUS

(1) Accounting for VAT

Understand the process of accounting for VAT and completing a VAT Return. Be able to:

- explain the need for a business to register for VAT
- identify the form and content of a VAT invoice
- define the terms
    - Input tax
    - Output tax
    - Standard rate
    - Zero Rate
    - Exempt Supplies
    - Tax Point
- account for VAT using a VAT control account
- explain the process of bad debt relief
- prepare a VAT Return

(2) The Cash Book and Petty Cash Book

Understand the purpose and need to record petty cash. Be able to:

- explain the purpose of the imprest system
- prepare and authorise petty cash vouchers
- code the expenditure
- record the transactions in the petty cash book
- balance off and restore the imprest
- post to ledger accounts

Understand the purpose and use of a three column cash book. Be able to:

- accurately record receipts and payments in a three-column cash book
- balance off cash and bank columns and bring down balances
- complete the double entry to main and subsidiary ledgers

ICB LEVEL II: MANUAL BOOKKEEPING

(3) Bank Reconciliation Statement

Understand the need to balance bank transactions and the bank reconciliation statement. Be able to:

- compare individual items on the bank statement with those in the cash book
- update the cash book
- prepare the bank reconciliation statement

(4) Control Accounts and Reconciliation of Sales and Purchase Ledger Accounts

Understand the purpose and use of control accounts. Be able to:

- prepare sales and purchase ledger control accounts
- total and balance off accounts in the subsidiary ledgers
- reconcile control accounts with the total from subsidiary ledger

(5) Correction of Errors and the Suspense Account

Understand the need to correct errors and use a suspense account until errors have been clearly identified. Be able to:

- open a suspense account
- correct errors through the journal
- prepare the suspense account

(6) Depreciation of Fixed Assets

Understand the need to depreciate fixed assets and calculate depreciation using appropriate rates and methods. Be able to:

- record Capital Expenditure in appropriate records
- calculate and record the charge for depreciation using both straight line and reducing balance method
- prepare a schedule of fixed assets showing clearly their net book value
- understand the effects of depreciation on the accounts

(7) Accruals and Prepayments

Understand the need for accruals and prepayments.

Apply the accruals or matching concept by:
- calculating accruals
- calculating pre-payments

- accounting for accruals and prepayments
- understand the effect of accruals and prepayments on final accounts

(8) Bad Debts

Understand the need to recognise and deal with writing off a bad debt. Be able to:

- recognise when a debt becomes classed as 'bad'
- prepare a journal entry to write off a bad debt
- post the transaction to both the bad debts accounts and the debtors account
- understand the effect of bad debts on final accounts

(9) Final Accounts of a Sole Trader

Prepare the Trading and Profit & Loss Accounts of a Sole Trader and be able to:

- explain the role and purpose of final accounts
- prepare a trading and profit and loss account from a trial balance to include adjustments for:
    - accruals and pre-payments
    - depreciation (straight line and reducing balance)
    - write off of a bad debt

Prepare a Balance Sheet in good (vertical) form showing clearly the main categories of assets and liabilities.

STUDY SKILLS

Preparing to study

Devise a study plan

Determine which times of the week you will study.

Split these times into sessions of at least one hour for study of new material. Any shorter periods could be used for revision or practice.

Put the times you plan to study onto a study plan for the weeks from now until the assessment and set yourself targets for each period of study – in your sessions make sure you cover the whole course, activities and the associated questions in the study text and revision kit.

If you are studying more than one unit at a time, try to vary your subjects as this can help to keep you interested and see subjects as part of wider knowledge.

When working through your course, compare your progress with your plan and, if necessary, re-plan your work (perhaps including extra sessions) or, if you are ahead, do some extra revision / practice questions.

Effective studying

Active reading

You are not expected to learn the text by rote, rather, you must understand what you are reading and be able to use it to pass the assessment and develop good practice.

A good technique is to use SQ3Rs – Survey, Question, Read, Recall, Review:

1 **Survey the chapter**

   Look at the headings and read the introduction, knowledge, skills and content, so as to get an overview of what the chapter deals with.

2 **Question**

   Whilst undertaking the survey ask yourself the questions you hope the chapter will answer for you.

3 Read

Read through the chapter thoroughly working through the activities and, at the end, making sure that you can meet the learning objectives shown within the summary.

4 Recall

At the end of each section and at the end of the chapter, try to recall the main ideas of the section / chapter without referring to the text. This is best done after short break of a couple of minutes after the reading stage.

5 Review

Check that your recall notes are correct.

You may also find it helpful to re-read the chapter to try and see the topic(s) it deals with as a whole.

Note taking

Taking notes is a useful way of learning, but do not simply copy out the text.

The notes must:

- be in your own words
- be concise
- cover the key points
- be well organised
- be modified as you study further chapters in this text or in related ones.

Trying to summarise a chapter without referring to the text can be a useful way of determining which areas you know and which you don't.

Three ways of taking notes

1 Summarise the key points of a chapter

2 Make linear notes

A list of headings, subdivided with sub-headings listing the key points.

If you use linear notes, you can use different colours to highlight key points and keep topic areas together.

Use plenty of space to make your notes easy to use.

3 Try a diagrammatic form

The most common of which is a mind map.

To make a mind map, put the main heading in the centre of the paper and put a circle around it.

Draw lines radiating from this to the main sub-headings which again have circles around them.

Continue the process from the sub-headings to sub-sub-headings.

Highlighting and underlining

You may find it useful to underline or highlight key points in your study text – but do be selective.

You may also wish to make notes in the margins.

Revision phase

Kaplan has produced material specifically designed for your final assessment preparation for this unit.

These include a bank of revision questions that both test your knowledge and allow you to practice questions similar to those you will face in the exam.

Further guidance on how to approach the final stage of your studies is given in these materials.

Double entry bookkeeping

ICB LEVEL II: MANUAL BOOKKEEPING

Introduction

A sound knowledge of double entry underpins many of the learning outcomes and skills required for Level II. A sound understanding of double entry bookkeeping is essential in order to pass this unit and candidates will be assessed on double entry bookkeeping in the examination and so this must be very familiar ground.

CONTENTS

1. Principles behind double entry bookkeeping
2. Double entry – cash transactions
3. Double entry – credit transactions
4. Balancing a ledger account
5. Ledger accounting and the trial balance

Principles behind double entry bookkeeping

1.1 Introduction

There are two main principles that underlie the process of double entry bookkeeping – these are the dual effect and the separate entity concept.

1.2 The dual effect

Definition

The principle of the dual effect is that each and **every** transaction that a business makes has **two** effects.

For example if a business buys goods for cash then the two effects are that cash has decreased and that the business now has some purchases. The principle of double entry bookkeeping is that each of these effects must be shown in the ledger accounts by a *debit entry* in one account and an equal *credit entry* in another account.

Each and every transaction that a business undertakes has *two equal and opposite effects.*

1.3 The separate entity concept

Definition

The separate entity concept is that the business is a completely separate accounting entity from the owner.

Therefore if the owner pays his personal money into a business bank account this becomes the capital of the business which is owed back to the owner. Similarly if the owner takes money out of the business in the form of drawings then the amount of capital owed to the owner is reduced.

The business itself is a completely separate entity in accounting terms from the owner of the business.

1.4 Rules for double entry bookkeeping

There are a number of rules that can help to determine which two accounts are to be debited and credited for a transaction:

- When money is paid out by a business this is a credit entry in the cash or bank account.
- When money is received by a business this is a debit entry in the cash or bank account.
- An asset or an increase in an asset is always recorded on the debit side of its account.
- A liability or an increase in a liability is always recorded on the credit side of its account.
- An expense is recorded as a debit entry in the expense account.
- Income is recorded as a credit entry in the income account.

The Golden Rule

Every debit has an equal and opposite credit.

Ledger account

A debit entry represents	A credit entry represents
An increase to an asset	An increase to a liability
A decrease to a liability	A decrease to an asset
An item of expense	An item of income

For increases we can remember this as DEAD CLIC

Ledger account

Debtors	Creditors
Expenses	Liabilities
Assets	Income
Drawings	Capital

2 Double entry – cash transactions

2.1 Introduction

For this revision of double entry bookkeeping we will start with accounting for cash transactions – remember that money paid out is a credit entry in the cash account and money received is a debit entry in the cash account.

Cash/Bank Account	
DEBIT	**CREDIT**
Money in	Money out

Example

Dan Baker decides to set up in business as a sole trader by paying £20,000 into a business bank account. The following transactions are then entered into:

(i) purchase of a van for deliveries by writing a cheque for £5,500;

(ii) purchase of goods for resale by a cheque for £2,000;

(iii) payment of shop rental in cash, £500;

(iv) sale of goods for cash of £2,500;

(v) Dan took £200 of cash for his own personal expenses.

Note that cash received or paid is normally deemed to pass through the bank account.

State the two effects of each of these transactions and record them in the relevant ledger accounts.

Solution

Money paid into the business bank account by Dan:
- increase in cash;
- capital now owed back to Dan.

   Double entry:
   - a debit to the bank account as money is coming in
   - a credit to the capital account

Bank account

	£		£
Capital	20,000		

Capital account

	£		£
		Bank	20,000

(i) Purchase of a van for deliveries by writing a cheque for £5,500;
- cash decreases
- the business has a fixed asset, the van

   Double entry:
   - a credit to the bank account as cash is being paid out
   - a debit to an asset account, the van account

Bank account

	£		£
Capital	20,000	Van	5,500

Van account

	£		£
Bank	5,500		

Double entry bookkeeping: Chapter 1

(ii) Purchase of goods for resale by a cheque for £2,000

- decrease in cash
- increase in purchases

Double entry:

- a credit to the bank account as money is paid out
- a debit to the purchases account, an expense account

Purchases of stock are always recorded in a purchases account and never in a stock account. The stock account is only dealt with at the end of each accounting period and this will be dealt with in a later chapter.

Bank account

	£		£
Capital	20,000	Van	5,500
		Purchases	2,000

Purchases account

	£		£
Bank	2,000		

(iii) Payment of shop rental in cash, £500

- decrease in cash
- expense incurred

Double entry:

- a credit to the bank account as money is paid out
- a debit to the rent account, an expense

Bank account

	£		£
Capital	20,000	Van	5,500
		Purchases	2,000
		Rent	500

Rent account

	£		£
Bank	500		

(iv) Sale of goods for cash of £2,500
- cash increases
- sales increase

Double entry:
- a debit to the bank account as money is coming in
- a credit to the sales account, income

Bank account

	£		£
Capital	20,000	Van	5,500
Sales	2,500	Purchases	2,000
		Rent	500

Sales account

	£		£
		Bank	2,500

(v) Dan took £200 of cash for his own personal expenses
- cash decreases
- drawings increase (money taken out of the business by the owner)

Double entry:
- a credit to the bank account as money is paid out
- a debit to the drawings account

Bank account

	£		£
Capital	20,000	Van	5,500
Sales	2,500	Purchases	2,000
		Rent	500
		Drawings	200

Drawings account

	£		£
Bank	200		

Double entry – credit transactions

3.1 Introduction

We will now introduce sales on credit and purchases on credit and the receipt of money from debtors and payment of money to creditors. For the sales and purchases on credit there is no cash increase or decrease therefore the cash account rule cannot be used. Remember though that increase in income (sales) is always a credit entry and an increase in an expense (purchases) is a debit entry.

Example

Dan now makes some further transactions:

(i) purchases are made on credit for £3,000
(ii) sales are made on credit for £4,000
(iii) Dan pays £2,000 to the credit suppliers
(iv) £2,500 is received from the credit customers
(v) Dan returned goods costing £150 to a supplier
(vi) goods were returned by a customer which had cost £200.

State the two effects of each of these transactions and write them up in the appropriate ledger accounts.

Solution

(i) Purchases are made on credit for £3,000

- increase in purchases
- increase in creditors

Double entry:

- a debit entry to the purchases account, an expense
- a credit to the creditors account

Purchases account

	£		£
Bank	2,000		
Creditors	3,000		

Creditors account

	£		£
		Purchases	3,000

(ii) Sales are made on credit for £4,000
- increase in sales
- increase in debtors

Double entry:
- a credit entry to the sales account, income
- a debit entry to the debtors account

Sales account

	£		£
		Bank	2,500
		Debtors	4,000

Debtors account

	£		£
Sales	4,000		

(iii) Dan pays £2,000 to the suppliers
- decrease in cash
- decrease in creditors

Double entry:
- a credit entry to the bank account as money is paid out
- a debit entry to creditors as they are reduced

Bank account

	£		£
Capital	20,000	Van	5,500
Sales	2,500	Purchases	2,000
		Rent	500
		Drawings	200
		Creditors	2,000

Creditors account

	£		£
Bank	2,000	Purchases	3,000

(iv) £2,500 is received from the credit customers

- increase in cash
- decrease in debtors

Double entry

- a debit entry in the bank account as money is received
- a credit entry to debtors as they are reduced

Bank account

	£		£
Capital	20,000	Van	5,500
Sales	2,500	Purchases	2,000
Debtors	2,500	Rent	500
		Drawings	200
		Creditors	2,000

Debtors account

	£		£
Sales	4,000	Bank	2,500

(v) Dan returned goods costing £150 to a supplier

- purchases returns increase
- creditors decrease

Double entry

- a debit entry to the creditors account as creditors are now decreasing
- a credit entry to the purchases returns account (the easiest way to remember this entry is that it is the opposite of purchases which are a debit entry)

Creditors account

	£		£
Bank	2,000	Purchases	3,000
Purchases returns	150		

Purchases returns account

	£		£
		Creditors	150

(vi) Goods were returned by a customer which had cost £200
- sales returns increase
- debtors decrease

Double entry:
- a credit entry to the debtors account as debtors are now decreasing
- a debit entry to sales returns (the opposite to sales which is a credit entry)

Debtors account

	£		£
Sales	4,000	Bank	2,500
		Sales returns	200

Sales returns account

	£		£
Debtors	200		

4 Balancing a ledger account

4.1 Introduction

Once all of the transactions for a period have been recorded in the ledger accounts then it is likely that the owner will want to know the answer to questions such as how much cash there is in the bank account or how much has been spent on purchases. This can be found by balancing the ledger accounts.

4.2 Procedure for balancing a ledger account

The following steps should be followed when balancing a ledger account:

Step 1

Total both the debit and credit columns to find the larger total – enter this figure as the total for both the debit and credit columns.

Step 2

For the side that does not add up to this total put in the figure that makes it add up and call it the balance carried down.

Double entry bookkeeping: Chapter 1

Step 3

Enter the balance brought down on the opposite side below the totals.

Example

We will now balance Dan's bank account.

Bank account

	£		£
Capital	20,000	Van	5,500
Sales	2,500	Purchases	2,000
Debtors	2,500	Rent	500
		Drawings	200
		Creditors	2,000

Bank account

	£		£
Capital	20,000	Van	5,500
Sales	2,500	Purchases	2,000
Debtors	2,500	Rent	500
		Drawings	200
		Creditors	2,000
		Balance c/d *Step 2*	14,800
Step 1	25,000	**Step 1**	25,000
Balance b/d *Step 3*	14,800		

ICB LEVEL II: MANUAL BOOKKEEPING

Activity 1

(a) Show by means of ledger accounts how the following transactions would be recorded in the books of Bertie Dooks, a seller of second-hand books:

- (i) paid in cash £5,000 as capital;
- (ii) took the lease of a stall and paid six months' rent – the yearly rental was £300;
- (iii) spent £140 cash on the purchase of books from W Smith;
- (iv) purchased on credit from J Fox books at a cost of £275;
- (v) paid an odd-job man £25 to paint the exterior of the stall and repair a broken lock;
- (vi) put an advertisement in the local paper at a cost of £2;
- (vii) sold three volumes containing The Complete Works of William Shakespeare to an American for £35 cash;
- (viii) sold a similar set on credit to a local schoolmaster for £3;
- (ix) paid J Fox £175 on account for the amount due to him;
- (x) received £1 from the schoolmaster;
- (xi) purchased cleaning materials at a cost of £2 and paid £3 to a cleaner;
- (xii) took £5 from the business to pay for his own groceries.

(b) Balance off the ledgers, clearly showing balance carried down (c/d) and balance brought down (b/d).

5 Ledger accounting and the trial balance

5.1 Introduction

Definition

A trial balance is the list of the balances on all of the ledger accounts in an organisation's main or general ledger.

KAPLAN PUBLISHING 13

5.2 Trial balance

The trial balance will appear as a list of debit balances and credit balances depending upon the type of account. If the double entry has been correctly carried out then the debit balance total should be equal to the credit balance total.

A trial balance lists all of the ledger account balances in the general ledger.

5.3 Preparing the trial balance

When all of the entries have been made in the ledger accounts for a period, the trial balance will then be prepared.

Step 1

Balance off each ledger account and bring down the closing balance.

Step 2

List each balance brought down as either a debit balance or a credit balance.

Step 3

Total the debit balances and the credit balances to see if they are equal.

Example

Given below are the initial transactions for Mr Smith, a sole trader. Enter the transactions in the ledger accounts using a separate account for each debtor and creditor. Produce the trial balance for this sole trader at the end of 12 January 20X1.

On 1 Jan 20X1	Mr Smith put £12,500 into the business bank account.
On 2 Jan 20X1	He bought goods for resale costing £750 on credit from J Oliver. He also bought on the same basis £1,000 worth from K Hardy.
On 3 Jan 20X1	Sold goods for £800 to E Morecombe on credit.
On 5 Jan 20X1	Mr Smith returned £250 worth of goods bought from J Oliver, being substandard goods.
On 6 Jan 20X1	Sold goods on credit to A Wise for £1,000.
On 7 Jan 20X1	Mr Smith withdrew £100 from the bank for his personal use.
On 8 Jan 20X1	Bought a further £1,500 worth of goods from K Hardy, again on credit.

ICB LEVEL II: MANUAL BOOKKEEPING

On 9 Jan 20X1   A Wise returned £200 worth of goods sold to him on the 6th

On 10 Jan 20X1   The business paid J Oliver £500 by cheque, and K Hardy £1,000 also by cheque.

On 12 Jan 20X1   Mr Smith banked a cheque for £800 received from E Morecombe.

Solution

Step 1

Enter the transactions into the ledger accounts and then balance off each ledger account. Use a separate ledger account for each debtor and creditor. (Note that in most examinations you will be required to complete the double entry for debtors and creditors in the sales ledger control account and purchase ledger control account as seen in Level I, but for practice we are using the separate accounts.)

Step 2

Balance off each of the ledger accounts as at 12th January.

Capital account

	£		£
		1 Jan Bank	12,500

Sales account

	£		£
		3 Jan E Morecombe	800
12 Jan Balance c/d	1,800	6 Jan A Wise	1,000
	1,800		1,800
		13 Jan Balance b/d	1,800

Purchases account

		£		£
2 Jan	J Oliver	750		
2 Jan	K Hardy	1,000		
8 Jan	K Hardy	1,500	12 Jan Balance c/d	3,250
		3,250		3,250
13 Jan Balance b/d		3,250		

Double entry bookkeeping: Chapter 1

Purchases returns account

	£		£
		5 Jan J Oliver	250

Sales returns account

	£		£
9 Jan A Wise	200		

Drawings account

	£		£
7 Jan Bank	100		

Bank account

	£		£
1 Jan Capital	12,500	7 Jan Drawings	100
12 Jan E Morecombe	800	10 Jan J Oliver	500
		K Hardy	1,000
		12 Jan Balance c/d	11,700
	13,300		13,300
13 Jan Balance b/d	11,700		

Debtor – E Morecombe account

	£		£
3 Jan Sales	800	12 Jan Bank	800

Debtor – A Wise account

	£		£
6 Jan Sales	1,000	9 Jan Sales returns	200
		12 Jan Balance c/d	800
	1,000		1,000
13 Jan Balance b/d	800		

Creditor – J Oliver account

	£		£
5 Jan Purchases returns	250	2 Jan Purchases	750
10 Jan Bank	500		
	750		750

Creditor – K Hardy account

	£		£
10 Jan Bank	1,000	2 Jan Purchases	1,000
12 Jan Balance c/d	1,500	8 Jan Purchases	1,500
	2,500		2,500
		13 Jan Balance b/d	1,500

Note that accounts with only one entry do not need to be balanced as this entry is the final balance on the account.

Step 3

Produce the trial balance by listing each balance brought down as either a debit balance or a credit balance.

Make sure that you use the balance brought down below the total line as the balance to list in the trial balance.

Step 4

Total the debit and credit columns to check that they are equal.

Double entry bookkeeping: **Chapter 1**

Trial balance as at 12 January 20X1 for Mr Smith

	Debits £	Credits £
Capital		12,500
Sales		1,800
Purchases	3,250	
Purchases returns		250
Sales returns	200	
Drawings	100	
Bank	11,700	
Debtor – A Wise	800	
Creditor – K Hardy		1,500
	16,050	16,050

5.4 Purpose of the trial balance

One of the main purposes of a trial balance is to serve as a check on the double entry. If the trial balance does not balance, i.e. the debit and credit totals are not equal then some errors have been made in the double entry.

The trial balance can also serve as the basis for preparing an extended trial balance (this is not part of the Level II syllabus) and finally the financial statements of the organisation.

 Activity 2

Enter the following details of transactions for the month of May 20X6 into the appropriate books of account. You should also extract a trial balance as at 1 June 20X6. Open a separate ledger account for each debtor and creditor, and also keep separate 'cash' and 'bank' ledger accounts. Balance off each account and prepare a trial balance.

20X6

1 May   Started in business by paying £6,800 into the bank.

3 May   Bought goods on credit from the following: J Johnson £400; D Nixon £300 and J Agnew £250.

5 May   Cash sales £300.

6 May   Paid rates by cheque £100.

KAPLAN PUBLISHING

8 May	Paid wages £50 in cash.
9 May	Sold goods on credit: K Homes £300; J Homes £300; B Hood £100.
10 May	Bought goods on credit: J Johnson £800; D Nixon £700.
11 May	Returned goods to J Johnson £150.
15 May	Bought office fixtures £600 by cheque.
18 May	Bought a motor vehicle £3,500 by cheque.
22 May	Goods returned by J Homes £100.
25 May	Paid J Johnson £1,000; D Nixon £500, both by cheque.
26 May	Paid wages £150 by cheque

5.5 Debit or credit balance?

When you are balancing a ledger account it is easy to see which side, debit or credit, the balance brought down is on. However if you were given a list of balances rather than the account itself then it is sometimes difficult to decide which side the balance should be shown in the trial balance, the debit or the credit?

There are some rules to help here:

- assets are debit balances;
- expenses are debit balances;
- liabilities are credit balances;
- income is a credit balance.

5.6 Debit or credit balance?

Another common problem area is determining whether settlement discounts allowed and received are debits or credits.

The double entry for a discount allowed to a customer is:

- debit to the discounts allowed account (an expense account);
- credit to the debtors account (reducing the amount owed by the customer).

Therefore the balance on the discounts allowed account is a debit balance. This is an expense of the business as it is the cost to the business of getting the money due into their bank account earlier.

Double entry bookkeeping: Chapter 1

The double entry for a discount received from a supplier is:

- debit to the creditors account (reducing the amount owed to the supplier);
- credit to the discounts received account (a form of sundry income).

Therefore the balance on the discounts received account is a credit balance. This is income as it means that the business has paid less for the goods than originally envisaged although the payment was made earlier.

Activity 3

The following balances have been extracted from the books of Fitzroy at 31 December 20X2:

Prepare a trial balance at 31 December 20X2.

	£	Debit	Credit
Capital on 1 January 20X2	106,149		
Freehold factory at cost	360,000		
Motor vehicles at cost	126,000		
Stocks at 1 January 20X2	37,500		
Debtors	15,600		
Cash in hand	225		
Bank overdraft	82,386		
Creditors	78,900		
Sales	318,000		
Purchases	165,000		
Rent and rates	35,400		
Discounts allowed	6,600		
Insurance	2,850		
Sales returns	10,500		
Purchase returns	6,300		
Loan from bank	240,000		
Sundry expenses	45,960		
Drawings	26,100		
TOTALS			

Activity 4

(1) The rental income account for January is as follows:

Rent Account

	£		£
Balance b/d	1,900	Bank account	7,000
Invoice	2,500		
Invoice	500		

At the end of the month there is a **debit/credit** balance of **£7,000/4,900/2,100**.

Circle the correct answer.

(2) True or false, to increase a liability a debit entry is made.

   True

   False

Select the correct answer for question 2.

Circle the correct answer for questions 3, 4, 5, 6 and 7.

(3) When a sole trader uses goods for resale for his own personal use the drawings account is **Debited / Credited** and the purchases account is **Debited / Credited**

(4) When a supplier is paid the bank account is **Debited / Credited** and the supplier account is **Debited / Credited**

(5) When goods are sold to a debtor, the sales account is **Debited / Credited** and the debtor account is **Debited / Credited**

(6) A bank overdraft is a **Debit / Credit** balance.

(7) Discounts received are a **Debit / Credit** balance.

6 Summary

The basic principles of double entry are of great importance for this unit and in particular all students should be able to determine whether a particular balance on an account is a debit or a credit balance in the trial balance.

Answers to chapter activities

Activity 1

Ledger accounts

Cash account

	£		£
Capital account (i)	5,000	Rent (six months) (ii)	150
Sales (vii)	35	Purchases (iii)	140
Debtors (x)	1	Repairs (v)	25
		Advertising (vi)	2
		Creditors (ix)	175
		Cleaning (xi)	5
		Drawings (xii)	5
		Balance c/d	4,534
	5,036		5,036
Balance b/d	4,534		

J Fox – Creditor account

	£		£
Cash (ix)	175	Purchases (iv)	275
Balance c/d	100		
	275		275
		Balance b/d	100

Schoolmaster – Debtor account

	£		£
Sales (viii)	3	Cash (x)	1
		Balance c/d	2
	3		3
Balance b/d	2		

Capital account

	£		£
Balance c/d	5,000	Cash (i)	5,000
	5,000		5,000
		Balance b/d	5,000

Sales account

	£		£
		Cash (vii)	35
Balance c/d	38	Schoolmaster (viii)	3
	38		38
		Balance b/d	38

Purchases account

	£		£
Cash (iii)	140	Balance c/d	415
J Fox (iv)	275		
	415		415
Balance b/d	415		

Rent account

	£		£
Cash (ii)	150	Balance c/d	150
	150		150
Balance b/d	150		

Repairs account

	£		£
Cash (v)	25	Balance c/d	25
	25		25
Balance b/d	25		

Advertising account

	£		£
Cash (vi)	2	Balance c/d	2
	2		2
Balance b/d	2		

Cleaning account

	£		£
Cash (xi)	5	Balance c/d	5
	5		5
Balance b/d	5		

Drawings account

	£		£
Cash (xii)	5	Balance c/d	5
	5		5
Balance b/d	5		

Activity 2

Cash account

		£			£
5 May	Sales	300	8 May	Wages	50
			31 May	Balance c/d	250
		300			300
1 June	Balance b/d	250			

Bank account

	£			£
1 May Capital	6,800	6 May	Rates	100
		15 May	Office fixtures	600
		18 May	Motor vehicle	3,500
		25 May	J Johnson	1,000
			D Nixon	500
		26 May	Wages	150
		31 May	Balance c/d	950
	6,800			6,800
1 June Balance b/d	950			

Creditor – J Johnson account

	£			£
11 May Purchase returns	150	3 May	Purchases	400
25 May Bank	1,000	10 May	Purchases	800
31 May Balance c/d	50			
	1,200			1,200
		1 June	Balance b/d	50

Creditor – D Nixon account

	£			£
25 May Bank	500	3 May	Purchases	300
31 May Balance c/d	500	10 May	Purchases	700
	1,000			1,000
		1 June	Balance b/d	500

Creditor – J Agnew account

		£			£
31 May	Balance c/d	250	3 May	Purchases	250
			1 June	Balance b/d	250

Debtor – K Homes account

		£			£
9 May	Sales	300	31 May	Balance c/d	300
		300			300
1 June	Balance b/d	300			

Debtor – J Homes account

		£			£
9 May	Sales	300	22 May	Sales returns	100
			31 May	Balance c/d	200
		300			300
1 June	Balance b/d	200			

Debtor – B Hood account

		£			£
9 May	Sales	100	31 May	Balance c/d	100
1 June	Balance b/d	100			

Capital account

		£			£
31 May	Balance c/d	6,800	1 May	Bank	6,800
			1 June	Balance b/d	6,800

Purchases account

		£			£
3 May	J Johnson	400			
	D Nixon	300			
	J Agnew	250			
10 May	J Johnson	800			
	D Nixon	700	31 May	Balance c/d	2,450
		2,450			2,450
1 June	Balance b/d	2,450			

Sales account

		£			£
			5 May	Cash	300
			9 May	K Homes	300
				J Homes	300
31 May	Balance c/d	1,000		B Hood	100
		1,000			1,000
			1 June	Balance b/d	1,000

Rates account

		£			£
6 May	Bank	100	31 May	Balance c/d	100
1 June	Balance b/d	100			

Wages account

		£			£
8 May	Cash	50			
26 May	Bank	150	31 May	Balance c/d	200
		200			200
1 June	Balance b/d	200			

Purchase returns account

		£			£
31 May	Balance c/d	150	11 May	J Johnson	150
			1 June	Balance b/d	150

Office fixtures account

	£		£
15 May Bank	600	31 May Balance c/d	600
1 June Balance b/d	600		

Motor vehicle account

	£		£
18 May Bank	3,500	31 May Balance c/d	3,500
1 June Balance b/d	3,500		

Sales returns account

	£		£
22 May J Homes	100	31 May Balance c/d	100
1 June Balance b/d	100		

Trial balance as at 30 May 20X6

	Dr £	Cr £
Cash	250	
Bank	950	
J Johnson		50
D Nixon		500
J Agnew		250
K Homes	300	
J Homes	200	
B Hood	100	
Capital		6,800
Purchases	2,450	
Sales		1,000
Rates	100	
Wages	200	
Purchase returns		150
Office fixtures	600	
Motor vehicles	3,500	
Sales returns	100	
	8,750	8,750

Activity 3

Trial balance at 31 December 20X2 of Fitzroy

	Dr £	Cr £
Capital on 1 January 20X2		106,149
Freehold factory at cost	360,000	
Motor vehicles at cost	126,000	
Stocks at 1 January 20X2	37,500	
Debtors	15,600	
Cash in hand	225	
Bank overdraft		82,386
Creditors		78,900
Sales		318,000
Purchases	165,000	
Rent and rates	35,400	
Discounts allowed	6,600	
Insurance	2,850	
Sales returns	10,500	
Purchase returns		6,300
Loan from bank		240,000
Sundry expenses	45,960	
Drawings	26,100	
	831,735	831,735

Activity 4

(1) The rental income account for January is as follows:

Rent Account

	£		£
Balance b/d	1,900	Bank account	7,000
Invoice	2,500		
Invoice	500		
Balance c/d	**2,100**		
	7,000		7,000
		Balance b/d	2,100

The correct answer is **CREDIT** of **£2,100**

(2) False.

(3) When a sole trader uses goods for resale for his own personal use the drawings account is **Debited** and the purchases account is **Credited**

(4) When a supplier is paid the bank account is **Credited** and the supplier account is **Debited**

(5) When goods are sold to a debtor, the sales account is **Credited** and the debtor account is **Debited**

(6) A bank overdraft is a **Credit** balance.

(7) Discounts received are a **Credit** balance.

Double entry bookkeeping: Chapter 1

7 Test your knowledge

Workbook Activity 5

Musgrave starts in business with capital of £20,000, in the form of cash £15,000 and fixed assets of £5,000.

- In the first three days of trading he has the following transactions:
- Purchases stock £4,000 on credit terms, supplier allows one month's credit.
- Sells some stock costing £1,500 for £2,000 and allows the customer a fortnight's credit.
- Purchases a motor vehicle for £6,000 and pays by cheque.

The accounting equation at the start would be:

Assets less Liabilities = Capital
£20,000 – £0 = £20,000

Required:

Restate in values the accounting equation after all the transactions had taken place.

Workbook Activity 6

Heather Simpson notices an amount of £36,000 on the trial balance of her business in an account called 'Capital'. She does not understand what this account represents.

Briefly explain what a capital account represents.

ICB LEVEL II: MANUAL BOOKKEEPING

Workbook Activity 7

Tony

Tony started a business selling tapes and CDs. In the first year of trading he entered into the following transactions:

(a) Paid £20,000 into a business bank account.
(b) Made purchases from Debbs for £1,000 cash.
(c) Purchased goods costing £3,000 from Gary for cash.
(d) Paid £200 for insurance.
(e) Bought storage units for £700 cash from Debbs.
(f) Paid £150 cash for advertising.
(g) Sold goods to Dorothy for £1,500 cash.
(h) Paid the telephone bill of £120 in cash.
(i) Sold further goods to Dorothy for £4,000 cash.
(j) Bought stationery for £80 cash.
(k) Withdrew £500 cash for himself.

Required:

Show how these transactions would be written up in Tony's ledger accounts, followed by balancing the accounts.

Workbook Activity 8

Dave

Dave had the following transactions during January 20X3:

1 Introduced £500 cash as capital.
2 Purchased goods on credit from A Ltd worth £200.
3 Paid rent for one month, £20.
4 Paid electricity for one month, £50.
5 Purchased a car for cash, £100.
6 Sold half of the goods on credit to X Ltd for £175.
7 Drew £30 for his own expenses.
8 Sold the remainder of the goods for cash, £210.

Required:

Write up the relevant ledger accounts necessary to record the above transactions.

Workbook Activity 9

Audrey Line

Audrey Line started in business on 1 March, opening a toy shop and paying £6,000 into a business bank account. She made the following transactions during her first six months of trading:

	£
Payment of six months' rent	500
Purchase of shop fittings	600
Purchase of toys on credit	2,000
Payments to toy supplier	1,200
Wages of shop assistant	600
Electricity	250
Telephone	110
Cash sales	3,700
Drawings	1,600

All payments were made by cheque and all stocks had been sold by the end of August.

Required:

Record these transactions in the relevant accounts.

ICB LEVEL II: MANUAL BOOKKEEPING

Accounting for sales – summary

Introduction

We have previously studied the double entry bookkeeping for sales and receipts in detail within Level I Certificate in Basic Bookkeeping. It is essential that you have completed and achieved Level I before you commence your studies for Level II.

When studying Level I we concentrated on the basic entries so that the double entry would be clear. It is now time to build on these basic entries and study these transactions again using more realistic material.

CONTENTS

1. The sales day book
2. The analysed sales day book
3. The sales returns day book
4. Posting to the sales ledger
5. The cash book
6. Document retention policies

Accounting for sales – summary: **Chapter 2**

1 The sales day book

The sales day book is a book of prime entry where credit sales are recorded. This example provides us with a recap of the material from our Level I studies.

Example

Given below are three invoices that have been sent out by your organisation today. You are required to record them in the sales day book

INVOICE

Invoice to:
T J Builder
142/148 Broadway
Oldham
OD7 6LZ

A.J. Broom & Company Limited
59 Parkway
Manchester
M2 6EG
Tel: 0161 560 3392
Fax: 0161 560 5322

Deliver to:
As above

Invoice no:	69489
Tax point:	23 August 20X3
Sales tax reg no:	625 9911 58
Delivery note no:	68612
Account no:	SL21

Code	Description	Quantity	VAT rate %	Unit price £	Amount excl of VAT £
874 KL7	Brown Brick Roof Tiles	40	20	43.95	1,758.00
					1,758.00
Trade discount 5%					87.90
					1,670.10
VAT					323.99
Total amount payable					1,994.09
Deduct discount of 3% if paid within 14 days					

INVOICE

A.J. Broom & Company Limited

Invoice to:
McCarthy & Sons
Shepherds Moat
Manchester M6 9LF

Deliver to:
As above

59 Parkway
Manchester
M2 6EG
Tel: 0161 560 3392
Fax: 0161 560 5322

Invoice no:	69490
Tax point:	28 August 20X3
Sales tax reg no:	625 9911 58
Delivery note no:	68610
Account no:	SL08

Code	Description	Quantity	VAT rate %	Unit price £	Amount excl of VAT £
617 BB8	Red Wall Bricks	400	20	2.10	840.00
294 KT6	Insulation Brick	3	20	149.90	449.70
					1,289.70
Trade discount 4%					51.58
					1,238.12
VAT					247.62
Total amount payable					1,485.74

Accounting for sales – summary: Chapter 2

INVOICE

A.J. Broom & Company Limited
59 Parkway
Manchester
M2 6EG
Tel: 0161 560 3392
Fax: 0161 560 5322

Invoice to:
Trevor Partner
Anderson House
Bank Street
Manchester M1 9FP

Deliver to:
As above

Invoice no:	69491
Tax point:	28 August 20X3
Sales tax reg no:	625 9911 58
Delivery note no:	68613
Account no:	SL10

Code	Description	Quantity	VAT rate %	Unit price £	Amount excl of VAT £
611 TB4	Bathroom Tiles	160	20	5.65	904.00
					904.00
Trade discount 2%					18.08
					885.92
VAT					173.64
Total amount payable					1,059.56
Deduct discount of 2% if paid within 21 days					

Solution

SALES DAY BOOK

Date	Invoice No	Customer name	Code	Total £	VAT £	Net £
28/08/X3	69489	T J Builder	SL21	1,994.09	323.99	1,670.10
28/08/X3	69490	McCarthy & Sons	SL08	1,485.74	247.62	1,238.12
28/08/X3	69491	Trevor Partner	SL10	1,059.56	173.64	885.92

2 The analysed sales day book

2.1 Introduction

Many organisations analyse their sales into different groups. This may be analysis by different products or by the geographical area in which the sale is made. If the sales are eventually to be analysed in this manner in the accounting records then they must be analysed in the original book of prime entry, the sales day book.

Example

You work for an organisation that makes sales to five different geographical regions. You are in charge of writing up the sales day book and you have listed out the details of the invoices sent out yesterday, 15 August 20X1. They are given below and must be entered into the sales day book and the totals of each column calculated. The VAT rate in use is 20%.

The invoice details are as follows:

	£
Invoice number 167 – France	
Worldwide News – (Code W5)	
Net total	2,500.00
VAT	500.00
Gross	3,000.00
Invoice number 168 – Spain	
Local News – (Code L1)	
Net total	200.00
VAT	40.00
Gross	240.00
Invoice number 169 – Germany	
The Press Today – (Code P2)	
Net total	300.00
VAT	60.00
Gross	360.00

Accounting for sales – summary: Chapter 2

Invoice number 170 – Spain	
Home Call – (Code H1)	
Net total	200.00
VAT	40.00
Gross	240.00
Invoice number 171 – France	
Tomorrow – (Code T1)	
Net total	100.00
VAT	20.00
Gross	120.00
Invoice number 172 – Russia	
Worldwide News – (Code W5)	
Net total	3,000.00
VAT	600.00
Gross	3,600.00

Solution

SALES DAY BOOK

Date	Invoice no	Customer name	Code	Total	VAT	Russia	Poland	Spain	Germany	France
				£	£	£	£	£	£	£
15/08/X1	167	Worldwide News	W5	3,000.00	500.00					2,500.00
	168	Local News	L1	240.00	40.00			200.00		
	169	The Press Today	P2	360.00	60.00				300.00	
	170	Home Call	H1	240.00	40.00			200.00		
	171	Tomorrow	T1	120.00	20.00					100.00
	172	Worldwide News	W5	3,600.00	600.00	3,000.00				
				7,560.00	1,260.00	3,000.00	–	400.00	300.00	2,600.00

When you have totalled the columns you can check your additions by 'cross-casting'. If you add together the totals of all of the analysis columns and the VAT column, they should total the figure in the 'Total' column. The terms 'Total' and 'Gross' both mean the amounts inclusive of VAT.

Activity 1

Sweepings Ltd is a wall covering manufacturer. It produces four qualities of wallpaper:

01 – Anaglypta

02 – Supaglypta

03 – Lincrusta

04 – Blown Vinyl

Francis is a sales ledger clerk and he is required to write up the sales day book each week from the batch of sales invoices he receives from the sales department.

He has just received this batch of sales invoices which show the following details. All sales are standard-rated for VAT.

Invoice no	Date	Customer	Description	Amount (incl VAT) £
1700	06.09.X1	Gates Stores	Anaglypta, 188 rolls	480.00
1701	06.09.X1	Texas	Blown Vinyl, 235 rolls	1,800.00
1702	07.09.X1	Dickens	Blown Vinyl, 188 rolls	1,440.00
1703	07.09.X1	Hintons DIY	Supaglypta, 470 rolls	1,920.00
1704	08.09.X1	Co-op Stores	Anaglypta, 94 rolls	240.00
1705	08.09.X1	B & Q Stores	Lincrusta, 125 rolls	1,200.00
1706	09.09.X1	Ferris Decor	Supaglypta, 235 rolls	960.00
1707	09.09.X1	Ferris Decor	Blown Vinyl, 94 rolls	720.00
1708	10.09.X1	Homestyle	Lincrusta, 25 rolls	240.00
1709	10.09.X1	Quick Style	Anaglypta, 47 rolls	120.00

Accounting for sales – summary: **Chapter 2**

Show how this information would appear in the sales day book given below, including the totals of the relevant columns.

SALES DAY BOOK

Date	Invoice	Customer	Code	Total	VAT	Group 01	Group 02	Group 03	Group 04
				£	£	£	£	£	£

Activity 2

Given below are the totals from the analysed sales day book for an organisation for a week.

Sales day book

	Gross	VAT	Sales Type 1	Sales Type 2
	£	£	£	£
Totals	8,652.00	1,442.00	4,320.00	2,890.00

You are required to post these totals to the main ledger accounts given below:

SLCA account

£	£

42   KAPLAN PUBLISHING

```
          Sales – Type 1 account
  £                          |                          £
                             |
                             |
                             |
          Sales – Type 2 account
  £                          |                          £
                             |
                             |
                             |
              VAT account
  £                          |                          £
                             |
                             |
                             |
```

3 The sales returns day book

3.1 Introduction

When goods are returned by customers and credit notes sent out then these credit notes are also recorded in their own book of prime entry, the sales returns day book.

3.2 Sales returns day book

The sales returns day book is effectively the reverse of the sales day book but will have the same entries, the total of the credit note, including VAT, the VAT element and the net amount, excluding the VAT.

Accounting for sales – summary: **Chapter 2**

Example

Given below are the totals from three credit notes that your organisation has sent out this week, the week ending 21 January 20X4. They are to be recorded in the sales returns day book. VAT is at 20%.

Credit note no:	03556	To: J Slater & Co	Code: SL67
		£	
Goods total		126.45	
VAT		25.29	
Credit note total		151.74	

Credit note no:	03557	To: Paulsons	Code: SL14
		£	
Goods total		58.40	
VAT		11.68	
Credit note total		70.08	

Credit note no:	03558	To: Hudson & Co	Code: SL27
		£	
Goods total		104.57	
VAT		20.91	
Credit note total		125.48	

Solution

Sales returns day book

Date	Credit note no	Customer name	Code	Total	VAT	Net
				£	£	£
21/01/X4	03556	J Slater & Co	SL67	151.74	25.29	126.45
21/01/X4	03557	Paulsons	SL14	70.08	11.68	58.40
21/01/X4	03558	Hudson & Co	SL27	125.48	20.91	104.57

3.3 Analysed sales returns day book

If the business keeps an analysed sales day book then it will also analyse its sales returns day book in exactly the same manner.

> **Example**
>
> In an earlier example we considered the sales day book for an organisation that makes sales to five different geographical regions. The sales returns day book would also be analysed into these geographical regions. The details of two credit notes issued this week are given and are to be written up in the sales returns day book. Today's date is 21 October 20X6. VAT in use is 20%.
>
> Credit note no: 0246 – Poland To: Russell & Sons Code: R3
>
> | | £ |
> |---|---|
> | Goods total | 85.60 |
> | VAT | 17.12 |
> | | 102.72 |
>
> Credit note no: 0247 – Germany To: Cleansafe Code: C7
>
> | | £ |
> |---|---|
> | Goods total | 126.35 |
> | VAT | 25.27 |
> | | 151.62 |
>
> **Solution**
>
> **Sales returns day book**
>
> | Date | Credit | Customer | Code | Total | VAT | Russia | Poland | Spain | Germany | France |
> |---|---|---|---|---|---|---|---|---|---|---|
> | 21/10/X6 | 0246 | Russell & Sons | R03 | 102.72 | 17.12 | | 85.60 | | | |
> | 21/10/X6 | 0247 | Cleansafe | C07 | 151.62 | 25.27 | | | | 126.35 | |
> | | | | | | | | | | | |

Accounting for sales – summary: **Chapter 2**

Activity 3

A business analyses its sales into Product 1 sales and Product 2 sales. During the week ending 14 March 20X4 the following credit notes were sent out to customers.

CN3066	£120.00 plus VAT	–	Product 2, Customer K Lilt, Code L04
CN3067	£16.00 plus VAT	–	Product 1, Customer J Davis, Code D07
CN3068	£38.00 plus VAT	–	Product 1, Customer I Oliver, Code O11
CN3069	£80.00 plus VAT	–	Product 2, Customer D Sharp, Code S02

Enter the credit notes in the analysed sales returns day book given below and total the day book for the week.

Sales returns day book

Date	Credit note no	Customer name	Code	Total £	VAT £	Product 1 £	Product 2 £

Activity 4

Given below are the totals from the analysed sales returns day book for an organisation for a week:

Date	Customer name	Credit note no	Code	Total £	VAT £	Sales Type 1 £	Sales Type 2 £
25/09/X2				601.80	100.30	327.00	174.50

Post these totals to the general ledger accounts.

4 Posting to the sales ledger

As well as posting the totals from the books of prime entry to the main ledger accounts each individual invoice and credit note must also be posted to the individual customer's account in the sales ledger. You must remember that the sales ledger is sometimes referred to as the subsidiary (sales) ledger.

Example

Here is an account from the sales ledger of Frosty Limited, a glass manufacturer which specialises in glassware for the catering trade.

Account name:		Account code:	
	£		£

You have taken over writing up the sales ledger because the ledger clerk has been ill for several months.

You have gathered together the following information about sales. The customer is a new customer whose name is Arthur Pickering. The account code will be SP05.

Sales invoices

Date	Invoice number	Gross	VAT	Net
		£	£	£
02/05/X1	325	598.06	99.67	498.39
03/06/X1	468	243.98	40.66	203.32
15/06/X1	503	115.84	19.30	96.54
16/06/X1	510	49.74	8.29	41.45
25/06/X1	CN048	28.32	4.72	23.60
17/07/X1	604	450.51	75.08	375.43

Solution

Account name: Arthur Pickering   **Account code: SP05**

		£			£
02/05/X1	Inv 325	598.06	25/06/X1	CN048	28.32
03/06/X1	Inv 468	243.98			
15/06/X1	Inv 503	115.84			
16/06/X1	Inv 510	49.74			
17/07/X1	Inv 604	450.51			

Remember that sales invoices are always entered on the debit side of the customer's account and credit notes on the credit side of the account.

5 The cash book

5.1 Introduction

One of the most important books used within a business is the cash book. There are various forms of cash book, a 'two column' and a 'three column' cash book. As part of the Level I syllabus, you are required to have the ability to create, update and interpret a two column cash book. A three column cash book is required knowledge for the Level II syllabus.

Definition

A cash book is a record of cash receipts and payments that confirms to the double entry system.

5.2 Two column cash book

A proforma two column cash book is shown below.

CASH BOOK

Date	Narrative	Cash £	Bank £	Date	Narrative	Cash £	Bank £

Notes:

(a) The left hand side of the cash book represents the debit side – money received.

(b) The right hand side of the cash book represents the credit side – money paid out.

(c) The date column contains the date of the transaction

(d) The narrative column describes the transactions – typically the name of the customer who is paying. It would also contain the sales ledger code of the debtor.

(e) The cash column on the debit side represents cash received, whereas the cash column on the credit side represents cash paid.

(f) The bank column on the debit side represents money received (by cheque or other bank payment) whereas the bank column on the credit side represents money paid (by cheque or other bank payment).

A business may operate a bank current account as a means to settle business transactions. Receipts may be made in the form of a cheque, cash may be deposited into the current account and payment may be made by drawing a cheque against the current account.

To be able to record these bank specific transactions, a separate column must be introduced to the cash book to account for them. This is what leads to the use of a two column cash book; a column for cash transactions and a column for transactions made through the bank current account. Each column represents a separate account, cash account and bank account, each with its own double entry.

Accounting for sales – summary: Chapter 2

As well as being aware of the use of two columns for bank and cash, you should also be aware that a cash book may have additional columns for the purpose of analysing the receipts and payments in terms of sources and types of income and expenditure.

Definition

An analysed cash book is a cash book with additional columns for analysing principal sources and payments for cash.

5.3 Three column cash book

The three-column cashbook incorporates the cash discounts for each relevant entry into a third column. At the end of a certain period of time, when the cashbook is balanced off, the totals from these discount columns would then be transferred to the discount accounts in the general ledger. Discounts received are entered in the discounts column on the credit side of the cashbook, and discounts allowed in the discounts column on the debit side of the cashbook.

A proforma three column cash book is shown below.

CASH BOOK									
Date	Narrative	Cash £	Bank £	Discount £	Date	Narrative	Cash £	Bank £	Discount £

The purpose of each of the columns is consistent to that of a two column cash book with the addition of the discount columns in both the receipts (debit) side and the payments (credit) side. It is important to note that cash books can be in different formats with different numbers of analysis columns.

We will now focus on the cash receipts book. The cash payments book will be reviewed in the chapter that follows.

5.4 The cash receipts book

In order to revise the layout of the cash receipts book consider the following example.

Cash receipts book for the week commencing 15 September 20X4

Date	Narrative	Total	VAT	SLCA	Cash/cheque sales	Discount allowed
		£	£	£	£	£
15 Sept	Paying-in slip 584	653.90		653.90		
16 Sept	Paying-in slip 585	864.60		864.60		
17 Sept	Paying-in slip 586	954.98	11.24	887.54	56.20	
18 Sept	Paying-in slip 587	559.57		559.57		
19 Sept	Paying-in slip 588	238.18	31.69	48.00	158.49	
		3,271.23	42.93	3,013.61	214.69	

The bankings are a mixture of cash sales and cheques from debtors. The VAT is just the VAT on the cash/cheque sales. There are no discounts.

Check that the three analysis column totals add back to the total column total.

Example

Returning to the cash receipts book, post the totals to the general ledger accounts.

Cash receipts book

Date	Narrative	Total	VAT	Debtors	Cash/cheque sales	Discount allowed
		£	£	£	£	£
15 Sept	Paying-in slip 584	653.90		653.90		
16 Sept	Paying-in slip 585	864.60		864.60		
17 Sept	Paying-in slip 586	954.98	11.24	887.54	56.20	
18 Sept	Paying-in slip 587	559.57		559.57		
19 Sept	Paying-in slip 588	238.18	31.69	48.00	158.49	
		3,271.23	42.93	3,013.61	214.69	

Accounting for sales – summary: Chapter 2

Solution

The double entry for posting the cash receipts book totals is:

		£	£
DR	Bank account	3,271.23	
CR	VAT account		42.93
	Sales ledger control account		3,013.61
	Sales account		214.69

Bank account

	£		£
Cash receipts book (CRB)	3,271.23		

VAT account

	£		£
		CRB	42.93

Sales ledger control account

	£		£
		CRB	3,013.61

Sales account

	£		£
		CRB	214.69

Note that the description of each transaction is the primary record that it came from, the cash receipts book, shortened to CRB.

ICB LEVEL II: MANUAL BOOKKEEPING

Activity 5

The cheques received from customers of Passiflora Products Ltd, a small company which produces herbal remedies and cosmetics and supplies them to shops and beauty parlours, for a week are given below:

Cheques received:

	Paying-in slip/customer	Amount £	Discount allowed £
01/5/X6	Paying-in slip 609		
	Natural Beauty	11,797.05	176.95
	Grapeseed	417.30	6.26
	New Age Remedies	6,379.65	95.69
	The Aromatherapy Shop	9,130.65	136.96
03/5/X6	Paying-in slip 610		
	Comfrey Group	5,689.20	85.34
	Natural Elegance	2,056.89	30.85
08/5/X6	Paying-in slip 611		
	The Herbalist	8,663.45	129.95
12/5/X6	Paying-in slip 612		
	Edwards Pharmacy	106.42	
	Healthworks	17,213.94	258.21
19/5/X6	Paying-in slip 613		
	The Beauty Box	11,195.85	167.94
	Crystals	54.19	
25/5/X6	Paying-in slip 614		
	The Village Chemist	7,662.55	114.94
29/5/X6	Paying-in slip 615		
	Brewer Brothers	2,504.61	37.57
30/5/X6	Paying-in slip 616		
	Lapis Lazuli	112.58	
31/5/X6	Paying-in slip 617		
	Lorelei	5,618.40	84.27
	Spain & Co, Chemists	197.93	

Required:

(a) Enter the totals for each paying-in slip (including discounts) into the cash receipts book given below.

(b) Total the cash receipts book and post the totals for the month to the general ledger accounts given.

Accounting for sales – summary: Chapter 2

(a) **Cash receipts book**

Date	Narrative	Total £	VAT £	SLCA £	Other £	Discount £

(b) **General ledger**

Sales ledger control account

£	£

Discount allowed account

£	£

ICB LEVEL II: MANUAL BOOKKEEPING

Activity 6

Given below are the details of paying-in slip 609 from the previous activity, Passiflora Products Ltd. You are required to enter the details in the sales ledger accounts given.

Paying-in slip 609

	Amount	Discount allowed
	£	£
Natural Beauty	11,797.05	176.95
Grapeseed	417.30	6.26
New Age Remedies	6,379.65	95.69
The Aromatherapy Shop	9,130.65	136.96

Natural Beauty

	£		£
Opening balance	17,335.24		

The Aromatherapy Shop

	£		£
Opening balance	12,663.42		

New Age Remedies

	£		£
Opening balance	6,475.34		

Grapeseed

	£		£
Opening balance	423.56		

Accounting for sales – summary: Chapter 2

Activity 7

Cash book – Debit side

Date	Details	Discount £	Bank £
30 Nov	Balance b/f		10,472
30 Nov	SMK Ltd	300	12,000

(a) What will be the TWO entries in the sales ledger?

Sales Ledger

Account name	Amount £	Debit / Credit

(b) What will be the THREE entries in the general ledger?

General Ledger

Account name	Amount £	Debit / Credit

6 Document retention policies

6.1 Introduction

Throughout the studies for Level I and Level II we will have seen many documents that businesses produce. It is a legal requirement that all financial documents, and some non-financial documents, must be kept by a business for six years. Therefore it is essential that a business has a secure and organised method of filing such information, to ensure that they can be located easily.

6.2 Reasons for document retention

Documents must be kept for three main reasons:

- in order that they could be inspected by HM Revenue and Customs in a tax inspection;
- in order that they could be inspected by HM Revenue and Customs in a VAT inspection;
- in order that they could be used as evidence in any legal action.

7 Summary

In this chapter we have pulled together into one place all the main documents and double entry for the sales cycle. If you have had any trouble with any of these points, you should refer again to the relevant chapters of the textbook for Level I where the double entry is explained in basic terms. Level II is building on our knowledge from Level I.

Accounting for sales – summary: **Chapter 2**

Answers to chapter activities

Activity 1

SALES DAY BOOK

Date	Invoice	Customer	Code	Total £	VAT £	Group 01 £	Group 02 £	Group 03 £	Group 04 £
06/09/X1	1700	Gates Stores		480.00	80.00	400.00			
06/09/X1	1701	Texas		1,800.00	300.00				1,500.00
07/09/X1	1702	Dickens		1,440.00	240.00				1,200.00
07/09/X1	1703	Hintons DIY		1,920.00	320.00		1,600.00		
08/09/X1	1704	Co-op Stores		240.00	40.00	200.00			
08/09/X1	1705	B & Q Stores		1,200.00	200.00			1,000.00	
09/09/X1	1706	Ferris Decor		960.00	160.00		800.00		
09/09/X1	1707	Ferris Decor		720.00	120.00				600.00
10/09/X1	1708	Homestyle		240.00	40.00			200.00	
10/09/X1	1709	Quick Style		120.00	20.00	100.00			
				9,120.00	1,520.00	700.00	2,400.00	1,200.00	3,300.00

Activity 2

SLCA

	£		£
SDB	8,652.00		

Sales – Type 1 account

	£		£
		SDB	4,320.00

Sales – Type 2 account

	£		£
		SDB	2,890.00

VAT account

	£		£
		SDB	1,442.00

ICB LEVEL II: MANUAL BOOKKEEPING

Activity 3

SALES RETURNS DAY BOOK

Date	Credit note no	Customer name	Code	Total £	VAT £	Product 1 £	Product 2 £
14/3	3066	K Lilt	L04	144.00	24.00		120.00
14/3	3067	J Davis	D07	19.20	3.20	16.00	
14/3	3068	I Oliver	O11	45.60	7.60	38.00	
14/3	3069	D Sharp	S02	96.00	16.00		80.00
				304.80	50.80	54.00	200.00

Activity 4

Sales ledger control account

	£		£
		SRDB	601.80

Sales returns – Type 1

	£		£
SRDB	327.00		

Sales returns – Type 2

	£		£
SRDB	174.50		

VAT account

	£		£
SRDB	100.30		

Accounting for sales – summary: Chapter 2

Activity 5

(a) Cash receipts book

Date	Narrative	Total £	VAT £	SLCA £	Others £	Discount £
01/05/X6	Cheques – 609	27,724.65		27,724.65		415.86
03/05/X6	Cheques – 610	7,746.09		7,746.09		116.19
08/05/X6	Cheques – 611	8,663.45		8,663.45		129.95
12/05/X6	Cheques – 612	17,320.36		17,320.36		258.21
19/05/X6	Cheques – 613	11,250.04		11,250.04		167.94
25/05/X6	Cheques – 614	7,662.55		7,662.55		114.94
29/05/X6	Cheques – 615	2,504.61		2,504.61		37.57
30/05/X6	Cheques – 616	112.58		112.58		
31/05/X6	Cheques – 617	5,816.33		5,816.33		84.27
		88,800.66	–	88,800.66	–	1,324.93

(b) General ledger

Sales ledger control account

	£		£
		CRB	88,800.66
		CRB – discount allowed	1,324.93

Discount allowed account

	£		£
CRB	1,324.93		

Activity 6

Natural Beauty

	£		£
Opening balance	17,335.24	CRB	11,797.05
		CRB – discount	176.95

The Aromatherapy Shop

	£		£
Opening balance	12,663.42	CRB	9,130.65
		CRB – discount	136.96

New Age Remedies

	£		£
Opening balance	6,475.34	CRB	6,379.65
		CRB – discount	95.69

Grapeseed

	£		£
Opening balance	423.56	CRB	417.30
		CRB – discount	6.26

Activity 7

Cashbook – Debit side

Date	Details	Discount £	Bank £
30 Nov	Balance b/f		10,472
30 Nov	SMK Ltd	300	12,000

(a) What will be the TWO entries in the sales ledger?

Sales Ledger

Account name	Amount £	Debit / Credit
SMK Ltd	12,000	Credit
SMK Ltd	300	Credit

(b) What will be the THREE entries in the general ledger?

General Ledger

Account name	Amount £	Debit / Credit
SLCA	12,000	Credit
Discount allowed	300	Debit
SLCA	300	Credit

Accounting for sales – summary: **Chapter 2**

8 Test your knowledge

Workbook Activity 8

Your organisation receives a number of cheques from debtors through the post each day and these are listed on the cheque listing. It also makes some cash sales each day which include VAT at the standard rate.

Today's date is 28 April 20X1 and the cash sales today were £240.00 including VAT at 20%. The cheque listing for the day is given below:

Cheque listing 28 April 20X1

G Heilbron	£108.45
L Tessa	£110.57 – settlement discount of £3.31 taken
J Dent	£210.98 – settlement discount of £6.32 taken
F Trainer	£ 97.60
A Winter	£105.60 – settlement discount of £3.16 taken

An extract from the customer file shows the following:

Customer	Sales ledger code
J Dent	SL17
G Heilbron	SL04
L Tessa	SL15
F Trainer	SL21
A Winter	SL09

Required:

(a) Write up the cash receipts book given below; total each of the columns of the cash receipts book and check that they cross-cast

(b) Post the totals of the cash receipts book to the general ledger accounts.

(c) Post the individual receipts to the sales ledger.

ICB LEVEL II: MANUAL BOOKKEEPING

Cash receipts book

Narrative	SL Code	Discount £	Cash £	Bank £	VAT £	Cash Sales £	SLCA £

Workbook Activity 9

There are 5 receipts to be entered into Longley Ltd's cash receipts book.

Cash receipts

From Irlam Transport – £468.00 (inc VAT)

From Paulson Haulage – £216.00 (inc VAT)

From Mault Motors – £348.00 (inc VAT)

Cheques received from credit customers

From James John Ltd – £579.08 (discount of £24.39 taken)

From Exilm & Co – £456.74 (discount of £19.80 taken)

Required:

Write up the cash receipts book given below; total each of the columns of the cash receipts book and check that they cross cast.

Accounting for sales – summary: Chapter 2

Cash receipts book

Narrative	Discount £	Cash £	Bank £	VAT £	Cash Sales £	SLCA £

Workbook Activity 10

Indicate whether each of the following statements is true or false.

	True/False
Documents can be disposed of as soon as the year end accounts are prepared	
Documents cannot be inspected by anyone outside the business	
Documents can be used as legal evidence in any legal actions	
Businesses must keep an aged debtor analysis as part of their financial documents	
Businesses do not need to keep copies of invoices	
Businesses need to keep copies of their bank statements available for inspection	

Accounting for purchases – summary

Introduction

As well as recapping accounting for sales as seen in previous chapter, we also need to recap on the techniques learned in Bookkeeping Level I for purchases.

CONTENTS

1. The purchases day book
2. Returns of goods
3. Accounting entries in the general ledger
4. Accounting entries in the purchases ledger
5. The impact of value added tax
6. Cash (settlement) discounts
7. The cash payments book

Accounting for purchases – summary: **Chapter 3**

1 The purchases day book

1.1 Introduction

In the purchases day book, the purchase invoices are normally given an internal invoice number and are also recorded under the supplier's purchase ledger code and possibly the type of purchase.

1.2 Authorisation stamp

This is often done by stamping an authorisation stamp or grid stamp onto the invoice once it has been thoroughly checked and the relevant details entered onto the authorisation stamp. A typical example of an authorisation stamp is shown below:

Purchase order no	04618
Invoice no	04821
Cheque no	
Account code	PL06
Checked	L Finn
Date	23/02/X2
GL account	07

1.3 Entries on the authorisation stamp

At this stage of entering the invoice in the purchases day book it has been checked to the purchase order and the delivery note, therefore the purchase order number is entered onto the authorisation stamp.

The purchase invoice will then be allocated an internal invoice number which will be sequential and therefore the next number after the last invoice entered into the purchases day book.

At this stage the invoice will not necessarily have been authorised for payment, therefore the cheque number will not yet be entered onto the authorisation stamp.

The purchase invoice details such as trade and settlement discounts should have been checked to the supplier's file to ensure that the correct percentages have been used and at this point the supplier's purchases ledger code can be entered onto the authorisation stamp.

The person checking the invoice should then sign and date the authorisation stamp to show that all details have been checked.

ICB LEVEL II: MANUAL BOOKKEEPING

Finally, the general ledger account code should be entered. We have seen that in some businesses a simple three column purchases day book will be used with a total, VAT and net column. In such cases all of the invoices will be classified as 'purchases' and will have the general ledger code for the purchases account.

However, if an analysed purchases day book is used then each analysis column will be for a different type of expense and will have a different general ledger code.

If your organisation does have an authorisation stamp procedure then it is extremely important that the authorisation is correctly filled out when the invoice has been checked. Not only is this evidence that the invoice is correct and is for goods or services that have been received, it also provides vital information for the accurate accounting for this invoice.

Example

Given below are three purchase invoices received and the authorisation stamp for each one. They are to be entered into the purchases day book. Today's date is 25 April 20X1.

INVOICE

Anderson Wholesale
Westlife Park
Gripton
M7 1ZK
Tel: 0161 439 2020
Fax: 0161 439 2121

Invoice to:
Keller Bros
Field House
Winstead
M16 4PT

Deliver to:
Above address

Invoice no: 06447
Tax point: 20 April 20X1
VAT reg no: 432 1679 28
Account no: SL14

Code	Description	Quantity	VAT rate %	Unit price £	Amount excl of VAT £
PT417	Grade A Compost	7 tonnes	20	15.80	110.60
					110.60
Trade discount 5%					5.53
					105.07
VAT					21.01
Total amount payable					126.08

KAPLAN PUBLISHING

67

Accounting for purchases – summary: Chapter 3

Purchase order no	34611
Invoice no	37240
Cheque no	
Account code	PL14
Checked	C Long
Date	25/04/X1
GL account	020

INVOICE

Invoice to:
Keller Bros
Field House
Winstead
M16 4PT

Deliver to:
Above address

Better Gardens Ltd
Broom Nursery
West Lane
Farforth M23 4LL
Tel: 0161 380 4444
Fax: 0161 380 6128

Invoice no: 46114
Tax point: 21 April 20X1
VAT reg no: 611 4947 26
Account no: K03

Code	Description	Quantity	VAT rate %	Unit price £	Amount excl of VAT £
B4188	Tulip bulbs	28 dozen	20	1.38	38.64
B3682	Daffodil bulbs	50 dozen	20	1.26	63.00
					101.64
VAT					19.71
Total amount payable					121.35

Deduct discount of 3% if paid within 14 days

Purchase order no	34608
Invoice no	37241
Cheque no	
Account code	PL06
Checked	C Long
Date	25/04/X1
GL account	020

INVOICE

Winterton Partners
28/32 Coleman Road
Forest Dene
M17 3AT
Tel: 0161 224 6760
Fax: 0161 224 6761

Invoice to:
Keller Bros
Field House
Winstead
M16 4PT

Deliver to:
Above address

Invoice no:	121167
Tax point:	22 April 20X1
VAT reg no:	980 3012 74
Account no:	SL44

Code	Description	Quantity	VAT rate %	Unit price £	Amount excl of VAT £
A47BT	Seedlings	120	20	0.76	91.20
					91.20
Trade discount 7%					6.38
					84.82
VAT					16.62
Total amount payable					101.44
Deduct discount of 2% if paid within 14 days					

Purchase order no	34615
Invoice no	37242
Cheque no	
Account code	PL23
Checked	C Long
Date	25/04/X1
GL account	020

Accounting for purchases – summary: Chapter 3

Solution

Purchases day book

Date	Invoice no	Code	Supplier	Total £	VAT £	Net £
25/04/X1	37240	PL14	Anderson Wholesale	126.08	21.01	105.07
25/04/X1	37241	PL06	Better Gardens Ltd	121.35	19.71	101.64
25/04/X1	37242	PL23	Winterton Partners	101.44	16.62	84.82

Note that the net total is the invoice amount after deducting any trade discount as the trade discount is a definite reduction in the list price of the goods. At this stage any settlement discount is ignored as it will not necessarily have been decided whether or not to take advantage of the settlement discount.

Activity 1

You are a purchases clerk for Robins, a soft drink manufacturer. Here is part of the layout of the purchases day book. VAT is at 20%.

Purchases day book

Date	Invoice no	Code	Supplier	Total £	VAT £	01 £	02 £	03 £	04 £

01 represents purchases of parts or raw materials for manufacture

02 represents advertising expenditure

03 represents entertaining expenditure

04 represents purchases of fixed assets

Here are five documents that are to be written up in the purchases day book on 10.11.X2 as necessary.

ICB LEVEL II: MANUAL BOOKKEEPING

Document 1

No: 511 X

SALES INVOICE

Drip Farm
Lover's Lane
Norwich NO56 2EZ

To: Robins Ltd
Softdrink House
Wembley
London
NW16 7SJ

Tax point: 7.11.X2
VAT Reg No: 566 0122 10

Quantity	Description	VAT rate	Price/unit	Total
50 litre drum	Apple juice (inferior)	20%	£2/litre	100.00
			VAT	20.00
				120.00

Grid stamp on reverse of invoice

Invoice no	4221
Account code	DF2
Checked	R Robins
Date	9.11.X2
GL account	01

Document 2

Sales Invoice   Inv No: 5177

DAILY NEWS PLC

Europe Way
Southampton
SO3 3BZ

Tax point 5.11.X2
VAT Reg No: 177 0255 01

To: Robins Ltd
Softdrink House
London
NW16 7SJ

Sale details:
4 line advertisement   £
3 weeks   04.10.X2 @ £100/week
                  11/10.X2   Net price   300.00
                  18.10.X2   VAT 20%   60.00
                                                                       360.00

KAPLAN PUBLISHING

Accounting for purchases – summary: Chapter 3

Grid stamp on reverse of invoice.

Invoice no	4222
Account code	DN1
Checked	R Robins
Date	9.11.X2
GL account	02

Document 3

RECEIPT

Yellow River Restaurant

9/11/12

Received with thanks the sum of £17.50

T W Wang

Document 4

SALES ORDER 562		
		Robins Ltd
BTEB Stores		Softdrink House
Gateshead		Wembley
		LONDON
		NW16 7SJ
Quantity	Description	Price
20 cases	0.75 bottles of Norfolk apple juice	£2/bottle

Document 5

```
                    SALES INVOICE P261
                      STANDARD MACHINES
                 Starlight Boulevard, Milton Keynes
                            MK51 7LY

To:  Robins Ltd
     Softdrink House
     Wembley
     LONDON                  Tax point: 6.11.X2
     NW16 7SJ
                             VAT Reg No: 127 0356 02
```

Quantity	Description	VAT	Price (£)/unit
1	Bottling machine	20%	2,000
		VAT	400
			2,400

Grid stamp on reverse of invoice.

Invoice no.	4223
Account code	SM4
Checked	R Robins
Date	9.11.X2
GL account	04

Activity 2

A newsagents shop has received the following invoices. Write them up in the purchases day book using the format provided. The last internal invoice number to be allocated to purchase invoices was 114.

1.1.X1	Northern Electric – invoice	£120 including VAT
	Northern Gas – invoice	£230 (no VAT)
2.1.X1	Post Office Ltd – invoice	£117.00 (no VAT)
	Northern Country – invoice	£48 including VAT
3.1.X1	South Gazette – invoice	£360 including VAT

Accounting for purchases – summary: Chapter 3

The supplier codes are as follows:

Northern Country (a newspaper)	N1
Northern Electric	N2
Northern Gas	N3
Post Office Ltd	P1
South Gazette (a newspaper)	S1

Purchases day book

Date	Invoice no	Code	Supplier	Total	VAT	Goods for resale	Heat and light	Postage and stationery
				£	£	£	£	£

2 Returns of goods

2.1 Introduction

Returns may be made for various reasons, e.g.
- faulty goods;
- excess goods delivered by supplier;
- unauthorised goods delivered.

All returned goods must be recorded on a returns outwards note.

2.2 Credit notes

The return should not be recorded until the business receives a credit note from the supplier. This confirms that there is no longer a liability for these goods. A credit note from a supplier is sometimes requested by the organisation issuing a debit note.

The credit note should be checked for accuracy against the returns outwards note. The calculations and extensions on the credit note should also be checked in just the same way as with an invoice.

2.3 Purchases returns day book

When credit notes are received from suppliers they are normally recorded in their own primary record, the purchases returns day book. This has a similar layout to a purchases day book. If the purchases day book is analysed into the different types of purchase that the organisation makes then the purchases returns day book will also be analysed in the same manner.

Example

Today, 5 February 20X5, three credit notes have been passed as being checked. The details of each credit note and the authorisation stamp are given below. The credit note details are to be entered into the purchases returns day book.

From Calderwood & Co	£
Goods total	16.80
VAT	3.36
Credit note total	20.16

Purchase order no	41120
Credit note	C461
Cheque no	–
Account code	053
Checked	J Garry
Date	05/02/X5
GL account	02

From Mellor & Cross	£
Goods total	104.50
Less: Trade discount 10%	10.45
	94.05
VAT	18.81
Credit note total	112.86

Accounting for purchases – summary: Chapter 3

Purchase order no	41096
Credit note	C462
Cheque no	–
Account code	259
Checked	J Garry
Date	05/02/X5
GL account	02

From Thompson Bros Ltd	**£**
Goods total	37.60
Less: Trade discount 5%	1.88
	35.72
VAT	7.14
Credit note total	42.86

Purchase order no	41103
Credit note	C463
Cheque no	–
Account code	360
Checked	J Garry
Date	05/02/X5
GL account	01

Solution

Purchases returns day book									
Date	Credit note no	Code	Supplier	Total £	VAT £	01 £	02 £	03 £	04 £
05/02/X5	C461	053	Calderwood & Co	20.16	3.36		16.80		
05/02/X5	C462	259	Mellor & Cross	112.86	18.81		94.05		
05/02/X5	C463	360	Thompson Bros Ltd	42.86	7.14	35.72			

Note that it is the credit note total which is entered into the total column and the VAT amount into the VAT column. The amount entered into the analysis columns is the goods total less the trade discount. The analysis column is taken from the general ledger code on the authorisation stamp.

KAPLAN PUBLISHING

3 Accounting entries in the general ledger

3.1 Introduction

The accounting entries that are to be made in the general ledger are the same as those that have been considered in Bookkeeping Level I and are made from the totals of the columns in the purchases day book and purchases returns day book.

3.2 Analysed purchases day book

If an analysed purchases day book is being used then there will be a debit entry in an individual purchases or expense account for each of the analysis column totals.

Remember that these totals are the net of VAT purchases/expenses totals.

Example

Reproduced below is a purchases day book for the first week of February 20X5. Each column has been totalled and it must be checked that the totals of the analysis columns agree to the 'Total' column. Therefore you should check the following sum:

	£
01	744.37
02	661.23
03	250.45
04	153.72
VAT	338.43
	2,148.20

Accounting for purchases – summary: Chapter 3

Purchases day book

Date	Invoice no	Code	Supplier	Total £	VAT £	01 £	02 £	03 £	04 £
20X5									
1 Feb	3569	265	Norweb	151.44	25.24	126.20			
2 Feb	3570	053	Calderwood & Co	98.60			98.60		
3 Feb	3571	259	Mellor & Cross	675.15	112.52		562.63		
4 Feb	3572	360	Thompson Bros Ltd	265.71	44.28	221.43			
5 Feb	3573	023	Cooplin Associates	18.90				18.90	
	3574	056	Heywood Suppliers	277.86	46.31			231.55	
	3575	395	William Leggett	46.33	7.72				38.61
	3576	271	Melville Products	374.29	62.38	311.91			
	3577	301	Quick-Bake	101.79	16.96	84.83			
	3578	311	Roger & Roebuck	138.13	23.02				115.11
				2,148.20	338.43	744.37	661.23	250.45	153.72

The totals of the purchases day book will now be posted to the general ledger accounts.

Solution

Purchase ledger control account

	£		£
		PDB	2,148.20

VAT account

	£		£
PDB	338.43		

Purchases – 01 account

	£		£
PDB	744.37		

Purchases – 02 account

	£		£
PDB	661.23		

Purchases – 03 account

	£		£
PDB	250.45		

Purchases – 04 account

	£		£
PDB	153.72		

3.3 Purchases returns day book

The purchases returns day book is kept in order to record credit notes received by the business. The totals of this must also be posted to the general ledger.

Example

Given below is a purchases returns day book for the week. The totals are to be posted to the general ledger accounts. VAT is at 20%.

Purchases day book

Date	Credit note no	Code	Supplier	Total £	VAT £	01 £	02 £	03 £	04 £
20X3									
4 May	CN 152	PL21	Julian R Partners	132.00	22.00		110.00		
6 May	CN 153	PL07	S T Trader	81.60	13.60			68.00	
8 May	CN 154	PL10	Ed Associates	70.32	11.72		58.60		
8 May	CN 155	PL03	Warren & Co	107.52	17.92	89.60			
				391.44	65.24	89.60	168.60	68.00	–

Solution

First, check that each of the column totals add back to the total column total:

	£
VAT	65.24
01	89.60
02	168.60
03	68.00
04	–
	391.44

Then post the totals to the general ledger accounts:

Purchases ledger control account

	£		£
Purchases return day book (PRDB)	391.44		

VAT account

	£		£
		PRDB	65.24

Accounting for purchases – summary: **Chapter 3**

Purchases returns – 01

£		£
	PRDB	89.60

Purchases returns – 02

£		£
	PRDB	168.60

Purchases returns – 03

£		£
	PRDB	68.00

If the purchases returns day book is analysed then there will be an account in the general ledger for each different category of purchases returns.

Activity 3

Given below is the purchases day book. You are required to check the total of each analysis column and that the total of each analysis column agrees to the total column, and then to enter the totals in the correct general ledger accounts.

Purchases day book

Date	Invoice no	Code	Supplier	Total £	VAT £	Goods for sale £	Heat and light £	Postage and stationery £
01.01.X1	115	N2	Northern Electric	120.00	20.00		100.00	
	116	N3	Northern Gas	230.00			230.00	
02.01.X1	117	P1	Post Office	117.00				117.00
	118	N1	Northern Country	48.00	8.00	40.00		
03.01.X1	119	S1	South Gazette	360.00	60.00	300.00		
				875.00	88.00	340.00	330.00	117.00

4 Accounting entries in the purchases ledger

4.1 Purchases ledger

As well as posting the totals from the books of prime entry to the general ledger accounts, each individual invoice and credit note must also be posted to the individual supplier's account in the purchases ledger (also referred to as the subsidiary (purchases) ledger.

Example

Here is an account from the purchases ledger of Frosty Limited.

Account name:			Code:		
Date	Transaction	£	Date	Transaction	£

We will write up the account for Jones Brothers, account number PJ06. This is a new supplier.

Frosty Limited has only been trading for a short time and is not yet registered for VAT.

Purchase invoices and credit notes

02.5.X1	9268	£638.26
06.6.X1	9369	£594.27
15.6.X1	9402	£368.24
17.6.X1	C Note 413	£58.62
19.6.X1	9568	£268.54

Solution

Account name: Jones Brothers   **Account number:** PJ06

Date	Transaction	£	Date	Transaction	£
17.6.X1	Credit note 413	58.62	02.5.X1	Invoice 9268	638.26
			06.6.X1	Invoice 9369	594.27
			15.6.X1	Invoice 9402	368.24
			19.6.X1	Invoice 9568	268.54

Accounting for purchases – summary: **Chapter 3**

Each purchase invoice from the Purchases Day Book must be entered on the credit side of that individual suppliers account in the purchases ledger. Any credit notes recorded in the Purchases Returns Day Book must be recorded on the debit side of the supplier's account. Where there is VAT involved the amount to be recorded for an invoice or credit note is the gross amount or VAT inclusive amount.

5 The impact of value added tax

5.1 Introduction

Having looked at the accounting for purchase invoices and credit notes, we will now move on to consider the accounting for payments to suppliers. First we will consider the impact of VAT in this area.

When writing up the payments side of the cash book VAT must be considered.

Any payments to suppliers or creditors included in the Purchases ledger column need have no analysis for VAT as the VAT on the purchase was recorded in the purchases day book when the invoice was initially received.

However any other payments on which there is VAT must show the gross amount in the Total column, the VAT in the VAT column and the net amount in the relevant expense column.

Example

Peter Craddock is the cashier for a business which manufactures paper from recycled paper. The payments that were made for one week in September are as follows:

15 September	Cheque no 1151 to K Humphrey (credit supplier)	£1,034.67
	Cheque no 1152 to Y Ellis (credit supplier)	£736.45
	Cheque no 1153 to R Phipps (credit supplier)	£354.45
	Standing order for rent	£168.15
	Direct debit to the electricity company	£130.98
	(including VAT of £22.92)	

ICB LEVEL II: MANUAL BOOKKEEPING

16 September	Cheque no 1154 to L Silton (credit supplier)	£1,092.75
	Cheque no 1155 to the insurance company	£103.18
17 September	Cheque no 1156 to F Grange (credit supplier)	£742.60
	Cheque no 1157 to Hettler Ltd for cash purchases	£504.00
	(including VAT at 20%)	
18 September	Cheque no 1158 to J Kettle (credit supplier)	£131.89
19 September	BACS payment of wages	£4,150.09
	Cheque no 1159 to Krane Associates for cash purchases	£223.20
	(including VAT at 20%)	

Enter these transactions into the cash payments book, total the columns and post the totals to the general ledger.

Solution

Date	Details	Cheque no	Total £	VAT £	PLCA £	Cash purchases £	Rent £	Electricity £	Wages £	Insurance £
15/9	K Humphrey	1151	1,034.67		1,034.67					
	Y Ellis	1152	736.45		736.45					
	R Phipps	1153	354.45		354.45					
	Rent	SO	168.15				168.15			
	Electricity	DD	130.98	22.92				108.06		
16/9	L Silton	1154	1,092.75		1,092.75					
	Insurance	1155	103.18							103.18
17/9	F Grange	1156	742.60		742.60					
	Hettler Ltd	1157	504.00	84.00		420.00				
18/9	J Kettle	1158	131.89		131.89					
	Wages	BACS	4,150.09						4,150.09	
19/9	Krane Ass	1159	223.20	37.20		186.00				
			9,372.41	144.12	4,092.81	606.00	168.15	108.06	4,150.09	103.18

The analysis column totals should add back to the Total column – this must always be done to check the accuracy of your totalling.

	£
VAT	144.12
Purchases ledger	4,092.81
Cash purchases	606.00
Rent	168.15
Electricity	108.06
Wages	4,150.09
Insurance	103.18
	9,372.41

Accounting for purchases – summary: **Chapter 3**

Purchase ledger control account

			£		£
19/9	CPB		4,092.81		

VAT account

			£		£
19/9	CPB		144.12		

Purchases account

			£		£
19/9	CPB		606.00		

Electricity account

			£		£
19/9	CPB		108.06		

Salaries account

			£		£
19/9	CPB		4,150.09		

Rent account

			£		£
19/9	CPB		168.15		

Insurance account

			£		£
19/9	CPB		103.18		

All of the entries in the general ledger accounts are debit entries. The credit entry is the total column of the cash payments book and these individual debit entries form the double entry.

6 Cash (settlement) discounts

6.1 Introduction

If a business takes advantage of cash discounts on items purchased, the discount is treated as income as it is a benefit to the business i.e. although the invoice is paid earlier, the amount paid is less than the invoice net amount due to the discount.

ICB LEVEL II: MANUAL BOOKKEEPING

Cash or settlement discounts are recorded in a memorandum column in the cash book. The memorandum column does not form part of the double entry. It requires an entire piece of double entry itself (see below).

The business must record these settlement discounts. Trade discounts are not recorded in the cash book.

An extra column is included in the analysed cash payments book. This should be the final right hand column.

Example

The following four payments have been made today, 12 June 20X6:

Cheque no. 22711 B Caro	Purchases ledger code CL13 £342.80 after taking a settlement discount of £14.20
Cheque no. 22712 S Wills	Cash purchases of £240.00 inclusive of VAT
Cheque no. 22713 P P & Co	Purchases ledger code CL22 £116.40
Cheque no. 22714 W Potts	Purchases ledger code CL18 £162.84

The relevant purchases ledger accounts are shown below:

B Caro (CL 13)

	£		£
		PDB Invoice	357.00

W Potts (CL 18)

	£		£
PRDB Credit note	10.00	PDB Invoice	172.84

P P & Co (CL 22)

	£		£
		PDB Invoice	116.40
		PDB Invoice	121.27

In this example we will:

- write up the cash payments book for the day;
- total the columns to check that they add back to the total of the Total column;
- enter the totals in the general ledger;
- write up each individual entry in the purchases ledger.

Accounting for purchases – summary: Chapter 3

Solution

Date	Details	Cheque	Code	Total £	VAT £	PLCA £	Cash purchases £	Other £	Discounts £
12 Jun	B Caro	22711	CL13	342.80		342.80			14.20
	S Wills	22712		240.00	40.00		200.00		
	PP&Co	22713	CL22	116.40		116.40			
	W Potts	22714	CL18	162.84		162.84			
				862.04	40.00	622.04	200.00	–	14.20

Total Check

	£
Purchases ledger	622.04
Cash purchases	200.00
VAT	40.00
	862.04

Note that the discount received column is not included in the total check as this is simply a memorandum column.

General ledger

Purchase ledger control account

	£		£
CPB	622.04		
CPB – discount	14.20		

Purchases account

	£		£
CPB	200.00		

VAT account

	£		£
CPB	40.00		

Discounts received account

	£		£
		CPB	14.20

ICB LEVEL II: MANUAL BOOKKEEPING

When posting the cash payments book to the general ledger there are two distinct processes. Firstly enter the totals of each of the analysis columns as debits in their relevant accounts in the general ledger. Then do the double entry for the discounts received – debit the purchase ledger control account and credit the discounts received account.

Purchases ledger

B Caro (CL 13)

			£			£
CPB	Payment		342.80	PDB	Invoice	357.00
CPB	Discount		14.20			

Note that the discount is entered here as well as the cash payment

W Potts (CL 18)

			£			£
PRDB	Credit note		10.00	PDB	Invoice	172.84
CPB	Payment		162.84			

P P & Co (CL 22)

			£			£
CPB	Payment		116.40	PDB	Invoice	116.40
				PDB	Invoice	121.27

Activity 4

Given below is a completed cash payments book. You are required to:

(a) Total each of the columns and check that the totals add across to the total column.
(b) Post the totals to the general ledger accounts given.
(c) Post the individual creditor entries to the creditors' accounts in the purchases ledger, also given.

Date	Details	Cheque no	Code	Total £	VAT £	PLCA £	Cash purchases £	Wages £
1/7	G Hobbs	34	PL14	325.46		325.46		
1/7	Purchases	35	GL03	68.40	11.40		57.00	
2/7	Purchases	36	GL03	50.59	8.43		42.16	
3/7	P Taylor	37	PL21	157.83		157.83		
3/7	S Dent	38	PL06	163.58		163.58		
4/7	K Smith	39	GL07	24.56				24.56

KAPLAN PUBLISHING

Accounting for purchases – summary: **Chapter 3**

7 The cash payments book

7.1 Introduction

We considered the difference between a two and three column cash book in the previous chapter. We must be aware that a cash book can be analysed in different ways. We have already reviewed the cash receipts book, we will now review the cash payments book.

A proforma analysed cash payments book is shown below.

CASH PAYMENTS BOOK

Date	Narrative	Reference	Total £	VAT £	PLCA £	Cash purchases £	Admin £	Rent and rates £	Discount received £
		TOTALS							

Notes:

(a) The date column contains the date of the transaction.

(b) The narrative column describes the transactions.

(c) The total column contains the total cash paid (including any VAT).

(d) The VAT column contains the VAT on the transaction but not if the VAT has already been entered in the purchases day book. This is a tricky point but is in principle exactly the same as the treatment of VAT that we studied for the cash receipts book.

(e) The PLCA column contains any cash paid that has been paid to a supplier. The total paid including VAT is entered in this column.

(f) The cash purchases column contains cash paid for purchases that are not bought on credit.

(g) We saw with the analysed cash receipts book that nearly all receipts come from debtors or cash sales. In the case of payments, there is a great variety of suppliers who are paid through the cash book; rent and rates, telephone, electricity, marketing, etc. The business will have a separate column for the categories of expense that it wishes to analyse. There may be as many or as little as a business wishes.

(h) The discount received column is a memorandum column that contains details of any cash/settlement discounts received. These discounts will need to be entered into the ledger accounts as we shall see.

Activity 5

Cashbook – Credit side

Date	Details	VAT £	Bank £
30 Nov	Motor expenses	40	240
30 Nov	Wages		6,200
30 Nov	HMRC		4,750

What will be the FOUR entries in the general ledger?

General Ledger

Account name	Amount £	Debit / Credit

8 Summary

In this chapter we have pulled together into one place all the general documents and double entry for the purchases cycle. If you have had any trouble with any of these points, you should refer again to the Bookkeeping Level I Study Text where the double entry is explained.

Accounting for purchases – summary: Chapter 3

Answers to chapter activities

Activity 1

Purchases day book

Date	Invoice no	Code	Supplier	Total £	VAT £	01 £	02 £	03 £	04 £
10/11/X2	4221	DF2	Drip Farm	120.00	20.00	100.00			
10/11/X2	4222	DN1	Daily News plc	360.00	60.00		300.00		
10/11/X2	4223	SM4	Standard Machines	2,400.00	400.00				2,000.00
				2,880.00	480.00	100.00	300.00	–	2,000.00

Document 3 receipt is not a purchase invoice, it is a receipt for cash paid.

Document 4 is a sales order to supply 20 cases of bottled juice. It is not a purchase invoice so would not appear in the purchases day book.

Activity 2

Purchases day book

Date	Invoice no	Code	Supplier	Total £	VAT £	Goods for resale £	Heat and light £	Postage and stationery £
01.01.X1	115	N2	Northern Electric	120.00	20.00		100.00	
	116	N3	Northern Gas	230.00	–		230.00	
02.01.X1	117	P1	Post Office Ltd	117.00	–			117.00
	118	N1	Northern Country	48.00	8.00	40.00		
03.01.X1	119	S1	South Gazette	360.00	60.00	300.00		
				875.00	88.00	340.00	330.00	117.00

Activity 3

	£
Goods for resale	340.00
Heat and light	330.00
Postage and stationery	117.00
VAT	88.00
Total	875.00

Purchases (goods for resale)

	£		£
PDB	340.00		

Heat and light

	£		£
PDB	330.00		

Postage and stationery

	£		£
PDB	117.00		

VAT

	£		£
PDB	88.00		

Purchases ledger control account

	£		£
		PDB	875.00

Accounting for purchases – summary: **Chapter 3**

Activity 4

(a) Cash payments book

Date	Details	Cheque no	Code	Total £	VAT £	PLCA £	Cash purchases £	Wages £
1/7	G Hobbs	34	PL14	325.46		325.46		
1/7	Purchases	35	GL03	68.40	11.40		57.00	
2/7	Purchases	36	GL03	50.59	8.43		42.16	
3/7	P Taylor	37	PL21	157.83		157.83		
3/7	S Dent	38	PL06	163.58		163.58		
4/7	K Smith	39	GL07	24.56				24.56
				790.42	19.83	646.87	99.16	24.56

Check that totals add across:

	£
VAT	19.83
Purchases ledger	646.87
Cash purchases	99.16
Wages	24.56
	790.42

(b) General ledger accounts

Purchases ledger control account

	£		£
CPB	646.87		

Cash purchases account

	£		£
CPB	99.16		

Wages account

	£		£
CPB	24.56		

VAT account

	£		£
CPB	19.83		

ICB LEVEL II: MANUAL BOOKKEEPING

(c) **Purchases ledger**

G Hobbs			PL14
	£		£
CPB	325.46		

P Taylor			PL21
	£		£
CPB	157.83		

S Dent			PL06
	£		£
CPB	163.58		

Activity 5

Cashbook – Credit side

Date	Details	VAT £	Bank £
30 Nov	Motor expenses	40	240
30 Nov	Wages		6,200
30 Nov	HMRC		4,750

What will be the FOUR entries in the general ledger?

General Ledger

Account name	Amount £	Debit / Credit
Motor expenses	200	Debit
VAT	40	Debit
Wages	6,200	Debit
VAT control account	4,750	Debit

Accounting for purchases – summary: **Chapter 3**

9 Test your knowledge

Workbook Activity 6

Given below is the cheque listing for a business for the week ending 12 March.

Cheque payment listing

Supplier	Code	Cheque number	Cheque amount £	Discount taken £
Homer Ltd	PL12	03648	168.70	5.06
Forker & Co	PL07	03649	179.45	5.38
Print Associates	PL08	03651	190.45	
ABG Ltd	PL02	03652	220.67	6.62
G Greg	PL19	03654	67.89	

Cash purchases were made for £342.00 and £200.40.

The cash purchases include VAT at standard rate 20%.

You are required to:

- enter the payments into the cash payments book and total each of the columns;
- post the totals to the general ledger accounts given;
- post the individual entries to the purchases ledger accounts given.

CASH PAYMENTS BOOK

Date	Details	Code	Discount £	Cash £	Bank £	VAT £	PLCA £	Cash purchases £	Other £

General ledger

Purchases ledger control account

	£			£
		5/3	Balance b/d	4,136.24

VAT account

	£			£
		5/3	Balance b/d	1,372.56

Purchases account

		£		£
5/3	Balance b/d	20,465.88		

Discounts received account

	£			£
		5/3	Balance b/d	784.56

Purchases ledger

ABG Ltd — PL02

	£			£
		5.3	Balance b/d	486.90

Forker & Co — PL07

	£			£
		5/3	Balance b/d	503.78

Print Associates — PL08

	£			£
		5/3	Balance b/d	229.56

Homer Ltd — PL12

	£			£
		5/3	Balance b/d	734.90

G Greg — PL19

	£			£
		5/3	Balance b/d	67.89

Workbook Activity 7

There are 7 payments to be entered into JR Ltd's cash payments book.

Cash payments

To JD & Co – £96.00 (inc VAT at 20%)

To LJ Ltd – £240.00 (inc VAT at 20%)

To MK Plc – £60.00 (inc VAT at 20%)

Cheque payments

To credit supplier TB Ltd – £68.89 (discount of £2.52 taken)

To credit supplier CF Ltd – £156.72 (discount of £3.16 taken)

Electricity – £90.00 (ignore VAT)

Stationery – £84.00 (inc VAT at 20%)

Required:

Write up the cash payments book given below; total each of the columns of the cash payments book and check that they cross cast.

Cash payments book

Narrative	Discount £	Cash £	Bank £	VAT £	Cash Purchases £	PLCA £	Expenses £

ICB LEVEL II: **MANUAL BOOKKEEPING**

Ledger balances and control accounts

Introduction

In this chapter we will be finding the correct ledger account balances by revising balancing off ledger accounts as the basis for drafting an initial trial balance (covered in Bookkeeping Level I and in chapter 1). In particular, we will be looking at ways of ensuring the accuracy of the balances for debtors (sales ledger control account) and creditors (purchases ledger control account).

CONTENTS

1. Balancing ledger accounts
2. Opening balances
3. Accounting for debtors
4. Sales ledger control account reconciliation
5. Accounting for creditors
6. Purchases ledger control account reconciliation
7. Cause of the difference
8. Batch control
9. The VAT control account

Ledger balances and control accounts: Chapter 4

1 Balancing ledger accounts

1.1 Introduction

The purpose of maintaining double entry ledger accounts is to provide information about the transactions and financial position of a business. Each type of transaction is gathered together and recorded in the appropriate ledger account, for example all sales are recorded in the sales account. Then at intervals it will be necessary to find the total of each of these types of transactions.

This is done by balancing each ledger account. This has been covered earlier in your studies but is worth revising here, by attempting Activity 1.

Activity 1

You are required to balance off the following ledger accounts:

Sales ledger control account

	£		£
SDB – invoices	5,426.23	CRB	3,226.56
		Discounts allowed	315.57

VAT account

	£		£
PDB	846.72	SDB	1,036.54

Sales account

	£		£
		SDB	2,667.45
		SDB	1,853.92

2 Opening balances

2.1 Introduction

If an account has a balance on it at the end of a period then it will have the same balance at the start of the next period. This is known as an opening balance.

2.2 Debit or credit?

The key to determining whether an opening balance on a ledger account is a debit or a credit is to understand the general rules for debit and credit balances. This can be expressed in the assessment either as a journal, or by entering the amount directly onto the ledger account.

2.3 Debit and credit balance rules

Let's revise the mnemonic DEAD/CLIC from chapter 1 which will help you determine if an entry should be made on the debit side or on the credit side of a ledger account.

Ledger account	
DEBIT	**CREDIT**
• Debtors	• Creditors
• Expenses	• Liabilities
• Assets	• Income
• Drawings	• Capital

Ledger balances and control accounts: **Chapter 4**

Example

You are told that the opening balance on the sales ledger control account is £33,600, the opening balance on the purchases account is £115,200 and the opening balance on the purchases ledger control account is £12,700.

You are required to enter these into the relevant ledger accounts.

Solution

Sales ledger control account

	£		£
Balance brought forward	33,600		

Purchases account

	£		£
Balance brought forward	115,200		

Purchases ledger control account

	£		£
		Balance brought forward	12,700

Assets and expenses normally have opening debit balances. Liabilities and income normally have opening credit balances.

2.4 Journals

A journal entry is a written instruction to the bookkeeping to enter a double entry into the general ledger accounts. It is shown below in its most basic form, although the journal voucher itself is explained later in this chapter.

Example

Record the journal entries needed in the general ledger to account for the following balances.

Sales ledger control account	33,600
Purchases	115,200
Purchases ledger control account	12,700
Sales	138,240
Rent and Rates	2,140

Solution

Sales ledger control account	33,600	Debit
Purchases	115,200	Debit
Purchases ledger control account	12,700	Credit
Sales	138,240	Credit
Rent and Rates	2,140	Debit

The total of the debit entries should equal the total of the credit entries.

Activity 2

Would the balances on the following accounts be debit or credit balances?

(a) Sales account
(b) Discounts allowed account
(c) Discounts received account
(d) Wages expense account

Activity 3

The following are the opening balances for a new business. Complete the journal to record these balances.

Account name	Amount £	Debit / Credit
Bank overdraft	6,975	
Cash	275	
VAT payable	2,390	
Motor vehicles	10,500	
Plant and machinery	25,700	
Loan from bank	12,000	
Motor expenses	1,540	
Rent and rates	2,645	
Miscellaneous expenses	725	

Ledger balances and control accounts: Chapter 4

Activity 4

The following transactions all occurred on 1 December 20X1 and have been entered into the relevant books of prime entry (given below). However, no entries have yet been made into the ledger system. VAT has been calculated at a rate of 20%.

Purchases day book

Date	Details	Invoice no	Total £	VAT £	Purchases £	Stationery £
20X1						
1 Dec	Bailey Limited	T151	240	40	200	
1 Dec	Byng & Company	10965	960	160	800	
1 Dec	Office Supplies Ltd	34565	336	56		280
1 Dec	O'Connell Frames	FL013	5,040	840	4,200	
	Totals		6,576	1,096	5,200	280

Purchases returns day book

Date	Details	Invoice no	Total £	VAT £	Purchases returns £	Stationery £
20X1						
1 Dec	O'Connell Frames	CO11	2,160	360	1,800	
1 Dec	Office Supplies Ltd	CR192	48	8		40
	Totals		2,208	368	1,800	40

Sales day book

Date	Details	Invoice no	Total £	VAT £	Sales £
20X1					
1 Dec	Bentley Brothers	H621	1,680	280	1,400
1 Dec	J & H Limited	H622	4,320	720	3,600
1 Dec	Furniture Galore	H623	4,800	800	4,000
1 Dec	The Sofa Shop	H624	2,640	440	2,200
	Totals		13,440	2,240	11,200

ICB LEVEL II: MANUAL BOOKKEEPING

Opening balances

The following are some of the balances in the accounting records and are all relevant to you at the start of the day on 1 December 20X1:

	£
Credit Suppliers	
Bailey Limited	11,750
Byng & Company	1,269
Office Supplies Limited	4,230
O'Connell Frames	423
PLCA	82,006
SLCA	180,312
Purchases	90,563
Sales	301,492
Purchases returns	306
Stationery	642
Discounts received	50
VAT (credit balance)	17,800

Receipts on 1 December 20X1

	Total £
Lili Chang (cash sale including VAT)	528
Bentley Brothers (credit customer)	5,875

Cheque issued

	Total £
Bailey Limited (in full settlement of debt of £819)	799

Task 1

Enter the opening balances listed above into the following accounts, blanks of which are provided on the following pages:

Task 2

Using the data shown above, enter all the relevant transactions into the accounts in the purchases ledger and general ledger. Entries to the sales ledger for debtors are not required.

Ledger balances and control accounts: Chapter 4

Task 3

Enter the receipts and payments shown above into the cash book given on the following pages.

Task 4

Transfer any relevant sums from the cash book into the purchases ledger for creditors and general ledger.

Task 5

Balance off all of the accounts and the cash book, showing clearly the balances carried down. The opening cash balance was £3,006. Find the closing balance on the cash book.

Tasks 1, 2, 4 and 5

Purchases ledger

Bailey Limited

£	£

Byng & Company

£	£

Office supplies Limited

£	£

O'Connell Frames

£	£

General ledger

PLCA

	£		£

SLCA

	£		£

Purchases

	£		£

Sales

	£		£

Purchases returns

	£		£

Stationery

	£		£

Ledger balances and control accounts: Chapter 4

Discounts received

£		£

VAT

£		£

Tasks 3, 4 and 5

Cash receipts book

Date	Narrative	Total £	VAT £	SLCA £	Cash sales £	Discount allowed £

Cash payments book

Date	Details	Cheque no	Code	Total £	VAT £	PLCA £	Cash purchases £	Other £	Discounts received £

3 Accounting for debtors

3.1 Sales ledger control account

Within the general ledger the total amount outstanding from debtors is shown in the sales ledger control account.

The totals of credit sales (from the sales day book), returns from customers (from the sales returns day book) and cash received and discounts (from the analysed cash book) are posted to this account. This account therefore shows the total debtors outstanding. It does not give details about individual customers' balances. This is available in the sales ledger for debtors.

However, as both records are compiled from the same sources, the total balances on the customers' individual accounts should equal the outstanding balance on the control account at any time.

3.2 Double entry system

The double entry system operates as follows.

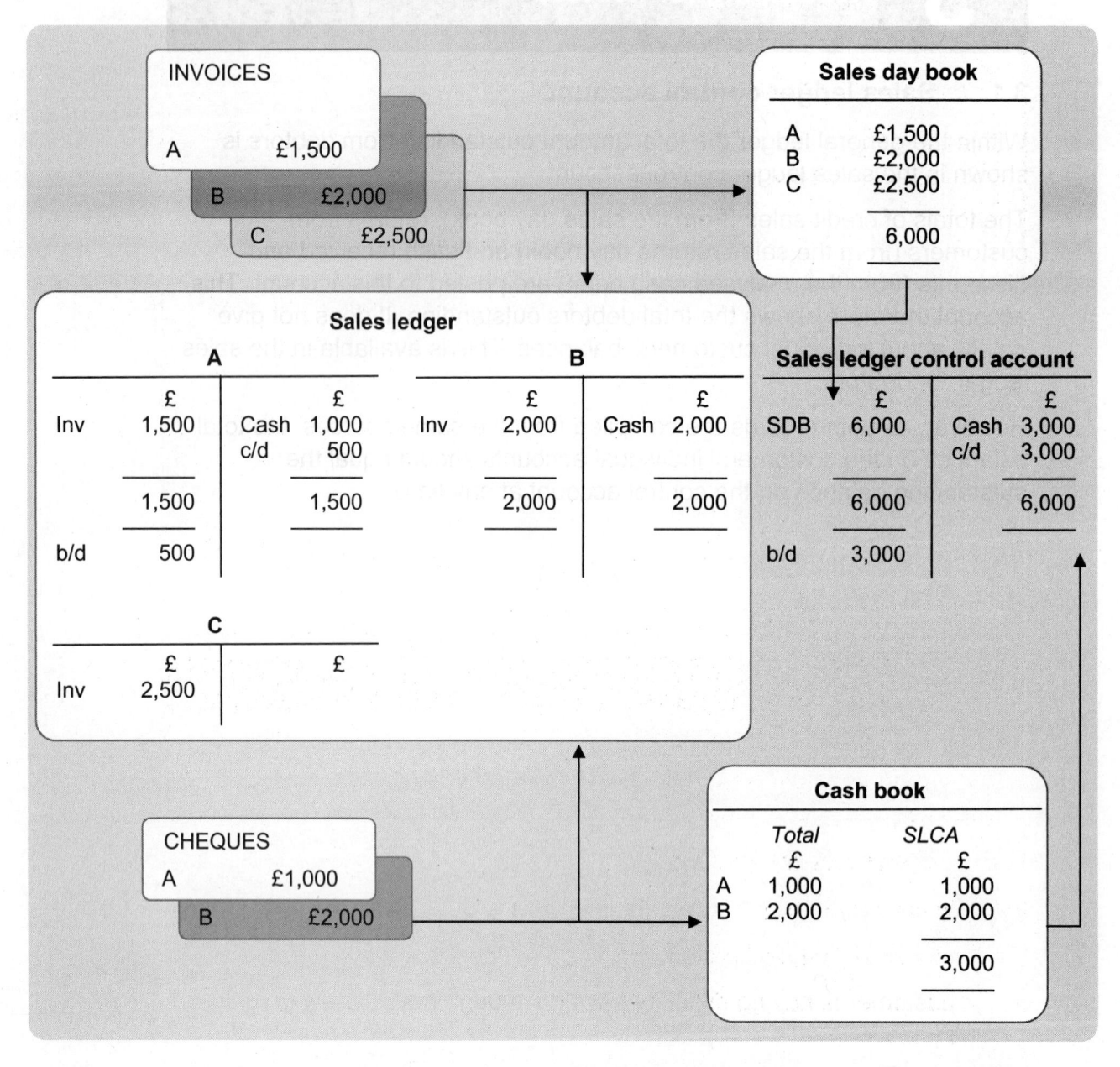

INVOICES
- A £1,500
- B £2,000
- C £2,500

Sales day book
	£
A	1,500
B	2,000
C	2,500
	6,000

Sales ledger

A
	£		£
Inv	1,500	Cash	1,000
		c/d	500
	1,500		1,500
b/d	500		

B
	£		£
Inv	2,000	Cash	2,000
	2,000		2,000

C
	£		£
Inv	2,500		

Sales ledger control account
	£		£
SDB	6,000	Cash	3,000
		c/d	3,000
	6,000		6,000
b/d	3,000		

CHEQUES
- A £1,000
- B £2,000

Cash book
	Total £	SLCA £
A	1,000	1,000
B	2,000	2,000
		3,000

Notice that the remaining balance on the control account (£3,000) is equal to the sum of the remaining balances on the individual debtors' accounts (A £500 + C £2,500).

If all of the accounting entries have been made correctly then the balance on the sales ledger control account should equal the total of the balances on each of the individual debtors' accounts in the sales ledger.

3.3 Proforma sales ledger control account

A sales ledger control account normally appears like this.

Sales ledger control account			
	£		£
Balance b/d	X	Returns per sales day book	X
Sales per sales day book	X	* Cash from debtors	X
		* Discounts allowed	X
		Bad debt written off	X
		Contra entry	X
		Balance c/d	X
	X		X
Balance b/d			

* Per cash receipts book

3.4 Bad debts

Definition

A bad debt is a debt which is not likely to be received; it is therefore not prudent for the business to consider this debt as an asset.

3.5 Reasons for bad debts

A business may decide that a debt is bad for a number of reasons:

- customer is in liquidation – no cash will be received;
- customer is having difficulty paying although not officially in liquidation;
- customer disputes the debt and refuses to pay all or part of it.

Ledger balances and control accounts: Chapter 4

3.6 Accounting for bad debts

The business must make an adjustment to write off the bad debt from the customer's account in the sales ledger and to write it off in the general ledger. The double entry in the general ledger is:

DR   Bad debt expense

    CR   Sales ledger control account

Notice that the bad debt becomes an expense of the business. Writing off bad debts decreases the profits made by a business, but is not deducted from sales. The sale was made in the anticipation of receiving the money but, if the debt is not to be received, this does not negate the sale it is just an added expense of the business.

The bad debt must also be written off in the individual debtor's account in the sales ledger by crediting the customer's account as this amount is not going to be received.

When you invoiced the customer you will have recorded the VAT and paid it to HMRC. Once the debt is more than 6 months old and it has been determined that the customer is not going to pay you, you can reclaim that VAT back from HMRC.

DR   Bad debt expense   Net amount
DR   VAT control account   VAT amount
    CR   Sales ledger control account   Gross amount

3.7 Contra entries

A further type of adjustment that may be required to sales ledger and purchases ledger control accounts is a contra entry.

3.8 Why a contra entry is required

In some instances a business will be both a debtor and a creditor of another business as it both buys from the business and sells to it. If this is the case then there will be money owed to the business and money owing from it. This can be simplified by making an adjustment known as a contra entry.

Example

James Associates has a customer, X Brothers. X Brothers also sells goods to James Associates. Therefore X Brothers is both a debtor and a creditor of James Associates. The subsidiary ledger accounts of James Associates show the following position:

Sales ledger – debtors

X Brothers

	£		£
Balance b/d	250		

Purchases ledger – creditors

X Brothers

	£		£
		Balance b/d	100

The problem here is that X Brothers owes James Associates £250 and is owed £100 by James Associates. If both parties are in agreement it makes more sense to net these two amounts off and to say that X Brothers owes James Associates just £150. This is achieved in accounting terms by a contra entry.

Solution

Step 1 Take the smaller of the two amounts and debit the purchases ledger account for the creditor and credit the sales ledger account for the debtor with this amount.

Sales ledger – debtors

X Brothers

	£		£
Balance b/d	250	Contra	100

Purchases ledger – creditors

X Brothers

	£		£
Contra	100	Balance b/d	100

Ledger balances and control accounts: Chapter 4

Step 2 Balance off the accounts in the subsidiary ledgers.

Sales ledger – debtors

X Brothers

	£		£
Balance b/d	250	Contra	100
		Balance c/d	150
	___		___
	250		250
	___		___
Balance b/d	150		

Purchases ledger – creditors

X Brothers

	£		£
Contra	100	Balance b/d	100
	___		___

This now shows that X Brothers owes £150 to James Associates and is owed nothing by James Associates.

Step 3 The double entry must also be carried out in the general ledger accounts. This is:

    DR Purchases ledger control account

        CR Sales ledger control account

When a contra entry is made you must remember not just to deal with the entries in the subsidiary ledgers but also to put through the double entry in the general ledger accounts, the sales ledger and purchases ledger control accounts.

3.9 General ledger and sales ledger

We will now return to the relationship between the sales ledger control account in the general ledger and the individual accounts for debtors in the sales ledger.

Example

James has been trading for two months. He has four credit customers. James is not registered for VAT. Here is the day book for the first two months:

Sales day book (SDB)

Date	Customer	Invoice	£
02.2.X4	Peter Brown	01	50.20
05.2.X4	Ian Smith	02	80.91
07.2.X4	Sid Parsons	03	73.86
23.2.X4	Eva Lane	04	42.30
	Total		247.27
09.3.X4	Ian Smith	05	23.96
15.3.X4	Sid Parsons	06	34.72
20.3.X4	Peter Brown	07	12.60
24.3.X4	Sid Parsons	08	93.25
31.3.X4	Total		164.53

Here is the receipts side of the analysed cash book for March 20X4 (no cash was received from debtors in February).

Cash receipts book (CRB)

Date	Narrative	Total £	Cash sales £	Sales ledger £	Rent £
01.3.X4	Peter Brown	50.20		50.20	
03.3.X4	Clare Jones	63.80	63.80		
04.3.X4	Molly Dell	110.00			110.00
12.3.X4	Sid Parsons	50.00		50.00	
13.3.X4	Emily Boyd	89.33	89.33		
20.3.X4	Frank Field	92.68	92.68		
25.3.X4	Eva Lane	42.30		42.30	
31.3.X4	Total	498.31	245.81	142.50	110.00

We will write up the sales ledger and the sales ledger control account and compare the balances.

Solution

Sales ledger – debtors

Peter Brown

			£				£
02.2.X4	01		50.20	28.2.X4	c/d		50.20
			50.20				50.20
01.3.X4	b/d		50.20	01.3.X4	Cash		50.20
20.3.X4	07		12.60	31.3.X4	c/d		12.60
			62.80				62.80
01.4.X4	b/d		12.60				

Eva Lane

			£				£
23.2.X4	04		42.30	28.2.X4	c/d		42.30
			42.30				42.30
01.3.X4	b/d		42.30	25.3.X4	Cash		42.30

Sid Parsons

			£				£
07.2.X4	03		73.86	28.2.X4	c/d		73.86
			73.86				73.86
01.3.X4	b/d		73.86	12.3.X4	Cash		50.00
15.3.X4	06		34.72	31.3.X4	c/d		151.83
24.3.X4	08		93.25				
			201.83				201.83
01.4.X4	b/d		151.83				

Ian Smith

		£			£
05.2.X4	02	80.91	28.2.X4	c/d	80.91
		80.91			80.91
01.3.X4	b/d	80.91	31.3.X4	c/d	104.87
09.3.X4	05	23.96			
		104.87			104.87
01.4.X4	b/d	104.87			

Sales ledger control account

		£			£
28.2.X4	SDB	247.27	28.2.X4	c/d	247.27
		247.27			247.27
01.3.X4	b/d	247.27	31.3.X4	CRB	142.50
31.3.X4	SDB	164.53	31.3.X4	c/d	269.30
		411.80			411.80
01.4.X4	b/d	269.30			

Let us compare balances at 31 March 20X4.

Subsidiary ledger – debtors

	£
Peter Brown	12.60
Eva Lane	–
Sid Parsons	151.83
Ian Smith	104.87
	269.30
Sales ledger control account	269.30

As the double entry has been correctly carried out, the total of the balances on the individual debtors' accounts in the sales ledger is equal to the balance on the sales ledger control account.

Ledger balances and control accounts: **Chapter 4**

4 Sales ledger control account reconciliation

4.1 Introduction

Comparing the sales ledger control account balance with the total of the sales ledger accounts is a form of internal control. The reconciliation should be performed on a regular basis by the sales ledger clerk and reviewed and approved by an independent person.

If the total of the balances on the sales ledger do not equal the balance on the sales ledger control account then an error or errors have been made in either the general ledger or sales ledger, and these must be discovered and corrected.

4.2 Journal entries

We saw earlier how a journal can be used to enter opening balances to start a new period of accounts. Journal entries are also used for unusual items that do not appear in the primary records, or for the correction of errors or making of adjustments to ledger accounts.

A typical journal entry to write off a bad debt is shown below:

JOURNAL ENTRY		No: 06671		
Prepared by:	P Freer			
Authorised by:	P Simms			
Date:	3 October 20X2			
Narrative:				
To write off bad debt from L C Hamper				
Account	Code	Debit	Credit	
Bad debts expense	GL28	102.00		
Debtors' control	GL06		102.00	
TOTALS		102.00	102.00	

Authorisation

Description of why double entry is necessary

Double entry

Sequential journal number

Equal totals as journal must balance

116   **KAPLAN** PUBLISHING

Example

The total sales for the month was posted from the sales day book as £4,657.98 instead of £4,677.98. This must be corrected using a journal entry.

Solution

The journal entry to correct this error will be as follows:

JOURNAL ENTRY		No: 97		
Prepared by:	A Graimm			
Authorised by:	L R Ridinghood			
Date:	23.7.X3			
Narrative:				
To correct error in posting from SDB				
Account		Code	Debit	Credit
Sales ledger control		GL11	20	
Sales		GL56		20
TOTALS			20	20

The adjustment required is to increase debtors and sales by £20 therefore a debit to sales ledger control and a credit to sales is needed.

4.3 Adjustments in the subsidiary ledger

Adjustments in the subsidiary ledger do not need to be shown in a journal entry. Journal entries are only required for adjustments to the general ledger.

These adjustments should be recorded in memorandum form, with proper authorisation.

Ledger balances and control accounts: Chapter 4

4.4 Procedure for a sales ledger control account reconciliation

(1) The balances on the sales ledger accounts for debtors are extracted, listed and totalled.

(2) The sales ledger control account is balanced.

(3) If the two figures differ, then the reasons for the difference must be investigated.

Reasons may include the following:
- An error in the casting of the day book. (The total is posted to the control account whereas the individual invoices are posted to the individual accounts and, therefore, if the total is incorrect, a difference will arise.)
- A transposition error (the figures are switched around, e.g. £87 posted as £78) which could be made in posting either:
    (a) to the control account (the total figure); or
    (b) to the individual accounts (the individual transactions).
- A casting error in the cash book column relating to the control account. (The total is posted.)
- A balance omitted from the list of individual accounts.
- A credit balance on an individual account in the sales ledger for debtors which has automatically and wrongly been assumed to be a debit balance.

(4) Differences which are errors in the control account should be corrected in the control account.

(5) Differences which are errors in the individual accounts should be corrected by adjusting the list of balances and, of course, the account concerned.

Activity 5

Would the following errors cause a difference to occur between the balance of the sales ledger control account and the total of the balances in the sales ledger?

(a) The total column of the sales day book was overcast by £100.

(b) In error H Lambert's account in the sales ledger was debited with £175 instead of M Lambert's account.

(c) An invoice for £76 was recorded in the sales day book as £67.

ICB LEVEL II: MANUAL BOOKKEEPING

Example

The balance on the sales ledger control account for a business at 31 March 20X3 is £14,378.37. The total of the list of sales ledger balances for debtors is £13,935.37.

The difference has been investigated and the following errors have been identified:

- the sales day book was overcast by £1,000;
- a credit note for £150 was entered into an individual debtor's account as an invoice;
- discounts allowed of £143 were correctly accounted for in the sales ledger but were not entered into the general ledger accounts;
- a credit balance on one debtor's account of £200 was mistakenly listed as a debit balance when totalling the individual debtor accounts in the sales ledger.

Prepare the reconciliation between the balance on the sales ledger control account and the total of the individual balances on the sales ledger accounts.

Solution

Step 1 Amend the sales ledger control account for any errors that have been made.

Sales ledger control account

	£		£
Balance b/d	14,378.37	SDB overcast	1,000.00
		Discounts allowed	143.00
		Balance c/d	13,235.37
	14,378.37		14,378.37
Balance b/d	13,235.37		

Ledger balances and control accounts: Chapter 4

Step 2 Correct the total of the list of balances in the sales ledger.

		£
Original total		13,935.37
Less:	Credit note entered as invoice (2 × 150)	(300.00)
	Credit balance entered as debit balance (2 × 200)	(400.00)
		13,235.37

Activity 6

The balance on Diana's sales ledger control account at 31 December 20X6 was £15,450. The balances on the individual accounts in the sales ledger have been extracted and total £15,705. On investigation the following errors are discovered:

(a) a debit balance of £65 has been omitted from the list of balances;

(b) discounts totalling £70 have been recorded in the individual accounts but not in the control account;

(c) the sales day book was 'overcast' by £200;

(d) a contra entry for £40 has not been entered into the control account; and

(e) an invoice for £180 was recorded correctly in the sales day book but was posted to the debtors' individual account as £810.

Prepare the sales ledger control account reconciliation.

5 Accounting for creditors

5.1 Introduction

As we have previously seen, the total amount payable to creditors is recorded in the general ledger in the purchases ledger control account. The total of credit purchases from the purchases day book, returns to suppliers from the purchases returns day book and the total payments to creditors and discounts received taken from the cash payments book are all posted to this account.

The purchases ledger control account shows the total amount that is payable to creditors but it does not show the amount owed to individual suppliers. This information is provided by the purchases ledger which contains an account for each individual creditor.

Each individual invoice from the purchases day book and each individual credit note from the purchases returns day book is posted to the relevant creditor's account in the purchases ledger. Similarly each individual payment to creditors and discounts received are posted from the cash payments book to the individual creditors' accounts in the purchases ledger.

5.2 Relationship between the purchases ledger control account and the balances in the purchases ledger

The information that is being posted to the purchases ledger control account in total and to the individual accounts in the purchases ledger as individual entries are from the same sources and should in total be the same figures.

Therefore, just as with the sales ledger control account, if the double entry and entries to the purchases ledger have been correctly carried out then the balance on the purchases ledger control account should be equal to the total of the list of balances on the individual creditors' accounts in the purchases ledger.

Ledger balances and control accounts: **Chapter 4**

5.3 Proforma purchases ledger control account

A purchases ledger control account normally appears like this.

Purchases ledger control account			
	£		£
Payments to suppliers per analysed cash book		Balance b/d	X
Cash	X	Purchases per purchases day book	X
Discount received	X		
Returns per purchases returns day book	X		
Contra entry	X		
Balance c/d	X		
	X		X
		Balance b/d	X

If all of the accounting entries have been correctly made then the balance on this purchases ledger control account should equal the total of the balances on the individual supplier accounts in the purchases ledger.

6 Purchases ledger control account reconciliation

6.1 Introduction

At each month end the purchases ledger clerk must reconcile the purchases ledger control account and the purchases ledger, just as the sales ledger clerk performed the sales ledger control account reconciliation.

Remember that as well as investigating and discovering the differences, the control account and the individual accounts in the purchases ledger must also be amended for any errors.

6.2 Adjustments to the purchases ledger control account

Any corrections or adjustments made to the purchases ledger control account can be documented as a journal entry.

Example

The total purchases for the month were posted from the purchases day book as £2,547.98 instead of £2,457.98. Prepare a journal to correct this error.

Solution

The journal entry to correct this error will be as follows:

JOURNAL ENTRY		No: 253		
Prepared by:	P Charming			
Authorised by:	U Sister			
Date:	29.8.X5			
Narrative:				
To correct error in posting to creditors' control account				
Account		Code	Debit	Credit
Purchase ledger control		GL56	90	
Purchases		GL34		90
TOTALS			90	90

In this case both PLCA and purchases need to be reduced by £90. Therefore a debit to the purchases ledger control and a credit to purchases are required.

6.3 Adjustments in the purchases ledger

Adjustments in the purchases ledger do not need to be documented in a journal entry. Journal entries are only required for adjustments to the general ledger.

Ledger balances and control accounts: Chapter 4

Example

The balance on the purchases ledger control account for a business at 30 June was £12,309. The total of the balances on the individual creditors' accounts in the purchases ledger was £19,200. VAT is at 20%.

The following errors were also found:

- the cash payments book had been undercast by £20;
- an invoice from Thomas Ltd, a credit supplier, for £2,400 was correctly entered in the purchases ledger but had been missed out of the addition of the total in the purchases day book;
- an invoice from Fred Singleton for £2,000 plus VAT was included in his individual account in the purchases ledger at the net amount;
- an invoice from Horace Shades for £6,000 was entered into the individual account in the purchases ledger twice;
- the same invoice is for £6,000 plus VAT but the VAT had not been included in the purchases ledger;
- returns to Horace Shades of £111 had been omitted from the purchases ledger.

You are required to reconcile the purchases ledger control account with the balances on the purchases ledger accounts at 30 June.

Solution

Step 1 Amend the purchases ledger control account to show the correct balance.

Purchases ledger control account

	£		£
Undercast of CPB	20	Balance b/d	12,309
Balance c/d	14,689	Invoice omitted from PDB	2,400
	14,709		14,709
		Amended balance b/d	14,689

Step 2 Correct the total of the list of purchases ledger balances.

	£
Original total	19,200
Add: Fred Singleton VAT	400
Less: Horace Shades invoice included twice	(6,000)
Add: Horace Shades VAT	1,200
Less: Horace Shades returns	(111)
Amended total of list of balances	14,689

Remember that invoices from suppliers should be included in the individual suppliers' accounts in the purchases ledger at the gross amount, including VAT.

Activity 7

How would each of the following be dealt with in the purchases ledger control account reconciliation?

(a) A purchase invoice for £36 from P Swift was credited to P Short's account in the subsidiary ledger.

(b) A purchase invoice for £96 not entered in the purchases day book.

(c) An undercast of £20 in the total column of the purchases day book.

(d) A purchase invoice from Short & Long for £42 entered as £24 in the purchases day book.

7 Cause of the difference

You may sometimes be asked to say what has caused the difference between the control account and the list of balances. If you are asked to do this, the difference will usually be caused by just one error.

An example will illustrate this.

Example

XYZ Ltd has made the following entries in the sales ledger control account.

	£
Opening balance 1 April 20X7	49,139
Credit sales posted from the sales day book	35,000
Discounts allowed	328
Bad debt written off	127
Cash received from debtors	52,359

The list of balances from the sales ledger totals £31,579.

(a) Calculate the closing balance on the SLCA at 31 April 20X7.

(b) State one reason for the difference between the SLCA balance and the total of the list of balances.

Solution

(a) The SLCA

Sales ledger control account

	£		£
Balance b/d	49,139	Discount allowed	328
SDB – sales	35,000	Bad debt	127
		Cash received	52,359
		Balance c/d	31,325
	84,139		84,139

(b) Total of sales ledger balances   31,579
    Balance of SLCA at 30 April 20X7   31,325
                                                 ──────
    Difference   254
                                                 ──────

Note: You have to look for the fairly obvious clues and also make some assumptions

(i) It's reasonable to assume that the control account is correct – it may not be, so be careful.

(ii) Calculate the difference and determine whether the list total is larger than the SLCA balance or vice versa.

(iii) See if one of the figures given in the question is the same as the difference or double the difference.

If a figure given is the same as the difference then it is likely that a number has been left out of an account.

If a figure given is double the difference then it is likely that a number has been entered on the wrong side of an account, or possibly entered twice.

- In the above question, the difference is £254.
- The total of the list of ledger balances is bigger than the SLCA balance.
- £254 is not a figure given in the question but the amount £127 is given and the difference is twice this figure.

One possible reason for this is that the bad debt write off (£127) was entered on the debit side of a ledger account in the sales ledger – that would have made the total of the list £254 larger. Of course there are a million possible reasons – perhaps there was an invoice for £254 and it was entered twice in a sales ledger account – that would have caused the difference, but the assessor is looking for something obvious in the figures given to you – not some speculative reason.

8 Batch control

8.1 Introduction

Throughout this chapter we have been dealing with control accounts in the general ledger and individual debtors and creditors accounts in the subsidiary ledgers. We have noted that there will sometimes be a discrepancy between the balance on the control account in the general ledger and the total of the balances in the subsidiary ledgers. Sometimes this difference is caused by correctly entered items that can be reconciled. However, sometimes the difference is caused by an error in the entering of the data. These latter errors can be eliminated or minimised by the use of batch control.

8.2 How a lack of batch control causes problems

Consider the situation where a small business has received 40 cheques from debtors and is going to post these into the accounts for the week. A typical system might be as follows.

(a) John writes the cheques into the total and SLCA columns of the analysed cash received book. John then totals the cash received book for the week and posts the total of the SLCA column to the sales ledger control account. He then writes out the bank paying-in slip and pays the cheques into the bank.

(b) George writes up the individual accounts in the sales ledger from the entries in the main cash book.

The above is a fairly typical system and of course all sorts of things can go wrong.

(a) A cheque could go missing and not be paid into the bank, causing a discrepancy between the entries in the cash book and the bank statement.

(b) John could write the values of one or more of the cheques incorrectly in the cash book, causing the cash book total and the sales ledger control account entry to be incorrect.

(c) George could also write the values of the cheques incorrectly in the sales ledger.

8.3 How batch control helps reduce errors

To improve the system the company employs a system of batch control.

(a) Before the cheques are entered in the cash book, a person unconnected with entering the cheques in the books (Jemima) will total the cheques using a computer spreadsheet such as Excel. She will not disclose the total of the cheques.

(b) John will now write the cheques into the cash book and total the cash book as before. He will then compare his total with Jemima's total. If the totals are different, Jemima and John will both check their work until they can agree on a total. This clearly minimises any errors that are likely to be made when entering the cheques in the books of account.

(c) George will write up the sales ledger as before. As a further check, the sales ledger could be passed to another person who would total the entries that George has just made and then compare that total with Jemima's total.

As you can see, by batching the cheques together and producing a total of their value before any entries are made in the books, the company has an excellent check on the accuracy of the entries that are made.

Of course nothing is foolproof. The accountants could enter incorrect amounts in the ledger which compensate for each other thereby still giving the correct total. Alternatively, a cheque might be lost thereby giving an incorrect banking total. But at least the possibility of human error is reduced.

9 The VAT control account

Within Level I we learned about the operation of VAT to enable us to calculate the amount we would charge on our sales, and the amounts we would reclaim on our purchases. We now need to consider how these transactions would look within the third control account within the general ledger, the VAT control account, and to appreciate that it is the difference between these two amounts that must be paid to or received from HMRC.

Ledger balances and control accounts: Chapter 4

Example

The following VAT figures have been extracted from your day books. Complete the VAT control account, and find the balance.

Sales day book	22,436
Sales returns day book	674
Purchases day book	15,327

Solution

VAT account

Details	Amount £	Details	Amount £
Sales returns (SRDB)	674	Sales (SDB)	22,436
Purchases (PDB)	15,327		
Balance c/d	6,435		
	22,436		22,436

The VAT from the sales daybook is payable to HMRC, whereas the VAT from the sales returns and the purchases daybooks can be reclaimed. It is the net effect that is payable to HMRC.

Businesses are required to complete a VAT return, usually on a quarterly basis, to show the amount payable to or reclaimed from HMRC. We look at the completion of a VAT return later in this study text.

Activity 8

The following VAT figures have been extracted from the books of prime entry.

Sales day book	60,200
Sales returns day book	980
Purchases day book	34,300
Purchases returns day book	2,660
Cash receipts book	112

(a) What will be the entries in the VAT control account to record the VAT transactions in the quarter

(b) The VAT return has been completed and shows an amount owing from HMRC of £27,692. Is the VAT return correct?

VAT account

Details	Amount £	Details	Amount £

10 Summary

We started this chapter with a revision of balancing accounts and extended this to entering opening balances in the ledger accounts. Then the chapter moved on to aspects of control and the use of control accounts and control account reconciliations in order to determine the accuracy of the figures in the ledger accounts. The reconciliations, sales ledger and purchases ledger are important and you should ensure that you are happy with the subject matter in this chapter.

Answers to chapter activities

Activity 1

Sales ledger control account

	£		£
SDB – invoices	5,426.23	CRB	3,226.56
		Discounts allowed	315.57
		Balance c/d	1,884.10
	5,426.23		5,426.23
Balance b/d	1,884.10		

VAT account

	£		£
PDB	846.72	SDB	1,036.54
Balance c/d	189.82		
	1,036.54		1,036.54
		Balance b/d	189.82

Sales account

	£		£
		SDB	2,667.45
Balance c/d	4,521.37	SDB	1,853.92
	4,521.37		4,521.37
		Balance b/d	4,521.37

Activity 2

(a) Credit balance
(b) Debit balance
(c) Credit balance
(d) Debit balance

Activity 3

Account name	Amount £	Debit / Credit
Bank overdraft	6,975	Credit
Cash	275	Debit
VAT payable	2,390	Credit
Motor vehicles	10,500	Debit
Plant and machinery	25,700	Debit
Loan from bank	12,000	Credit
Motor expenses	1,540	Debit
Rent and rates	2,645	Debit
Miscellaneous expenses	725	Debit

Activity 4

Purchases ledger

Bailey Limited

		£			£
01 Dec	Bank	799	01 Dec	Balance b/d	11,750
01 Dec	Discount received	20	01 Dec	Purchases	240
01 Dec	Balance c/d	11,171			
		11,990			11,990
			02 Dec	Balance b/d	11,171

Ledger balances and control accounts: Chapter 4

Byng & Company

	£			£
		01 Dec	Balance b/d	1,269
01 Dec Balance c/d	2,229	01 Dec	Purchases	960
	2,229			2,229
		02 Dec	Balance b/d	2,229

Office Supplies Limited

	£			£
01 Dec Purchases returns	48	01 Dec	Balance b/d	4,230
01 Dec Balance c/d	4,518	01 Dec	Purchases	336
	4,566			4,566
		02 Dec	Balance b/d	4,518

O'Connell Frames

	£			£
01 Dec Purchases returns	2,160	01 Dec	Balance b/d	423
01 Dec Balance c/d	3,303	01 Dec	Purchases	5,040
	5,463			5,463
		02 Dec	Balance b/d	3,303

General ledger

PLCA

	£			£
01 Dec Purchases returns	2,208	01 Dec	Balance b/d	82,006
01 Dec Bank	799	01 Dec	Purchases	6,576
01 Dec Discounts received	20			
01 Dec Balance c/d	85,555			
	88,582			88,582
		02 Dec	Balance b/d	85,555

SLCA

		£			£
01 Dec	Balance b/d	180,312	01 Dec	Bank	5,875
01 Dec	Sales	13,440	01 Dec	Balance c/d	187,877
		193,752			193,752
02 Dec	Balance b/d	187,877			

Purchases

		£			£
01 Dec	Balance b/d	90,563			
01 Dec	PLCA	5,200	01 Dec	Balance c/d	95,763
		95,763			95,763
02 Dec	Balance b/d	95,763			

Sales

		£			£
			01 Dec	Balance b/d	301,492
			01 Dec	SLCA	11,200
01 Dec	Balance c/d	313,132	01 Dec	Bank	440
		313,132			313,132
			02 Dec	Balance b/d	313,132

Purchases returns

		£			£
			01 Dec	Balance b/d	306
01 Dec	Balance c/d	2,106	01 Dec	PLCA	1,800
		2,106			2,106
			02 Dec	Balance b/d	2,106

Ledger balances and control accounts: Chapter 4

Stationery

		£			£
01 Dec	Balance b/d	642	01 Dec	PLCA	40
01 Dec	PLCA	280	01 Dec	Balance c/d	882
		922			922
02 Dec	Balance b/d	882			

Discounts received

		£			£
			01 Dec	Balance b/d	50
01 Dec	Balance c/d	70	01 Dec	Creditors	20
		70			70
			02 Dec	Balance b/d	70

VAT

		£			£
01 Dec	PLCA	1,096	01 Dec	Balance b/d	17,800
			01 Dec	PLCA	368
			01 Dec	SLCA	2,240
01 Dec	Balance c/d	19,400	01 Dec	Bank	88
		20,496			20,496
			02 Dec	Balance b/d	19,400

Cash receipts book

Date	Narrative	Total £	VAT £	SLCA £	Other £	Discount £
20X1						
01 Dec	Lili Chang	528	88		440	
01 Dec	Bentley Brothers	5,875		5,875		
		6,403	88	5,875	440	–

NB: The VAT rate in use is 20%

ICB LEVEL II: MANUAL BOOKKEEPING

Cash payments book

Date	Details	Cheque no	Code	Total £	VAT £	PLCA £	Cash purchases £	Other £	Discount received £
20X1 01 Dec	Bailey Ltd			799	–	799	–	–	20

	£
Opening balance	3,006
Add: Receipts	6,403
Less:	(799)
Closing balance	8,610

Activity 5

(a) Yes, because the correct detailed individual entries in the sales day book are posted to the sales ledger accounts and the incorrect total used in the control account.

(b) No, because the arithmetical balance is correct even though the wrong account is used. No imbalance would occur.

(c) No, because the total posted to the SLCA will include the £67 and the entry in the sales ledger will also be for £67. They are both wrong.

Activity 6

- We must first look for those errors which will mean that the sales ledger control account is incorrectly stated. The control account is then adjusted as follows:

Sales ledger control account

	£		£
Balance b/d	15,450	Discounts allowed	70
		Overcast of sales day book	200
		Contra with PLCA	40
		Adjusted balance c/d	15,140
	15,450		15,450
Balance b/d	15,140		

- We must then look for errors in the total of the individual balances per the sales ledger. The extracted list of balances must be adjusted as follows:

	£
Original total of list of balances	15,705
Debit balance omitted	65
Transposition error (810 – 180)	(630)
	15,140

- As can be seen, the adjusted total of the list of balances now agrees with the balance per the control account.

Activity 7

(a) This does not affect the reconciliation. A correction would simply be made in the subsidiary ledger.

(b) This must be adjusted for in the purchase ledger control account and in the purchases ledger.

(c) This is just an adjustment to the purchase ledger control account.

(d) This will require alteration in both the control account and the purchases ledger.

Activity 8

(a) **VAT account**

Details	Amount £	Details	Amount £
Sales Returns (SRDB)	980	Sales (SDB)	60,200
Purchases (PDB)	34,300	Purchases returns (PRDB)	2,660
Balance c/d	27,692	Cash sales (CRB)	112
	62,972		**62,972**

(b) **No.** The amount of £27,692 is payable to HMRC.

Ledger balances and control accounts: Chapter 4

11 Test your knowledge

Workbook Activity 9

Record the journal entries needed in the accounts in the general ledger to deal with the opening entries listed below:

Account name	Amount £	Dr ✓	Cr ✓
Cash	2,350		
Capital	20,360		
Motor Vehicles	6,500		
Electricity	800		
Office expenses	560		
Loan from bank	15,000		
Cash at bank	6,400		
Factory equipment	14,230		
Rent	2,500		
Insurance	1,000		
Miscellaneous expenses	1,020		

Workbook Activity 10

The following totals are taken from the books of a business:

	£
Credit balance on purchases ledger control account	5,926
Debit balance on sales ledger control account	10,268
Credit sales	71,504
Credit purchases	47,713
Cash received from credit customers	69,872
Cash paid to creditors	47,028
Sales ledger balances written off as bad debts	96
Sales returns	358
Purchases returns	202
Discounts allowed	1,435
Discounts received	867
Contra entry	75

ICB LEVEL II: MANUAL BOOKKEEPING

Required:

(a) Prepare the purchases ledger control account and balance at the end of the month.

(b) Prepare the sales ledger control account and balance at the end of the month.

Workbook Activity 11

The balance on the sales ledger control account of Robin & Co on 30 September 20X0 amounted to £3,825 which did not agree with the net total of the list of sales ledger balances at that date of £3,362.

The errors discovered were as follows:

1. Debit balances in the sales ledger, amounting to £103, had been omitted from the list of balances.

2. A bad debt amounting to £400 had been written off in the sales ledger but had not been posted to the bad debts expense account or entered in the control accounts.

3. An item of goods sold to Sparrow, £250, had been entered once in the sales day book but posted to his account twice.

4. No entry had been made in the control account in respect of the transfer of a debit of £70 from Quail's account in the sales ledger to his account in the purchases ledger (a contra entry).

5. The discount allowed column in the cash account had been undercast by £140.

Required:

(a) Make the necessary adjustments in the sales ledger control account and bring down the balance.

(b) Show the adjustments to the net total of the original list of balances to reconcile with the amended balance on the sales ledger control account.

Ledger balances and control accounts: Chapter 4

Workbook Activity 12

When carrying out the purchases ledger control account reconciliation the following errors were discovered:

(a) the purchases day book was overcast by £1,000;

(b) the total of the discount received column in the cash payments book was posted to the general ledger as £89 instead of £98;

(c) a contra entry of £300 had been entered in the subsidiary ledger but not in the general ledger.

Required:

Produce journal entries to correct each of these errors.

Workbook Activity 13

(a) Show whether each entry will be a debit or credit in the Sales ledger control account in the general ledger.

Details	Amount £	Dr ✓	Cr ✓
Balance of debtors at 1 July	60,580		
Goods sold on credit	18,950		
Payments received from credit customers	20,630		
Discounts allowed	850		
Bad debt written off	2,400		
Goods returned from credit customers	3,640		

(b) The following debit balances were in the sales ledger on 1 August:

	Amount £
Rock 'n Roll Ltd	10,700
Cavern Ltd	18,420
Tunnel Plc	2,400
Studio 51 Ltd	7,680
Hacienda Ltd	9,955
Warehouse Company	5,255

ICB LEVEL II: MANUAL BOOKKEEPING

Required:

Calculate the balance brought down on the sales ledger control account on 1 August using the information from part (a). Then reconcile the balances shown above with the sales ledger control account balance.

	Amount £
Sales ledger control account balance as at 31 July	
Total of sales ledger accounts as at 31 July	
Difference	

(c) What may have caused the difference calculated above?

	✓
Goods returned may have been omitted from the sales ledger	
Bad debt written off may have been omitted from the sales ledger	
Goods returned may have been entered twice in the sales ledger	
Bad debt written off may have been entered twice in the sales ledger	

Workbook Activity 14

(a) Show whether each entry will be a debit or credit in the Purchases ledger control account in the general ledger.

Details	Amount £	Dr ✓	Cr ✓
Balance of creditors at 1 July	58,420		
Goods bought on credit	17,650		
Payments made to credit suppliers	19,520		
Discounts received	852		
Contra entry with sales ledger control	600		
Goods returned to credit suppliers	570		

(b) The following credit balances were in the purchases ledger on 1 August:

	Amount £
Price & Co	9,570
Andre Ltd	12,478
Hayes Plc	6,895
Lucas Ltd	7,950
Millers & Co	8,546
Griffiths Ltd	7,560

Required:

Calculate the balance brought down on the purchases ledger control account on 1 August using the information from part (a). Then reconcile the balances shown above with the purchases ledger control account balance.

	Amount £
Purchases ledger control account balance as at 31 July	
Total of purchase ledger accounts as at 31 July	
Difference	

(c) What may have caused the difference calculated above?

	✓
Payments made to suppliers may have been understated in the purchase ledger	
Goods returned to suppliers may have been overstated in the purchase ledger	
Goods bought on credit may have been overstated in the purchase ledger	
Contra entry may have been omitted from the purchase ledger	

Accounting for VAT

Introduction

Level II requires an understanding of the accounting for VAT and the completion of a VAT return. We will consider the need to register for VAT, the requirements of a VAT invoice, common terms used, the use of a VAT control account, bad debt relief and the preparation of a VAT return.

In this chapter we consider how to complete a VAT return correctly. Businesses must complete a VAT return (a VAT 100 form) at the end of each quarter. The purpose of a VAT return is to summarise the transactions of a business for a period.

CONTENTS

1. Accounting for VAT
2. Form and content of a VAT invoice
3. The VAT return

1 Accounting for VAT

1.1 Introduction

This chapter will begin with just a brief reminder of how the VAT system operates.

1.2 What is VAT?

VAT is:

- an indirect tax
- charged on most goods and services supplied within the UK,
- is borne by the final consumer, and
- collected by businesses on behalf of HM Revenue and Customs.

VAT is an indirect tax because it is paid indirectly when you buy most goods and services, rather than being collected directly from the taxpayer as a proportion of their income or gains.

VAT is charged by **taxable persons** when they make **taxable supplies** in the course of their business. VAT is not generally charged on non business transactions.

1.3 Taxable persons

> **Definition**
>
> Taxable persons are businesses which are (or should be) registered for VAT.

1.4 Registration and non-registration for VAT

When a business reaches a set annual turnover level, in 2011-2012 this is £73,000, then it must register for VAT. If turnover is below this limit, the business can, if it wishes, register voluntarily. If a business is registered it must:

- charge VAT on its sales or services to its customers;
- recover the VAT charged on its purchases and expenses rather than having to bear these costs as part of the business.

In such cases, as the VAT charged and incurred is neither revenue nor expense, the revenues and costs of the business are entered in books at their value net of VAT, and the VAT is entered in the VAT account.

If the business is not registered for VAT then the cost of purchases and expenses must include the VAT as these amounts are said to be irrecoverable. Thus, the costs of the business are entered in the books at their gross, VAT inclusive, value and there is no VAT account.

1.5 Taxable supplies

Taxable supplies or outputs, are most sales made by a taxable person. Taxable supplies can also include gifts and goods taken from the business for personal use.

1.6 Output VAT

> **Definition**
>
> The VAT charged on sales or taxable supplies is called **output VAT**.

1.7 Input VAT

When a business buys goods or pays expenses (inputs), then it will also be paying VAT on those purchases or expenses.

> **Definition**
>
> VAT paid by a business on purchases or expenses is called **input VAT**.

Businesses are allowed to reclaim their input tax. They do this by deducting the input tax they have paid from the output tax which they owe, and paying over the net amount only. If the input tax exceeds the output tax, then the balance is recoverable from HMRC.

1.8 Rates of VAT

VAT is currently charged at the standard rate of 20% and the zero rate 0%. The zero rate of VAT applies to items such as food, drink, books, newspapers, children's clothes and most transport.

1.9 Standard rated activities

Any taxable supply which is not charged at the zero or reduced rates is charged at the standard rate.

This is calculated by taking the VAT exclusive amount and multiplying by 20%.

Accounting for VAT: Chapter 5

If you are given the VAT inclusive figure then to calculate the VAT element, multiply this figure by the "VAT fraction", which is 1/6 or 20/120 for a rate of 20%. The following VAT structure can also be used to calculate VAT, VAT inclusive or VAT exclusive figures.

	£	%
VAT inclusive	120	120
VAT	20	20
VAT Exclusive	100	100

Example

Suppose that a business makes sales on credit of £1,000 and purchases on credit of £400 (both amounts exclusive of any VAT). How would these be accounted for in the ledger accounts. Assume a VAT rate of 20%.

Solution

The sales and purchases must be shown net and the VAT entered in the VAT account. As the sales and purchases were on credit the full double entry would be as follows:

DR Debtors account   £1,200
CR Sales account   £1,000
CR VAT control account   £200

DR Purchases account   £400
DR VAT control account   £80
CR Creditors account   £480

Sales account

	£		£
		Debtors	1,000

Debtors account

	£		£
Sales and VAT	1,200		

Purchases account

	£		£
Creditors	400		

Creditors account

	£		£
		Purchases	480

VAT control account

	£		£
Creditors	80	Debtors	200
Balance c/d	120		
	200		200
		Balance b/d	120

The amount due to HM Revenue and Customs is the balance on the VAT account, £120.

If a business is not registered for VAT then it will not charge VAT on its sales, and its expenses must be recorded at the gross amount (inclusive of VAT).

If a business is registered for VAT then it will charge VAT on its sales, although they will be recorded as sales at their net amount, and its expenses will also be recorded at the net amount.

The output and input VAT is recorded in the VAT account and the difference paid over to HM Revenue and Customs.

1.10 Zero-rated activities

If a business is registered for VAT and sells zero-rated products or services then it charges no VAT on the sales but can still reclaim the input VAT on its purchases and expenses. Such a business will normally be owed VAT by HM Revenue and Customs each quarter.

Accounting for VAT: **Chapter 5**

> **Example**
>
> Suppose that a business makes sales on credit of £1,000 plus VAT and purchases on credit of £400 plus VAT. How would these be accounted for if the rate of VAT on the sales was zero, whereas the purchases were standard rated? Standard rate is at 20%.
>
> **Solution**
>
> | DR | Debtors (£1,000 at 0%) | £1,000 |
> |---|---|---|
> | CR | Sales (£1,000 at 0%) | £1,000 |
> | DR | Purchases | £400 |
> | DR | VAT (£400 at 20%) | £80 |
> | CR | Creditors | £480 |
>
> This would leave a debit balance on the VAT account which is the amount that can be claimed back from HM Revenue and Customs by the business.

1.11 Exempt activities

Certain supplies are exempt from VAT such as financial and postal services.

If a business sells such services then not only is no VAT charged on the sales of the business but also no input VAT can be reclaimed on purchases and expenses.

> **Example**
>
> Suppose that a business makes sales on credit of £1,000 plus VAT and purchases on credit of £400 plus VAT. How would these be accounted for if the sales are exempt activities, whereas the purchases were standard-rated? (VAT rate is 20%)
>
> **Solution**
>
> | DR | Debtors | £1,000 |
> |---|---|---|
> | CR | Sales | £1,000 |
> | DR | Purchases | £480 |
> | CR | Creditors | £480 |
>
> There is no VAT on sales due to HM Revenue and Customs and the business cannot claim the £80 from HM Revenue and Customs. However, the seller of the purchases should pay the £80 of VAT over to HM Revenue and Customs.

ICB LEVEL II: MANUAL BOOKKEEPING

Activity 1

A business that is registered for VAT makes credit sales of £110,000 in the period and credit purchases of £75,000. Each of these figures is net of VAT at the standard rate of 20%.

Show how these transactions should be entered into the ledger accounts and state how much VAT is due to HM Revenue and Customs.

1.12 Differences between zero rated and exempt supplies

You must be careful to distinguish between traders making zero rated and exempt supplies.

	Exempt	Zero rated
Can register for VAT?	No	Yes
Charge output VAT to customers?	No	Yes at 0%
Can recover input tax?	No	Yes

Activity 2

Robbie's business bank account shows administrative expenses of £27,216 which is inclusive of VAT at the standard rate 20%.

1. Calculate the administrative expenses to be included in the trial balance.

2. Calculate the VAT figure on administrative expenses for inclusion in the VAT control account.

3. Update the VAT control account below and find the closing balance figure for VAT.

VAT control account

	£		£
VAT on purchases	35,000	Balance b/d	5,000
Paid to HMRC	5,000	VAT on sales	26,250

KAPLAN PUBLISHING

1.13 Tax point (time of supply)

> **Definition**
>
> The **tax point** is the date on which the liability for output tax arises – it is the date on which a supply is recorded as taking place for the purposes of the tax return. It is also referred to as the time of supply.

Most taxable persons make a VAT return each quarter. The return must include all supplies whose tax points fall within that quarter.

1.14 The basic tax point

The **basic tax point** for goods is the date when goods are 'removed' which usually means the date of delivery of those goods or the date the customer takes the goods away.

A tax point also occurs if goods are not 'removed' but are made available to a customer – for example if a specialist installer is constructing a new machine for a customer on site in their factory, the tax point will occur when the machine is handed over and not when all the materials are delivered to the site.

For services, the tax point is the date the services are performed or completed.

> **Example**
>
> Queue Ltd received an order for goods from a customer on 14 March. The goods were despatched on 18 March and the customer paid on 15 April when they received their invoice dated 13 April.
>
> State the basic tax point date.
>
> **Solution**
>
> The tax point is 18 March, i.e. the date of despatch.

1.15 Actual tax point

The basic tax point is amended in two situations.

Earlier tax point	Later tax point
• A tax invoice is issued or a payment is received before the basic tax point	• A tax invoice is issued within 14 days after the basic tax point (14 day rule)
• In these circumstances the date of invoice or payment is the time when the supply is treated as taking place	• In these circumstances the date of issue of the invoice is the time when the supply is treated as taking place

Provided that written approval is received from the local VAT office, the 14 day rule can be varied.

For example, it can be extended to accommodate a supplier who issues all of his invoices each month on the last day of the month and would like the month end invoice date to be the tax point date.

Note that the 14 day rule cannot apply to invoices which are only for zero rated goods as these are not tax invoices.

Most exports are zero rated so the tax point for these goods is always the earlier of the supply of goods and the receipt of payment.

1.16 Deposits received in advance

If a business receives a deposit or part payment in advance then this creates a tax point when the deposit is received. However, this is only for the deposit, not the whole supply. The business must account for the VAT included in the deposit.

No tax point is created for a returnable deposit, e.g. a deposit required to ensure the safe return of a hired item, where the deposit will be returned to the customer when they bring the item back safely.

Example

Ahmed receives a £60 deposit from a customer on 1 July. The total cost of the item is £210 including VAT at 20% and the customer pays the balance of £150 on 12 September when they collect the goods.

On 15 September Ahmed issues an invoice to his customer which he marks as paid in full.

How is VAT accounted for on this transaction?

Solution

The deposit of £60 creates a tax point on 1 July.

The amount of VAT is £10 (£60 × 20/120) and this must be entered in the VAT return which includes 1 July.

When the goods are collected and paid for on 12 September this creates a further tax point. The VAT is £25 (£150 × 20/120) and this must be included in the VAT return which includes 12 September.

2 Form and content of a VAT invoice

2.1 Introduction

All businesses that are registered for VAT must provide evidence to VAT registered customers of the VAT they have been charged.

In order to do this the supplier must give or send to the purchaser a VAT invoice **within 30 days** of the earlier of:

- supply of the goods or services or
- receipt of the payment.

VAT invoices are not required:

- if the purchaser is not VAT registered or
- if the supply is wholly zero rated.

In practice it is impossible to tell if a purchaser is VAT registered or not, so traders normally issue a VAT invoice anyway.

If they are retailers selling to the public they have special rules (see below).

Similarly, traders will normally issue invoices for zero rated sales which show the same details as for other supplies, but technically this is not a VAT invoice.

The original VAT invoice is sent to the customer and forms their evidence for reclaiming input VAT. A copy must be kept by the supplier to support the calculation of output VAT.

2.2 Form of a VAT invoice

There is **no standard format for invoices**. The exact design is the choice of the business, but it must show the following details (unless the invoice is a **less detailed tax invoice** that you will see later):

- identifying number which must follow a sequence (if an invoice is spoilt or cancelled it must be kept as a VAT officer may wish to inspect it)
- date of supply (tax point) and the date of issue of the invoice
- supplier's name and address and registration number
- name and address of customer, i.e. the person to whom the goods or services are supplied
- type of supply
  - sale
  - hire purchase, credit sale, conditional sale or similar transaction
  - loan
  - exchange
  - hire, lease or rental
  - process (making goods using the customer's own materials)
  - sale on commission (e.g. an estate agent)
  - supply on sale or return
- description of the goods or services
- quantity of goods or extent of services
- rate of tax and amount payable (in sterling) excluding VAT for each separate description
- total amount payable (excluding VAT) in sterling
- rate of any cash discount offered (these are also called settlement discounts)
- separate rate and amount of VAT charged for each rate of VAT
- total amount of VAT chargeable.

2.3 VAT and discounts

The treatment of discounts and VAT was included in Level I. By way of revision, the basic principles are:

- if a **trade discount** is given then this is deducted before VAT is calculated,
- if a **settlement discount** is offered, then the VAT is always calculated as if the customer takes the maximum discount.

Accounting for VAT: **Chapter 5**

> ### Example
>
> Joachim is in business manufacturing angle brackets which he sells to retailers.
>
> He offers a 5% discount if goods are paid for within 10 days and a 2% discount if goods are paid for within 21 days.
>
> He sells angle brackets with a pre-discount price of £1,000 to Kim Ltd.
>
> How much VAT should he charge on the invoice assuming that the rate of VAT is 20%?
>
> **Solution**
>
> VAT should be calculated on the lowest amount a customer could pay. It does not matter whether the customer takes the discount or not. Accordingly, the VAT is £190 (£1,000 × 95% × 20%).

> ### Activity 3
>
> An invoice is issued for standard rated goods with a list price of £380.00 (excluding VAT).
>
> A 10% trade discount is given and a 4% settlement or cash discount is offered.
>
> How much VAT at the standard rate of 20% should be included on the invoice?
>
> A   £76.00
> B   £65.66
> C   £68.40
> D   £72.96

Sometimes a business will offer to pay a customer's VAT. This is really just another form of discount.

> ### Example
>
> XY Ltd sells beds with a normal retail price of £240 (including VAT at 20% of £40). They run a promotional offer to pay the customers' VAT for them and hence the customer pays £200.
>
> XY Ltd must treat the £200 paid as a VAT inclusive price and account for VAT of £33.33 (£200 × 20/120).

2.4 Example of a VAT invoice

> **Example**
>
> **MICRO TRAINING GROUP LTD**
> Unit 34
> Castlewell Trading Estate
> Manchester
> M12 5RHF
>
> To:
> Slough Labels Ltd   Sales invoice number: 35
> Station Unit   VAT registration number: 234 5566 87
> Slough   Date of issue: 30 September 20X0
> SL1 3EJ   Tax point: 12 September 20X0
>
> **Sales:**
>
> | Quantity | Description and price | Amount excl VAT £ p | VAT rate | VAT £ p |
> |---|---|---|---|---|
> | 6 | Programmable calculators FR34 at £24.76 | 148.56 | 20% | |
> | 12 | Programmable calculators GT60 at £36.80 | 441.60 | 20% | |
> | | | 590.16 | | 115.67 |
> | | Delivery | 23.45 | 20% | 4.69 |
> | | | 613.61 | | 120.36 |
> | VAT | | 120.36 | | |
> | TOTAL | | 733.97 | | |
>
> Terms: Net 30 days.
> Cash discount of 2% on goods if paid within 10 days

Note that on this invoice the VAT is calculated after applying the discount of 2% to the **goods** element of the invoice as the discount is not given on the delivery charge.

Accounting for VAT: Chapter 5

2.5 Rounding VAT

Usually, the amount of VAT calculated will not be a whole number of pounds and pence. You will therefore need a rounding adjustment.

The rules governing this adjustment are quite tricky, and permit more than one method.

However, for assessment purposes you only need to know the basic rounding rule – that is that the total amount of VAT payable on an invoice can be rounded down to the nearest penny.

Activity 4

Calculate the total VAT to be charged in respect of each of the three VAT invoices below.

Invoice	Description and price	Net of VAT £ p	VAT rate	VAT £ p
1	16 × 6 metre hosepipes @ £3.23 each	51.68	20%	
2	24 × bags of compost @ £5.78 each	138.72	20%	
3	Supply of kitchen units	1,084.57	20%	

2.6 Less detailed (simplified) VAT invoices

Retailers (selling to the public), do not have to issue a detailed VAT invoice every time they make a sale as this would make trading in a busy shop very difficult.

If the total amount of the supply **(including VAT)** by the retailer does not exceed £250, then **when a customer requests a tax invoice** a retailer may issue a **less detailed tax invoice**. However, if requested by a customer a full VAT invoice must be issued.

The details required on the less detailed invoice are:

- supplier's name and address
- supplier's VAT registration number
- date of supply
- description sufficient to identify the goods or services
- amount payable (including VAT) for each rate (standard and zero)
- the VAT rate applicable.

The main differences between the less detailed invoice and the full invoice are that the customer's name and address can be omitted, and the total on the invoice includes the VAT without the VAT itself being shown separately.

Although this invoice shows less detail, it is still a valid tax invoice. This means that if the purchaser is a VAT registered business they can use the invoice to support a claim for input VAT.

Example

Delta Office Supplies
46, Central Mall, Glastonbury, Somerset
G34 7QT
Telephone: 01392 43215
15 April 20X0

1 box of 50 blank DVD-R
Total including VAT @ 20%   £25.85

VAT registration number: 653 7612 44

If the business accepts credit cards they can use the sales voucher given to the cardholder as a less detailed invoice.

However, it must still contain the details above.

Exempt supplies must not be included in a less detailed invoice.

Retailers **do not have to keep** copies of the less detailed VAT invoices that they issue, whereas non retailers must keep copies of all sales invoices issued.

This is because retailers generally calculate their VAT from their **daily gross takings** rather than from individual invoices.

2.7 Modified invoices

If a trader sells goods or a service for more than £250 including VAT, and the customer agrees, they may issue a modified VAT invoice.

This shows the VAT inclusive amount for each item sold and then at the bottom of the invoice the following amounts must be shown:

- the overall VAT inclusive total
- the total amount of VAT included in the total
- the total value of the supplies net of VAT
- the total value of any zero-rated and exempt supplies.

Accounting for VAT: Chapter 5

This only saves the trader from including the individual cost net of VAT and the VAT rate for each item. All other details must be the same as for a full VAT invoice.

3 The VAT return

3.1 Introduction

The tax period for VAT is **three months**, or one month for taxpayers who choose to make monthly returns (normally taxpayers who receive regular refunds).

The taxpayer must complete a **VAT return at the end of each quarter**. The return summarises all the transactions for the period.

3.2 Timing of the VAT return

The taxpayer must submit the return within one month of the end of the tax period. The taxable person must send the amount due at the same time (i.e. output tax collected less input tax deducted).

If VAT is due from HMRC the VAT return must still be completed and submitted within one month of the end of the quarter in order to be able to reclaim the amount due.

3.3 What a VAT return looks like

An example of a paper VAT return is given below in section 3.4 although very few businesses will use these.

Most businesses have to file their returns online rather than on paper, however the boxes and numbers used for the electronic form are exactly the same.

3.4 Paper VAT return

Value Added Tax Return
For the period

For Official Use

Registration number | Period

You could be liable to a financial penalty if your completed return and all the VAT payable are not received by the due date.

Due date:

For Official Use

Your VAT Office telephone number is 0123 4567

Before you fill in this form please read the notes on the back and the VAT Leaflet *'Filling in your VAT return'*. Fill in all boxes clearly in ink and write 'none' where necessary. Don't put a dash or leave any box blank. If there are no pence write '00' in the pence column. Do not enter more than one amount in any box

For official use			
	VAT due in this period on sales and other options	1	
	VAT due in this period on acquisitions from other EC Member states	2	
	Total VAT due (the sum of boxes 1 and 2)	3	
	VAT reclaimed in this period on purchases and other inputs (including acquisitions from the EC)	4	
	Net VAT to be paid to Customs or reclaimed by you (Difference between boxes 3 and 4)	5	
	Total value of sales and all other outputs excluding any VAT. Include your box 8 figure	6	00
	Total value of purchases and all other inputs excluding any VAT. Include your box 9 figures.	7	00
	Total value of all supplies of goods and related services excluding any VAT to other EC Member States	8	00
	Total value of all supplies of goods and related services excluding any VAT, from other EC Member States	9	00

Retail schemes. If you have used any of the schemes in the period covered by this return, enter the relevant letter(s) in this box.

If you are enclosing a payment please tick this box ☐

DECLARATION You or someone on your behalf must sign below.

I .... declare that the information given
    (Full name of signatory in BLOCK LETTERS)
above is true and complete.
Signature .... Date   20
A false declaration can result in prosecution.

3.5 VAT return – online template

		£
VAT due in this period on **sales** and other outputs	Box 1	
VAT due in this period on **acquisitions** from other EC Member States	Box 2	
Total VAT due **(the sum of boxes 1 and 2)**	Box 3	
VAT reclaimed in the period on **purchases** and other inputs, including acquisitions from the EC	Box 4	
Net VAT to be paid to HM Revenue & Customs or reclaimed by you **(Difference between boxes 3 and 4)**	Box 5	
Total value of **sales** and all other outputs excluding any VAT. **Include your box 8 figure**	Box 6	
Total value of purchases and all other inputs excluding any VAT. **Include your box 9 figure**	Box 7	
Total value of all **supplies** of goods and related costs, excluding any VAT, to other **EC Member States**	Box 8	
Total value of all **acquisitions** of goods and related costs, excluding any VAT, from other **EC Member States**	Box 9	

As you will see there are nine boxes to complete with the relevant figures.

Boxes 2, 8 and 9 are to do with supplies of goods and services to other European Community (EC) Member States and acquisitions from EC Member States.

3.6 Completing the VAT return

The main source of information for the VAT return is the VAT account which must be maintained to show the amount that is due to or from HMRC at the end of each quarter.

It is important to realise that the balance on the VAT account should agree to the balance of VAT payable/reclaimable on the VAT return.

3.7 How the VAT account should look

Given below is a pro-forma of a VAT account as suggested by the VAT Guide.

---

1 April 20X5 to 30 June 20X5

VAT deductible – input tax	£ p	VAT payable – output tax	£ p
VAT on purchases		VAT on sales	
April	X	April	X
May	X	May	X
June	X	June	X
VAT on imports	X		
VAT on acquisition from EC	X	VAT on acquisition from EC	X

Adjustments of previous errors

(if within the error limit – Chapter 6)

Net under claim	X	Net over claim	X
Bad debt relief (section 2.6)	X		
Less: Credit notes received	(X)	Less: Credit notes issued	(X)
Total tax deductible	X	Total tax payable	X
		Less: Total tax deductible	(X)
		Payable to HMRC	X

You will note that the VAT shown is not strictly a double entry account as the VAT on credit notes received is deducted from input tax and the VAT on credit notes issued is deducted from output tax instead of being credited and debited respectively.

3.8 Information required for the VAT return

Boxes 1 to 4 of the VAT return can be fairly easily completed from the information in the VAT account. However, Boxes 6 and 7 require figures for total sales and purchases excluding VAT.

This information will need to be extracted from the totals of the accounting records such as sales day book and purchases day book totals. It is also possible that information relating to VAT could be shown in a journal.

Boxes 8 and 9 require figures, excluding VAT, for the value of supplies to other EC Member States and acquisitions from other EC Member States.

Therefore the accounting records should be designed in such a way that these figures can also be easily identified.

Activity 5

Panther

You are preparing the VAT return for Panther Alarms Ltd and you must first identify the sources of information for the VAT account.

Here is a list of possible sources of accounting information.

1. Sales day book
2. Sales returns day book
3. Bad and doubtful debts account
4. Purchase returns day book
5. Drawings account
6. Purchases day book
7. Cash book
8. Assets account
9. Petty cash book

Select from the list the best sources of information for the following figures by entering a number against each.

If you think the information will be in more than one place then give the number for both.

A   sales
B   cash sales
C   credit notes issued
D   purchases
E   cash purchases
F   credit notes received
G   capital goods sold
H   capital goods purchased
I   bad debt relief

ICB LEVEL II: MANUAL BOOKKEEPING

💡 Example

Given below is a VAT account for Thompson Brothers for the second VAT quarter of 20X5.

Thompson Brothers Ltd **1 April 20X5 to 30 June 20X5**

VAT deductible – input tax	£	VAT payable – output tax	£
VAT on purchases		*VAT on sales*	
April	700.00	April	1,350.00
May	350.00	May	1,750.00
June	350.00	June	700.00
	1,400.00		3,800.00

Other adjustments

	£		£
Less: Credit notes received	(20.00)	Less: Credit notes issued	(120.00)
Total tax deductible	1,380.00	Total tax payable	3,680.00
		Less: Total tax deductible	(1,380.00)
		Payable to HMRC	2,300.00

You are also given the summarised totals from the day books for the three-month period:

Sales Day Book

	Net £	VAT £	Total £
Standard rated	19,000.00	3,800.00	22,800.00
Zero rated	800.00	–	800.00

Sales Returns Day Book

	Net £	VAT £	Total £
Standard rated	600.00	120.00	720.00
Zero rated	40.00	–	40.00

Purchases Day Book

	Net £	VAT £	Total £
Standard rated	7,000.00	1,400.00	8,400.00
Zero rated	2,000.00	–	2,000.00

Purchases Returns Day Book

	Net £	VAT £	Total £
Standard rated	100.00	20.00	120.00
Zero rated	–	–	–

We are now in a position to complete the VAT return.

Solution

Step 1

Fill in Box 1 with the VAT on sales less the VAT on credit notes issued.

This can be taken either from the VAT account or from the day book summaries:
(£3,800 – £120) = £3,680.00.

Note that the figures in Boxes 1 – 5 should include pence so put '00' if there are no pence in the total.

Step 2

Fill in Box 2 with the VAT payable on acquisitions from other EC Member states – none here.

Step 3

Complete Box 3 with the total of Boxes 1 and 2:
(£3,680.00 + £Nil) = £3,680.00.

Step 4

Fill in Box 4 with the total of VAT on all purchases less the total VAT on any credit notes received. These figures can either be taken from the VAT account or from the day book totals:
(£1,400.00 – £20.00) = £1,380.00.

Step 5

Complete Box 5 by deducting the figure in Box 4 from the total in Box 3:
(£3,680.00 – £1,380.00) = £2,300.00.

This is the amount due to HMRC and should equal the balance on the VAT account.

If the Box 4 figure is larger than the Box 3 total then there is more input tax reclaimable than output tax to pay – this means that this is the amount being reclaimed from HMRC.

For a paper return, a negative figure like a repayment should be put in brackets. For an online return a negative figure should have a negative sign in front and no brackets.

Step 6

Fill in Box 6 with the VAT exclusive figure of all sales less credit notes issued – this information will come from the day books:
(£19,000 + £800 – £600 – £40) = £19,160

Note that this figure includes zero-rated supplies and any exempt supplies that are made.

Note that the figures in Boxes 6 – 9 should be whole pounds only (pence will already be completed as '00' on a paper return).

Step 7

Fill in Box 7 with the VAT exclusive total of all purchases less credit notes received – again this will be taken from the day books:
(£7,000 + £2,000 – £100) = £8,900

Step 8

Boxes 8 and 9 are for transactions with EU member states.

Note that if there is no entry for any box then 'none' should be written in the box for a paper return and 0 for an online return.

Step 9

If VAT is due to HMRC then payment must be made in accordance with the usual time limits. For assessment purposes you may be asked to state the payment date, or draft an email advising when this amount will be paid.

		£
VAT due in this period on **sales** and other outputs	Box 1	3,680.00
VAT due in this period on **acquisitions** from other EC Member States	Box 2	0.00
Total VAT due (**the sum of boxes 1 and 2**)	Box 3	3,680.00
VAT reclaimed in the period on **purchases** and other inputs, including acquisitions from the EC	Box 4	1,380.00
Net VAT to be paid to HM Revenue & Customs or reclaimed by you (**Difference between boxes 3 and 4**)	Box 5	2,300.00

Accounting for VAT: **Chapter 5**

Total value of **sales** and all other outputs excluding any VAT. **Include your box 8 figure**	Box 6	19,160
Total value of **purchases** and all other inputs excluding any VAT. **Include your box 9 figure**	Box 7	8,900
Total value of all **supplies** of goods and related costs, excluding any VAT, to other **EC Member States**	Box 8	0
Total value of all **acquisitions** of goods and related costs, excluding any VAT, from other **EC Member States**	Box 9	0

If the business makes sales or purchases for cash then the relevant net and VAT figures from the cash receipts and payments books should also be included on the VAT return.

Activity 6

Given below is a summary of the day books of a business for the three months ended 31 March 20X1.

The business is called Long Supplies Ltd and trades from Vale House, Lilly Road, Trent, TR5 2KL.

The VAT registration number of the business is 285 3745 12.

Sales Day Book	Net £	VAT £	Total £
Standard-rate	15,485.60	3,097.12	18,582.72
Zero-rated	1,497.56	–	1,497.56

Sales Returns Day Book	Net £	VAT £	Total £
Standard-rate	1,625.77	325.15	1,950.92
Zero-rated	106.59	–	106.59

Purchase Day Book	Net £	VAT £	Total £
Standard-rate	8,127.45	1,625.49	9,752.94
Zero-rated	980.57	–	980.57

Purchases Returns Day Book	Net £	VAT £	Total £
Standard-rate	935.47	187.09	1,122.56
Zero-rated	80.40	–	80.40

ICB LEVEL II: MANUAL BOOKKEEPING

Required:

(a) Write up the VAT account to reflect these figures.

(b) Complete the VAT return given.

Answer proformas

(a) **Proforma VAT account for completion**

	£ p		£ p
VAT on purchases		VAT on sales	
Less: Credit notes received		Less: Credit notes issued	
Total tax deductible		Total tax payable	
		Less: Total tax deductible	
		Payable to HMRC	

(b) **Proforma VAT return for completion**

		£
VAT due in this period on **sales** and other outputs	Box 1	
VAT due in this period on **acquisitions** from other EC **Member States**	Box 2	
Total VAT due (**the sum of boxes 1 and 2**)	Box 3	
VAT reclaimed in the period on **purchases** and other inputs, including acquisitions from the EC	Box 4	
Net VAT to be paid to HM Revenue & Customs or reclaimed by you (**Difference between boxes 3 and 4**)	Box 5	
Total value of **sales** and all other outputs excluding any VAT. Include your box 8 figure	Box 6	
Total value of purchases and all other inputs excluding any VAT. Include your box 9 figure	Box 7	

Total value of all **supplies** of goods and related costs, excluding any VAT, to other **EC Member States**	Box 8
Total value of all **acquisitions** of goods and related costs, excluding any VAT, from other **EC Member States**	Box 9

3.9 VAT: Adjustment of previous errors

You will notice in the pro-forma VAT account that there are entries for net under claims and net over claims.

Net errors made in previous VAT returns which are below the disclosure threshold can be adjusted for on the VAT return through the VAT account.

Errors can be corrected on the next VAT return if they are:

- No more than £10,000
- Between £10,000 and £50,000 but no more than 1% of turnover for the current return period (specifically the figure included in Box 6 of the return)

The one single figure for net errors will then be entered as additional input tax in Box 4 if there has been an earlier net under claim of VAT and as additional output tax in Box 1 if the net error was a net over claim in a previous return.

3.10 Errors above the threshold

The VAT office should be informed immediately either by a letter or on Form VAT 652. This is known as voluntary disclosure.

The information provided to the VAT office should be:

- how the error happened
- the amount of the error
- the VAT period in which it occurred
- whether the error was involving input or output tax
- how you worked out the error
- whether the error is in favour of the business or HMRC.

3.11 VAT: Bad debt relief

You will notice that there is an entry in the pro-forma VAT account for bad debt relief as additional input tax.

When a supplier invoices a customer for an amount including VAT, the supplier must pay the VAT to HMRC.

If the customer then fails to pay the debt, the supplier's position is that he has paid output VAT which he has never collected. This is obviously unfair, and the system allows him to recover such amounts.

Suppliers cannot issue credit notes to recover VAT on bad debts.

Instead, the business must make an **adjustment through the VAT return**. The business can reclaim VAT already paid over if:

- output tax was paid on the original supply
- six months have elapsed between the date payment was due (or the date of supply if later) and the date of the VAT return, and
- the debt has been written off as a bad debt in the accounting records
- the debt is less than 3 years and 6 months old
- the debt has not been sold to a factoring company
- you did not charge more than the selling price for the items.

If the business receives a **repayment of the debt later**, it must make an adjustment to the VAT relief claimed.

The bad debt relief is entered in Box 4 of the return along with the VAT on purchases.

Be very careful when computing the VAT on the bad debt.

The amount of the bad debt will be VAT inclusive, because the amount the debtor owes is the amount that includes VAT.

To calculate the VAT you have to multiply the bad debt by 20/120 (or 1/6) for the standard VAT rate of 20%.

Example

A business has made purchases of £237,000 (net of VAT) in the VAT quarter and has written off a bad debt of £750. They also have a net under claim of VAT of £1,250.00 from earlier periods.

Calculate the figure that will be entered on the VAT return for the quarter in Box 4.

Solution

	£	£ p
Purchases (net of VAT)	237,000	
VAT thereon (£237,000 × 0.20)		47,400.00
Bad debt	750	
VAT thereon (£750 × 20/120)		125.00
Net under claim of VAT		1,250.00
Total VAT for Box 4		48,775.00

Accounting for VAT: Chapter 5

4 Summary

For this unit you will need to be able to account for VAT and deal with the amount of VAT that is due either to or from HM Revenue and Customs.

In particular you must understand what is meant by the balance on the VAT control account in the trial balance.

This chapter has covered two important areas for VAT – invoicing and tax points.

The tax point for a supply of goods is important as this determines the VAT period in which the VAT on those goods is included. The basic tax point is the date on which goods are delivered or collected by a customer but there are also situations in which the tax point can be earlier or later. These rules must be understood.

VAT invoices must include certain details and in normal circumstances must be given or sent to a VAT registered purchaser. In practice this means that all purchasers will be provided with a VAT invoice whether they are registered or not. However retailers are allowed to issue less detailed or modified invoices.

A business should keep a VAT account which summarises all of the VAT from the accounting records and this can be used to complete the first five boxes on the VAT return. The figure for VAT due to or from HM Revenue and Customs on the VAT return should equal the balance on the VAT account.

Answers to chapter activities

Activity 1

Sales account

	£		£
		Sales ledger control account	110,000

Sales ledger control account

	£		£
Sales + VAT 110,000 + 22,000	132,000		

Purchases account

	£		£
Purchases ledger control account	75,000		

VAT control account

	£		£
Purchases ledger control account 75,000 × 20/100	15,000	Sales ledger control account 110,000 × 20/100	22,000
Balance c/d	7,000		
	22,000		22,000
		Balance b/d	7,000

Purchases ledger control account

	£		£
		Purchases + VAT 75,000 + 15,000	90,000

The amount due to HM Revenue and Customs is the balance on the VAT control account, £7,000.

Activity 2

1. The amount that should be included in the trial balance is the NET amount. As £27,216 is the VAT inclusive amount, the NET is calculated as follows:

    27,216 × 100/120 = 22,680

2. The VAT can be calculated using the gross figure £27,216 × 20/120 = £4,536

3. The VAT control would be completed as follows:

VAT control account

	£		£
VAT on purchases	35,000	Balance b/d	5,000
Paid to HMRC	5,000	VAT on sales	26,250
Vat on expenses	4,536	**Balance c/d**	**13,286**
	44,536		44,536
Balance b/d	**13,286**		

A debit balance represents a refund due from HMRC.

Activity 3

The correct answer is B.

	£ p
List price of goods	380.00
Less: 10% trade discount	(38.00)
	342.00
Less: 4% settlement discount	(13.68)
Amount on which VAT to be calculated	328.32
VAT (20% × £328.32)	65.66
Alternative calculation:	
VAT = (£380.00 × 90% × 96%) at 20%	65.66

Activity 4

1. VAT on 6 metre hosepipes = £10.33 (£51.68 × 20% = £10.336)
2. VAT on bags of compost = £27.74 (£138.72 × 20% = £27.744)
3. VAT on kitchen units = £216.91 (£1,084.57 × 20% = £216.914)

All rounded down to the nearest penny.

Activity 5

Panther

A	Sales	1
B	Cash sales	7
C	Credit notes issued	2
D	Purchases	6
E	Cash purchases	7 and 9
F	Credit notes received	4
G	Capital goods sold	8 or 1 (if it is an analysed sales day book)
H	Capital goods purchased	8 or 6 (if analysed)
I	Bad debt relief	3

Activity 6

(a)

Long Supplies Ltd
VAT account 1 January to 31 March 20X1

	£		£
VAT on purchases	1,625.49	VAT on sales	3,097.12
Less: Credit notes received	(187.09)	Less: Credit notes issued	(325.15)
Total tax deductible	1,438.40	Total tax payable	2,771.97
		Less: Total tax deductible	(1,438.40)
		Payable to HMRC	1,333.57

(b)

		£
VAT due in this period on **sales** and other outputs	Box 1	2,771.97
VAT due in this period on **acquisitions** from other EC Member States	Box 2	0.00
Total VAT due (**the sum of boxes 1 and 2**)	Box 3	2,771.97
VAT reclaimed in the period on **purchases** and other inputs, including acquisitions from the EC	Box 4	1,438.40
Net VAT to be paid to HM Revenue & Customs or reclaimed by you (**Difference between boxes 3 and 4**)	Box 5	1,333.57
Total value of **sales** and all other outputs excluding any VAT. **Include your box 8 figure**	Box 6	15,251
Total value of purchases and all other inputs excluding any VAT. **Include your box 9 figure**	Box 7	8,092

ICB LEVEL II: MANUAL BOOKKEEPING

Total value of all **supplies** of goods and related costs, excluding any VAT, to other **EC Member States**	Box 8	0
Total value of all **acquisitions** of goods and related costs, excluding any VAT, from other **EC Member States**	Box 9	0

Workings:

Box 1 £
VAT on sales 3,097.12
Less: VAT on credit notes (325.15)
  ―――――
  2,771.97
  ―――――

Box 4 £
VAT on purchases 1,625.49
Less: VAT on credit notes (187.09)
  ―――――
  1,438.40
  ―――――

Box 6 £
Standard-rated sales 15,485.60
Zero-rated sales 1,497.56
  ―――――
  16,983.16

Less: Credit notes
  Standard-rated (1,625.77)
  Zero-rated (106.59)
  ―――――
  15,250.80
  ―――――

Box 7 £
Standard-rated purchases 8,127.45
Zero-rated purchases 980.57
  ―――――
  9,108.02

Less: Credit notes
  Standard-rated (935.47)
  Zero-rated (80.40)
  ―――――
  8,092.15
  ―――――

Accounting for VAT: Chapter 5

5 Test your knowledge

Workbook Activity 7

A business that is registered for VAT has the following record relating to sales, purchases and expenses.

Sales for the quarter ending 31 March 20X4 of £236,100 (including VAT)

Purchases and expenses of £143,600 (excluding VAT).

At 1 January 20X4 there was an amount of £8,455 owing to HM Revenue and Customs and this was paid on 28 January 20X4.

Required:

Write up the VAT control account for the quarter ending 31 March 20X4. (VAT rate is 20%)

VAT control account

	£		£

Explain what the balance on the account represents.

ICB LEVEL II: MANUAL BOOKKEEPING

Workbook Activity 8

Indicate whether the following statements are true or false.

Tick one box on each line.

		True	False
1	Traders do not have to supply a VAT invoice unless their customer is VAT registered.		
2	Retailers can issue less detailed VAT invoices if the total amount of the supply, excluding VAT, does not exceed £250.		
3	The VAT invoice is used by a customer as their evidence for reclaiming input VAT.		
4	A VAT invoice must be issued to a customer within 30 days of the tax point.		

Workbook Activity 9

Calculate the amount of output VAT at the standard rate of 20% that should be charged on the following invoices (to the nearest pence).

Goods pre discount price £	Trade discount	Settlement discount	Output tax £ p
1,000	10%	2%	
2,000	Nil	5% if paid within 7 days. 2% if paid within 21 days	
750	8%	None	

Accounting for VAT: Chapter 5

Workbook Activity 10

Look at the following list of items.

Select by entering the appropriate number whether the items:

1. Should only be shown on a normal detailed VAT invoice; or
2. Should be shown on both a normal detailed VAT invoice and on a less detailed invoice; or
3. Should not be shown on either form of invoice.

	Item	Number (1, 2, or 3)
A	Identifying number	
B	Tax point date	
C	Delivery date	
D	Total amount of VAT payable	
E	Customer's registration number	

Workbook Activity 11

Which of the following statements about proforma invoices are FALSE?

Enter a tick in the final box for each false statement.

		False
A	A proforma invoice IS a valid tax invoice	
B	A proforma invoice IS NOT a valid tax invoice	
C	A customer receiving a proforma invoice can use it to reclaim the input tax shown	
D	A proforma invoice is really just a demand for payment	

Workbook Activity 12

In each of the following cases, state the tax point date.

		Tax point
1	Goods delivered to a customer on 15 August, invoice sent out on 20 August and payment received 30 August.	
2	Proforma invoice issued 3 June, payment received 10 June, goods delivered 30 June with a tax invoice dated on that day.	
3	Goods delivered to a customer on 4 March, invoice sent out on 25 March and payment received 15 April.	
4	Invoice sent to a customer on 10 December, goods delivered 18 December and payment received 27 December.	

Workbook Activity 13

A VAT registered business receives a £100 non refundable deposit on 19 October from a customer for the supply of goods which are despatched on 25 October.

The goods are invoiced on 31 October and the balance of £350 is paid on 10 November.

Both amounts are VAT inclusive.

1   What is the tax point for the deposit?

    A   19 October

    B   25 October

    C   31 October

    D   10 November

Accounting for VAT: Chapter 5

2   What is the output VAT on the deposit?

   A   £20.00

   B   £16.66

3   What is the tax point for the balance?

   A   19 October

   B   25 October

   C   31 October

   D   10 November

4   What is the output VAT on the balance?

   A   £70.00

   B   £58.33

Workbook Activity 14

You are a self-employed bookkeeper and Duncan Bye, a motor engineer, is one of your clients. He is registered for VAT.

His records for the quarter ended 30 June 20X1 showed the following:

Sales day book

	Gross £	Net £	VAT £
April	8,100.00	6,750.00	1,350.00
May	7,812.00	6,510.00	1,302.00
June	9,888.00	8,240.00	1,648.00
	25,800.00	21,500.00	4,300.00

Purchases day book

	Gross £	Net £	VAT £
April	3,780.00	3,150.00	630.00
May	3,924.00	3,270.00	654.00
June	3,216.00	2,680.00	536.00
	10,920.00	9,100.00	1,820.00

He also gives you some details of petty cash expenditure in the quarter.

	£ p
Net purchases	75.60
VAT	15.12
	90.72

Duncan understated his output VAT by £24 on his last return.

Prepare the following VAT form 100 for the period.

		£
VAT due in this period on **sales** and other outputs	Box 1	
VAT due in this period on **acquisitions** from other **EC Member States**	Box 2	
Total VAT due (**the sum of boxes 1 and 2**)	Box 3	
VAT reclaimed in the period on **purchases** and other inputs, including acquisitions from the EC	Box 4	
Net VAT to be paid to HM Revenue & Customs or reclaimed by you (**Difference between boxes 3 and 4**)	Box 5	
Total value of **sales** and all other outputs excluding any VAT. **Include your box 8 figure**	Box 6	
Total value of purchases and all other inputs excluding any VAT. **Include your box 9 figure**	Box 7	
Total value of all **supplies** of goods and related costs, excluding any VAT, to other **EC Member States**	Box 8	
Total value of all **acquisitions** of goods and related costs, excluding any VAT, from other **EC Member States**	Box 9	

Activity 15

You are provided with the following summary of Mark Ambrose's books and other information provided by Mark for the quarter ended 30 September 20X1.

MARK AMBROSE
Summary of day books and petty cash expenditure
Quarter ended 30 September 20X1

Sales day book

	Work done £	VAT £	Total £
July	12,900.00	2,580.00	15,480.00
August	13,200.00	2,640.00	15,840.00
September	12,300.00	2,460.00	14,760.00
	38,400.00	7,680.00	46,080.00

Purchase day book

	Net £	VAT £	Total £
July	5,250.00	1,050.00	6,300.00
August	5,470.00	1,094.00	6,564.00
September	5,750.00	1,150.00	6,900.00
	16,470.00	3,294.00	19,764.00

Petty cash expenditure for quarter (VAT inclusive)

July	£108.00
August	£96.00
September	£120.00

Bad debts list – 30 September 20X1

Date	Customer	Total (including VAT)
30 November 20X0	High Melton Farms	£300.00
3 January 20X1	Concorde Motors	£180.00
4 April 20X1	Bawtry Engineering	£120.00

These have now been written off as bad debts.

Complete boxes 1 to 9 of the VAT return for the quarter ended 30 September 20X1.

		£
VAT due in this period on **sales** and other outputs	Box 1	
VAT due in this period on **acquisitions** from other **EC Member States**	Box 2	
Total VAT due (**the sum of boxes 1 and 2**)	Box 3	
VAT reclaimed in the period on **purchases** and other inputs, including acquisitions from the EC	Box 4	
Net VAT to be paid to HM Revenue & Customs or reclaimed by you (**Difference between boxes 3 and 4**)	Box 5	
Total value of **sales** and all other outputs excluding any VAT. **Include your box 8 figure**	Box 6	
Total value of purchases and all other inputs excluding any VAT. **Include your box 9 figure**	Box 7	
Total value of all **supplies** of goods and related costs, excluding any VAT, to other **EC Member States**	Box 8	
Total value of all **acquisitions** of goods and related costs, excluding any VAT, from other **EC Member States**	Box 9	

Petty cash

Introduction

As well as making payments from the business bank account by cheque or other methods, most businesses will also carry a certain amount of cash on the premises known as petty cash. Petty cash is used to make small business payments, for which writing a cheque would not be appropriate, such as payment in the local shop for tea, coffee and milk for the staff kitchen. In this chapter we will consider how a petty cash system will work, the documentation required and how petty cash payments are accounted for.

CONTENTS

1. Petty cash
2. Petty cash systems
3. Maintaining petty cash records
4. Posting the petty cash book
5. Petty cash control account
6. Reconciling the petty cash

Petty cash: **Chapter 6**

1 Petty cash

> **Definition**
>
> Petty cash is the small amount of cash that most businesses hold in order to make small cash payments.

1.1 Petty cash box

Holding cash on business premises is a security risk and therefore it is important that the petty cash is secure. It should be kept in a locked petty cash box and usually this itself will be held in the safe. Only the person responsible for the petty cash should have access to the petty cash box.

1.2 Payment of petty cash

Petty cash is usually reimbursed to employees who have already incurred a small cash expense on behalf of the business, such as buying coffee and milk in the local shop or paying for a train fare. These payments should only be made for the incurrence of valid business expenses. For this reason, the petty cashier should only pay out to the employee on receipt of an authorised petty cash voucher and, where appropriate, VAT receipt.

> **Definition**
>
> A petty cash voucher is an internal document that details the business expenditure that an employee has incurred out of his own money.

This voucher must be authorised by an appropriate person before any amounts can be paid to that employee out of the petty cash box.

A typical petty cash voucher is shown below:

Signature of person authorising voucher →

PETTY CASH VOUCHER		
Authorised by F R Clarke	Received by *← Signature of claimant* L Kent	No 4173
Date	Description	Amount
4 April 20X1	Train Fare	12 50
	Total	12 50

Sequential voucher number →

Details of expenditure including the date and the nature of the expense →

Total paid to employee →

2 Petty cash systems

2.1 Introduction

There are two main types of petty cash systems that a business may use – an imprest system and a non-imprest system.

2.2 The imprest system

Many businesses use the imprest system for petty cash. Using an imprest system makes petty cash easier to control and therefore reduces the possibility of error and fraud.

The business decides on a fixed amount of petty cash (the imprest) which is just large enough to cover normal petty cash requirements for a period (usually a week). This amount of petty cash is withdrawn from the bank.

Claims are paid out of petty cash by a voucher being completed for each amount of petty cash paid out. The vouchers are kept in the petty cash box so that the amount of cash held decreases and is replaced by vouchers.

At any given time, the total contents of the box (i.e. petty cash plus amounts withdrawn represented by vouchers) should equal the amount of the imprest. At the end of the period, a cheque is drawn for the total of the vouchers which restores the petty cash float to the amount of the imprest. The vouchers are removed from the petty cash box and filed.

Example

The imprest amount for a petty cash system is £150, which is the amount paid into the petty cash box on 1 November. At the end of the week the total of the vouchers in the petty cash box is £125.05. How much cash is required in order to replenish the petty cash box to the imprest amount?

Solution

£125.05, the amount paid out on the basis of the petty cash vouchers is the amount that is required to be restored.

Activity 1

Allsports Limited maintains an imprest amount for the petty cash of £250. During the current period, the sum of £180 is paid out, supported by petty cash vouchers. At the end of the period, what amount should be drawn out of the bank to restore the imprest level?

2.3 Non-imprest petty cash system

An imprest petty cash system as in the previous example is the most common method of dealing with and controlling petty cash. However some businesses may use a non-imprest system. This might be where a set amount of cash is withdrawn each week and paid into the petty cash box no matter what the level of expenditure in that week.

For example it may be an organisation's policy to cash a cheque for £50 each Monday morning for use as petty cash for the week. The danger here is either that petty cash requirements are more than £50 in the week in which case the petty cash box will run out of money. Alternatively week after week expenditure is significantly less than £50 each week, leading to a large amount of cash building up in the petty cash box.

Activity 2

Give two ways in which the company might attempt to maintain security over petty cash.

3 Maintaining petty cash records

3.1 Introduction

Upon the petty cash vouchers being received and the employees being reimbursed, the details are recorded in their own book of prime entry which is known as the petty cash book. The petty cash book, similar to the cash receipts book and the cash payments book, is not only a primary record but can be kept as part of the main ledger double entry system.

3.2 Layout of the petty cash book

The petty cash book is normally set out as a large ledger account with a small receipts side and a larger analysed payments side. A typical petty cash book is set out below.

Receipts			Payments							
Date	Narrative	Total	Date	Narrative	Voucher no	Total	Postage	Cleaning	Tea & Coffee	Sundry	VAT
						£	£	£	£	£	£
1 Nov	Bal b/f	35.50									
1 Nov	Cheque 394	114.50	1 Nov	ASDA	58	23.50			23.50		
			2 Nov	Post Office Ltd	59	29.50	29.50				
			2 Nov	Cleaning materials	60	15.07		12.56			2.51
			3 Nov	Postage	61	16.19	16.19				
			3 Nov	ASDA	62	10.57		8.81			1.76
			4 Nov	Newspapers	63	18.90				18.90	
			5 Nov	ASDA	64	12.10				10.09	2.01

3.3 Receipts side of the petty cash book

The receipts side of the petty cash book only requires one column, as the only receipt into the petty cash box is the regular payment into the petty cash box of cash drawn out of the bank account.

From the example of a typical petty cash book (above), we can see that the balance brought forward was £35.50. The petty cash has then been restored up to £150 by paying in an additional £114.50.

Petty cash: Chapter 6

3.4 Payments side of the petty cash book

Payments out of petty cash will be for a variety of different types of expense and an analysis column is required for each type, in the same way as the cash payments book is analysed (as illustrated in the example above)

Note that a column is required for VAT; if an expense includes VAT this must be analysed out. In addition it is important to remember that any VAT included in an expense must be shown separately on the voucher.

Any VAT shown on the petty cash voucher must be analysed out into the VAT column and the net amount shown in the expense analysis column.

3.5 Writing up the petty cash book

When cash is originally paid into the petty cash book then this will be recorded on the receipts side (debit side) of the petty cash book.

Each petty cash voucher will then in turn be written up in the petty cash book on the payments side.

To ensure that no vouchers have been mislaid, petty cash vouchers are pre-numbered sequentially. Each voucher is then entered into the petty cash book in the correct order, with each item of expenditure being recorded in the correct expense analysis column.

Example

A business has just started to run a petty cash system with an amount of £100. £100 is withdrawn from the bank account and paid into the petty cash box on 3 April 20X1. During the first week the following authorised petty cash vouchers were paid. These transactions will now be recorded in the petty cash book.

PETTY CASH VOUCHER			
Authorised by T Smedley	Received by P Lannall	No	0001
Date	Description	Amount	
3 April 20X1	Tea/coffee/milk	4	73
	Total	4	73

PETTY CASH VOUCHER

Authorised by	Received by	No	0002
T Smedley	R Sellers		
Date	Description	Amount	
3 April 20X1	Train fare	14	90
	Total	14	90

PETTY CASH VOUCHER

Authorised by	Received by	No	0003
T Smedley	F Dorne		
Date	Description	Amount	
4 April 20X1	Stationery	4	00
	VAT	0	80
	Total	4	80

PETTY CASH VOUCHER

Authorised by	Received by	No	0004
T Smedley	P Dent		
Date	Description	Amount	
5 April 20X1	Postage costs	16	35
	Total	16	35

Petty cash: Chapter 6

PETTY CASH VOUCHER				
Authorised by T Smedley	Received by H Polly		No	0005
Date	Description		Amount	
7 April 20X1	Train fare		15	30
		Total	15	30

PETTY CASH VOUCHER				
Authorised by T Smedley	Received by P Lannall		No	0006
Date	Description		Amount	
8 April 20X1	Milk/biscuits		3	85
		Total	3	85

Solution

Petty cash book

Receipts			Payments								
Date	Narrative	Total	Date	Narrative	Voucher no	Total	Postage	Travel	Tea & coffee	Sundry	VAT
20X1		£	20X1			£	£	£	£	£	£
03/04	Cash	100.00	03/04	Tea/coffee	0001	4.73			4.73		
			03/04	Train fare	0002	14.90		14.90			
			04/04	Stationery	0003	4.80				4.00	0.80
			05/04	Postage	0004	16.35	16.35				
			07/04	Train fare	0005	15.30		15.30			
			08/04	Milk/biscuits	0006	3.85			3.85		

4 Posting the petty cash book

4.1 Introduction

Once the petty cash book has been written up, we must now post the totals of the petty cash book to the general ledger accounts.

When the petty cash book is not part of the double entry system, the accounting entries must show the impact on the expense accounts, the VAT account and the petty cash control account.

In the event of there being a top up to the petty cash, a separate entry will be required. We would need to show the money being withdrawn from the bank and deposited into petty cash.

When the petty cash book is part of the double entry accounting system as well as being a book of prime entry, there is no need for an entry to the petty cash control account as the petty cash book acts as the general ledger account and the closing balance on the account is taken from it when the trial balance is prepared.

4.2 Posting the petty cash receipt

The receipt into the petty cash box has come from cash being withdrawn from the bank account. This will have been done by writing out a cheque for cash and withdrawing this from the bank. Therefore the cheque should be recorded in the cash payments book as a payment when the cash payments book is written up.

The receipt of the cash into the petty cash box is recorded in the receipts side of the petty cash book, debit side.

As both the petty cash book and the cash payments book are normally part of the general ledger double entry system, the double entry has been completed. The debit is the entry into the petty cash book and the credit entry is the entry in the cash payments book.

4.3 Posting the petty cash payments

When the petty cash book is part of the general ledger double entry system the total column in the petty cash payments side is the credit entry to the petty cash account.

The only additional entries to make are the debits. These entries are taken from the totals of each of the analysis columns. The total from each analysis column is debited to the relevant general ledger account.

Petty cash: Chapter 6

Example

The petty cash book written up in an earlier example is given again below. This is to be posted to the general ledger accounts.

Petty cash book

Receipts			Payments							
Date	Narrative	Total	Date	Narrative	Voucher no	Total	Postage	Travel	Tea & coffee	Sundry	VAT
20X1		£	20X1			£	£	£	£	£	£
03/04	Cash	100.00	03/04	Tea/coffee	0001	4.73			4.73		
			03/04	Train fare	0002	14.90		14.90			
			04/04	Stationery	0003	4.80				4.00	0.80
			05/04	Postage	0004	16.35	16.35				
			07/04	Train fare	0005	15.30		15.30			
			08/04	Milk/biscuits	0006	3.85			3.85		

Solution

Step 1 Each of the columns in the petty cash payments side must be totalled.

The accuracy of your totalling should be checked by ensuring that all of the analysis column totals add back to the total of the 'total' column in the petty cash book payments side.

Petty cash book

Receipts			Payments							
Date	Narrative	Total	Date	Narrative	Voucher no	Total	Postage	Travel	Tea & coffee	Sundry	VAT
20X1		£	20X1			£	£	£	£	£	£
03/04	Cash	100.00	03/04	Tea/coffee	0001	4.73			4.73		
			03/04	Train fare	0002	14.90		14.90			
			04/04	Stationery	0003	4.80				4.00	0.80
			05/04	Postage	0004	16.35	16.35				
			07/04	Train fare	0005	15.30		15.30			
			08/04	Milk/biscuits	0006	3.85			3.85		
						59.93	16.35	30.20	8.58	4.00	0.80

Check the totals:

	£
Postage	16.35
Travel	30.20
Tea and coffee	8.58
Sundry	4.00
VAT	0.80
	59.93

Step 2 Each of the analysis column totals must now be entered into the general ledger accounts as debit entries.

VAT account

	£		£
Petty cash book (PCB)	0.80		

The entry has come from the petty cash book and this is the reference – this is now shortened to PCB.

Postage account

	£		£
PCB	16.35		

Travel account

	£		£
PCB	30.20		

Tea and coffee account

	£		£
PCB	8.58		

Sundry expenses account

	£		£
PCB	4.00		

Petty cash: Chapter 6

Activity 3

Summary of petty cash vouchers in hand at 31 October 20X7

Date	Description	Total £	VAT included at 20% £
1/10	Envelopes (Administration)	20.10	3.35
4/10	Cleaner (Administration)	8.75	
6/10	Food for staff lunch (Marketing)	17.13	
6/10	Taxi fares (Marketing)	16.23	
6/10	Rail fares (Marketing)	43.75	
10/10	Postage (Administration)	4.60	
15/10	Tea and coffee (Production)	4.39	
17/10	Light bulbs and refuse sacks (Distribution)	8.65	1.44
20/10	Flowers for reception (Administration)	21.23	
26/10	Cleaner (Administration)	8.75	

(a) Write up the payments side of the petty cash book for October 20X7 from the information given.

You should allocate a sequential voucher number to each entry in the petty cash book. The last voucher number to be allocated in September was 6578.

Use the blank petty cash book provided.

(b) Total each of the columns in the petty cash book and cross-cast them.

(c) Post the totals to the general ledger accounts given.

PETTY CASH BOOK – PAYMENTS

Date	Voucher no	Total £	Production £	Distribution £	Marketing £	Administration £	VAT £

Production expenses account

£	£

Distribution expenses account

£	£

Marketing expenses account

£	£

Administration expenses account

£	£

VAT account

£	£

5 Petty cash control account

5.1 Introduction

In most cases the petty cash book is not only a book of prime entry but also part of the general ledger. However in other businesses the petty cash book will be simply a book of prime entry and a petty cash control account will be maintained in the general ledger.

5.2 Petty cash control account

The petty cash control account summarises the information in the petty cash book and is posted from the petty cash book. When cash is put into the petty cash box the petty cash control account will be debited and the total of the petty cash payments for the period will be credited to the petty cash control account.

Example

A business runs a petty cash imprest system with an imprest amount of £100. At 1 May there was £32.56 remaining in the petty cash box and £67.44 of cash was withdrawn from the bank and put into the petty cash box to restore the imprest amount. During the month of May the total payments from the petty cash book were £82.16.

Write up the petty cash control account.

Solution

Petty cash control account

	£		£
Balance b/f	32.56	Payments	82.16
Receipt from bank	67.44	Balance c/d	17.84
	100.00		100.00
Balance b/d	17.84		

6 Reconciling the petty cash

6.1 Introduction

We saw earlier in the chapter that when an imprest system is being used for petty cash then at any point in time the amount of cash in the petty cash box plus the total of the vouchers in the petty cash box should equal the imprest amount.

At regular intervals, usually at the end of each week, this check will be carried out. If there is a difference then this must be investigated.

6.2 Possible causes of difference

If there is more cash in the petty cash box than the balance on the petty cash control account this could be due to an error in writing up the petty cash book (i.e. more has been recorded in payments than has actually been paid out). In this case the entries in the petty cash book should be checked to the underlying petty cash vouchers to discover the error.

If there is less cash in the petty cash box than the balance on the petty cash control account this could also be due to an error in writing up the petty cash book (i.e. less payments have been recorded in the petty cash control account than were actually made). This may be due to a petty cash voucher having been omitted from the petty cash book and therefore again the underlying petty cash vouchers should all be checked to their entries in the petty cash book.

If no accounting errors or posting errors can be found then the cause is likely to be one of the following:

- an error has been made in paying a petty cash voucher and more money was handed out than was recorded on the voucher;
- cash has been paid out of the petty cash box without a supporting voucher;
- cash could have been stolen from the petty cash box.

In such cases the matter should be investigated and security of the petty cash and petty cash procedures improved.

Example

The petty cash control account from the previous example is reproduced.

Petty cash control account

	£		£
Balance b/f	32.56	Payments	82.16
Receipt	67.44	Balance c/d	17.84
	100.00		100.00
Balance b/d	17.84		

What action should be taken if when the petty cash was counted at 31 May the amount held in the box was:

(a) £27.84

(b) £7.84

Solution

(a) If the amount of cash in the box was £27.84 then this is £10 more than expected. The following checks should be made:

Has the balance on the petty cash control account been correctly calculated?

Have the receipt and payments totals been correctly posted to the petty cash control account?

Have the payments in the petty cash book been correctly totalled?

Has each individual petty cash voucher been correctly recorded in the petty cash book?

(b) If the amount of cash in the box is only £7.84 then this is £10 less than expected. All of the above checks should be carried out and if no accounting errors can be found then it will have to be assumed that either £10 too much has been paid out on a petty cash voucher, £10 has been paid out of the petty cash box without a supporting voucher or that £10 has been stolen from the petty cash box.

6.3 Procedure for reconciling the petty cash box

The total amount of cash in the petty cash box will be counted. The vouchers that have been paid during the week are also in the petty cash box and they must also be totalled.

When the amount of cash is added to the total of the vouchers in the box they should equal the imprest amount.

The petty cash vouchers for the week will then be removed from the box and filed.

Example

The amount of cash remaining in a petty cash box at the end of a week is as follows:

Notes/coins	Quantity
£10	1
£5	2
£2	3
£1	7
50p	9
20p	11
10p	15
5p	7
2p	16
1p	23

The imprest amount is £100 and the vouchers in the petty cash box at the end of the week are as follows:

PETTY CASH VOUCHER			
Authorised by C Alexi	Received by P Trant	No	0467
Date	Description	Amount	
4 May 20X3	Window cleaner	15	00
	Total	15	00

PETTY CASH VOUCHER			
Authorised by C Alexi	Received by F Saint	No	0468
Date	Description	Amount	
5 May 20X3	Train fare	9	80
	Total	9	80

PETTY CASH VOUCHER			
Authorised by C Alexi	Received by A Paul	No	0469
Date	Description	Amount	
5 May 20X3	Stationery	8	00
	VAT	1	60
	Total	9	60

PETTY CASH VOUCHER			
Authorised by C Alexi	Received by P Peters	No	0470
Date	Description	Amount	
7 May 20X3	Postage	6	80
	Total	6	80

PETTY CASH VOUCHER			
Authorised by C Alexi	Received by C Ralph	No	0471
Date	Description	Amount	
5 May 20X3	Train fare	16	70
	Total	16	70

The cash and vouchers in the petty cash box at the end of the week are to be reconciled.

Solution

The petty cash must be totalled:

Notes/coins	Quantity	Amount £
£10	1	10.00
£5	2	10.00
£2	3	6.00
£1	7	7.00
50p	9	4.50
20p	11	2.20
10p	15	1.50
5p	7	0.35
2p	16	0.32
1p	23	0.23
		42.10

Now the vouchers must be totalled.

	£
0467	15.00
0468	9.80
0469	9.60
0470	6.80
0471	16.70
	57.90

Petty cash: Chapter 6

Finally, total the cash and the vouchers to ensure that they add back to the imprest amount.

	£
Cash	42.10
Vouchers	57.90
	100.00

Activity 4

Your business runs a petty cash box based upon an imprest amount of £60. This morning you have emptied the petty cash box and found the following notes, coins and vouchers.

Notes
£5 × 2

Coins
£1 × 3
50p × 5
20p × 4
10p × 6
5p × 7
2p × 10
1p × 8

Vouchers	£
2143	10.56
2144	3.30
2145	9.80
2146	8.44
2147	2.62
2148	6.31
2149	1.44

You are required to reconcile the cash and the vouchers in the petty cash box.

7 Summary

In this chapter we have considered the entire petty cash system. Cash is paid into the petty cash box in order to meet the requirements for actual cash in a business's life. This will normally be in the form of reimbursing employees for business expenses that they have incurred on their own behalf. In order to be reimbursed for the expense, the employee must fill out a petty cash voucher which will normally be accompanied by a receipt for the expense and must then be authorised. At this point the employee can be paid the cash out of the petty cash box.

All petty cash is recorded in the petty cash book which is normally both a book of prime entry and part of the general ledger. The cash paid into the petty cash box is recorded as a receipt in the petty cash book and as a payment in the cash payments book, an amount of cash being taken out of the bank account. The payments of petty cash vouchers are recorded as payments in the petty cash book and are analysed as to the type of payment. These payments are then recorded as debit entries in the appropriate expense account.

At the end of a period, a week or a month possibly, the cash in the petty cash box will be counted and reconciled to the vouchers in the box. In an imprest system the total of the vouchers in the box plus the total of the cash in the box should equal the imprest amount.

Petty cash: Chapter 6

Answers to chapter activities

Activity 1

£180

Activity 2

Any two from the following:

(i) Should be kept securely in a locked box or safe, etc.
(ii) All payments should be properly authorised.
(iii) Should be the responsibility of one person.
(iv) The amount of any one payment should be restricted.

Activity 3

(a), (b)

PETTY CASH BOOK – PAYMENTS

Date	Voucher no	Total £	Production £	Distribution £	Marketing £	Administration £	VAT £
01/10/X7	6579	20 10				16 75	3 35
04/10/X7	6580	8 75				8 75	
06/10/X7	6581	17 13			17 13		
06/10/X7	6582	16 23			16 23		
06/10/X7	6583	43 75			43 75		
10/10/X7	6584	4 60				4 60	
15/10/X7	6585	4 39	4 39				
17/10/X7	6586	8 65		7 21			1 44
20/10/X7	6587	21 23				21 23	
26/10/X7	6588	8 75				8 75	
		153 58	4 39	7 21	77 11	60 08	4 79

ICB LEVEL II: MANUAL BOOKKEEPING

(c)

Production expenses account

	£		£
PCB	4.39		

Distribution expenses account

	£		£
PCB	7.21		

Marketing expenses account

	£		£
PCB	77.11		

Administration expenses account

	£		£
PCB	60.08		

VAT account

	£		£
PCB	4.79		

Activity 4

Notes and coins

	£	£
£5 × 2	10.00	
£1 × 3	3.00	
50p × 5	2.50	
20p × 4	0.80	
10p × 6	0.60	
5p × 7	0.35	
2p × 10	0.20	
1p × 8	0.08	
		17.53

Petty cash: Chapter 6

Vouchers	
2143	10.56
2144	3.30
2145	9.80
2146	8.44
2147	2.62
2148	6.31
2149	1.44
	42.47
Imprest amount	60.00

8 Test your knowledge

Workbook Activity 5

Given below is a business' petty cash book for the week.

Petty cash book

Receipts			Payments							
Date	Narrative	Total	Date	Details	Voucher no	Amount £	Postage £	Staff welfare £	Stationery £	Travel expenses £	VAT £
5/1/X1	Bal b/d	150.00	12/1/X1	Postage	03526	13.68	13.68				
				Staff welfare	03527	25.00		25.00			
				Stationery	03528	15.12			12.60		2.52
				Taxi fare	03529	12.25				10.21	2.04
				Staff welfare	03530	6.40		6.40			
				Postage	03531	12.57	12.57				
				Rail fare	03532	6.80				6.80	
				Stationery	03533	8.16			6.80		1.36
				Taxi fare	03534	19.20				16.00	3.20
						119.18	26.25	31.40	19.40	33.01	9.12

Required:

Show what the entries in the general ledger will be:

Account name	Amount £	Dr ✓	Cr ✓

Workbook Activity 6

Given below is a completed petty cash book for transactions that took place on 12th April 20X1:

Petty cash book

Receipts			Payments							
Date	Narrative	Total	Date	Narrative	Voucher no	Total £	Postage £	Staff welfare £	Tea and coffee £	Travel expenses £	VAT £
12/04	Bal b/d	100.00	12/04	Coffee/milk	2534	4.68		4.68			
				Postage	2535	13.26	13.26				
				Stationery	2536	10.48			8.74		1.74
				Taxi fare	2537	15.32				12.77	2.55
				Postage	2538	6.75	6.75				
				Train fare	2539	7.40				7.40	
				Stationery	2540	3.94			3.29		0.65
						61.83	20.01	4.68	12.03	20.17	4.94

Required:

Post the required entries to the general ledger accounts:

Postage

	£		£
Balance b/f	231.67		

Staff welfare

	£		£
Balance b/f	334.78		

Tea and coffee

	£		£
Balance b/f	53.36		

Travel expenses

	£		£
Balance b/f	579.03		

VAT account

	£		£
		Balance b/f	967.44

Bank reconciliations

Introduction

Completion of this chapter will ensure we are able to correctly prepare the cash book, compare the entries in the cash book to details on the bank statement and then finally to prepare a bank reconciliation statement.

CONTENTS

1. Writing up the cash book
2. Preparing the bank reconciliation statement
3. Returned cheques

Bank reconciliations: **Chapter 7**

1 Writing up the cash book

1.1 Introduction

Most businesses will have a separate cash receipts book and a cash payments book which form part of the double entry system. If this form of record is used, the cash balance must be calculated from the opening balance at the beginning of the period, plus the receipts shown in the cash receipts book for the period and minus the payments shown in the cash payments book for the period.

1.2 Balancing the cash book

The following brief calculation will enable us to find the balance on the cash book when separate receipts and payments books are maintained.

	£
Opening balance per the cash book	X
Add: Receipts in the period	X
Less: Payments in the period	(X)
Closing balance per the cash book	X

Example

Suppose that the opening balance on the cash book is £358.72 on 1 June. During June the Cash Payments Book shows that there were total payments made of £7,326.04 during the month of June and the Cash Receipts Book shows receipts for the month of £8,132.76.

What is the closing balance on the cash book at the end of June?

Solution

	£
Opening balance at 1 June	358.72
Add: Receipts for June	8,132.76
Less: Payments for June	(7,326.04)
Balance at 30 June	1,165.44

ICB LEVEL II: MANUAL BOOKKEEPING

Take care if the opening balance on the cash book is an overdraft balance. Any receipts in the period will reduce the overdraft and any payments will increase the overdraft.

Suppose that the opening balance on the cash book is £631.25 overdrawn on 1 June. During June the Cash Payments Book shows that there were total payments made of £2,345.42 during the month of June and the Cash Receipts Book shows receipts for the month of £1,276.45

What is the closing balance on the cash book at the end of June?

Solution

	£
Opening balance at 1 June	(631.25)
Add: Receipts for June	1,276.45
Less: Payments for June	(2,345.42)
Balance at 30 June	(1,700.22)

Activity 1

The opening balance at 1 January in a business cash book was £673.42 overdrawn. During January payments totalled £6,419.37 and receipts totalled £6,488.20.

What is the closing balance on the cash book?

Example

The following transactions are to be written up in the cash book of Jupiter Limited and the balance at the end of the week calculated. The opening balance on the bank account on 28 June 20X1 was £560.61.

2 July   Received a cheque for £45.90 from Hill and French Limited (no settlement discount allowed) – paying in slip 40012.

2 July   Corrected a salary error by paying a cheque for £56.89 – cheque number 100107.

3 July   Paid £96.65 by cheque to Preston Brothers after deducting a settlement discount of £1.65 – cheque number 100108.

3 July   Banked £30 of cash held – paying in slip 40013.

KAPLAN PUBLISHING

Bank reconciliations: Chapter 7

4 July   Received a cheque from Green and Holland for £245.89. They were allowed a settlement discount of £3.68 – paying in slip 40014.

5 July   Reimbursed the petty cash account with £34.89 of cash drawn on cheque number 100109.

The cash receipts and payments books are to be written up and the closing balance calculated.

Solution

Step 1   Enter all of the transactions into the receipts and payments cash books.

Step 2   Total the cash book columns.

Cash receipts book

Date	Narrative		Total £	VAT £	SLCA £	Other £	Discount £
20X1							
2 July	Hill and French	40012	45.90		45.90		
3 July	Cash	40013	30.00			30.00	
4 July	Green and Holland	40014	245.89		245.89		3.68
			321.79	–	291.79	30.00	3.68

Cash payments book

Date	Details	Cheque	Code no	Total £	VAT £	PLCA £	Cash purchases £	Other £	Discount received £
20X1									
2 July	Salary error	100107		56.89				56.89	
3 July	Preston Bros	100108		96.65		96.65			1.65
5 July	Petty cash	100109		34.89				34.89	
				188.43	–	96.65	–	91.78	1.65

216   KAPLAN PUBLISHING

Step 3 Find the balance on the cash book at the end of the week.

		£
Opening balance at 1 July		560.61
Add:	Receipts total	321.79
Less:	Payments total	(188.43)
Balance at the end of the week		693.97

When totalling the cash book columns always check your additions carefully as it is easy to make mistakes when totalling columns of numbers on a calculator. Check that the totals of each analysis column (excluding the discounts columns) add back to the total of the total column.

2 Preparing the bank reconciliation statement

2.1 Introduction

At regular intervals (normally at least once a month) the cashier must check that the cash book is correct by comparing the cash book with the bank statement.

2.2 Differences between the cash book and bank statement

At any date the balance shown on the bank statement is unlikely to agree with the balance in the cash book for two main reasons.

(a) **Items in the cash book not on the bank statement**

Certain items will have been entered in the cash book but will not appear on the bank statement at the time of the reconciliation. Examples are:

- Cheques received by the business and paid into the bank which have not yet appeared on the bank statement, due to the time lag of the clearing system. These are known as **outstanding lodgements** (can also be referred to as "uncleared lodgements").

- Cheques written by the business but which have not yet appeared on the bank statement, because the recipients have not yet paid them in, or the cheques are in the clearing system. These are known as **unpresented cheques**.

- Errors in the cash book (e.g. transposition of numbers, addition errors).

(b) Items on the bank statement not in the cash book

At the time of the bank reconciliation certain items will appear on the bank statement that have not yet been entered into the cash book. These can occur due to the cashier not being aware of the existence of these items until receiving the bank statements. Examples are:

- Direct debit or standing order payments that are in the bank statement but have not yet been entered in the cash payments book.
- BACS or other receipts paid directly into the bank account by a customer.
- Bank charges or bank interest that are unknown until the bank statement has been received and therefore will not be in the cash book.
- Errors in the cash book that may only come to light when the cash book entries are compared to the bank statement.
- Returned cheques i.e. cheques paid in from a customer who does not have sufficient funds in his bank to pay the cheque (see later in this chapter).

2.3 The bank reconciliation

Definition

A bank reconciliation is simply a statement that explains the differences between the balance in the cash book and the balance on the bank statement at a particular date.

A bank reconciliation is produced by following a standard set of steps.

Step 1: Compare the cash book and the bank statement for the relevant period and identify any differences between them.

You should begin with agreeing the opening balances on the bank statement and cash book so that you are aware of any prior period reconciling items that exist.

This is usually done by ticking in the cash book and bank statement items that appear in both the cash book and the bank statement. Any items left unticked therefore only appear in one place, either the cash book or the bank statement. We saw in 2.2 above the reasons why this might occur.

ICB LEVEL II: MANUAL BOOKKEEPING

Step 2: Update the cash book for any items that appear on the bank statement that have not yet been entered into the cash book.

Tick these items in both the cash book and the bank statement once they are entered in the cash book.

At this stage there will be no unticked items on the bank statement.

(You clearly cannot enter on the bank statement items in the cash book that do not appear on the bank statement – the bank prepares the bank statement, not you. These items will either be unpresented cheques or outstanding lodgements – see 2.2 above.)

Step 3: Bring down the new cash book balance following the adjustments in step 2 above.

Step 4: Prepare the bank reconciliation statement.

This will typically have the following proforma.

Bank reconciliation as at 31.0X.200X

	£
Balance as per bank statement	X
Less unpresented cheques	(X)
Add outstanding lodgements	X
Balance as per cash book	X

Think for a moment to ensure you understand this proforma.

We deduct the unpresented cheques (cheques already entered in the cash book but not yet on the bank statement) from the bank balance, because when they are presented this bank balance will be reduced.

We add outstanding lodgements (cash received and already entered in the cash book) because when they appear on the bank statement they will increase the bank balance.

Bank reconciliations: Chapter 7

It is also useful to remember that the bank reconciliation can be performed the opposite way round as shown below:

Bank reconciliation as at 31.0X.200X

	£
Balance as per cash book	X
Add unpresented cheques	(X)
Less outstanding lodgements	X
Balance as per bank statement	X

If we start with the cash book balance, to reconcile this to the bank statement balance we add back the unpresented cheques as though they haven't been paid out of the cash book (as the bank statement has not recognised these being paid out).

We deduct outstanding lodgements as though we haven't recognised these in the cash book (as the bank statement has not recognised these receipts). The cash book balance should then agree to the bank statement balance i.e. we have reconciled these balances.

2.4 Debits and credits in bank statements

When comparing the cash book to the bank statement it is easy to get confused with debits and credits.

- When we pay money into the bank, we debit our cash book but the bank credits our account.

- This is because a debit in our cash book represents the increase in our asset 'cash'. For the bank, the situation is different: they will debit their cash book and credit our account because they now owe us more money; we are a payable.

- When our account is overdrawn, we owe the bank money and consequently our cash book will show a credit balance. For the bank an overdraft is a debit balance.

On the bank statement a credit is an amount of money paid into the account and a debit represents a payment. A bank statement conveys the transactions in the bank's point of view rather than the business' point of view.

ICB LEVEL II: MANUAL BOOKKEEPING

Example

Given below are the completed cash books for Jupiter Limited from the previous example.

Cash receipts book

Date	Narrative		Total £	VAT £	SLCA £	Other £	Discount £
20X1							
2 July	Hill and French	40012	45.90		45.90		
3 July	Cash	40013	30.00			30.00	
4 July	Green and Holland	40014	245.89		245.89		3.68
			321.79	–	291.79	30.00	3.68

Cash payments book

Date	Details	Cheque	Code no	Total £	VAT £	PLCA £	Cash purchases £	Other £	Discounts received £
20X1									
2 July	Salary error	100107		56.89				56.89	
3 July	Preston Bros	100108		96.65		96.65			1.65
5 July	Petty cash	100109		34.89				34.89	
				188.43	–	96.65	–	91.78	1.65

KAPLAN PUBLISHING

Bank reconciliations: Chapter 7

You have now received the bank statement for the week commencing 1 July 20X1 which is also shown below.

FIRST NATIONAL BANK
Cheque Account
SHEET NUMBER 012
ACCOUNT NUMBER 38 41 57 33794363

			Paid in £	Paid out £	Balance £
28 June	Balance brought forward				560.61
1 July	CT	A/C 38562959	123.90		684.51
4 July	CHQ	100107		56.89	
4 July	CR	40013	30.00		657.62
5 July	CR	40012	45.90		
5 July	DR	Bank charges		5.23	
5 July	DD	English Telecom		94.00	
5 July	CHQ	100109		34.89	569.40

CHQ	Cheque	CT	Credit transfer	CR	Payment in
DR	Payment out	DD	Direct debit		

You are required to compare the cash book and the bank statement and determine any differences. Tick the items in the bank statement and in the cash book above, then prepare the bank reconciliation statement at 5 July 20X1.

The balance on the cash book at 28 June was £560.61.

Solution

Step 1 The cash book, duly ticked, appears below.

Cash receipts book

Date	Narrative		Total £	VAT £	SLCA £	Other £	Discount £
20X1							
2 July	Hill and French	40012	45.90 ✓		45.90		
3 July	Cash	40013	30.00 ✓			30.00	
4 July	Green and Holland	40014	245.89		245.89		3.68
			321.79	–	291.79	30.00	3.68

Cash payments book

Date	Details	Cheque	Code no	Total £	VAT £	PLCA £	Cash purchases £	Other £	Discounts received £
20X1									
2 July	Salary error	100107		56.89 ✓				56.89	
3 July	Preston Bros	100108		96.65		96.65			1.65
5 July	Petty cash	100109		34.89 ✓				34.89	
				188.43	–	96.65	–	91.78	1.65

The bank statement should have been ticked as shown below.

FIRST NATIONAL BANK
Cheque Account
SHEET NUMBER 012
ACCOUNT NUMBER 38 41 57 33794363

				Paid in £	Paid out £	Balance £
28 June	Balance brought forward					560.61
1 July	CT	A/C 38562959		123.90		684.51
4 July	CHQ	100107			56.89 ✓	
4 July	CR	40013		30.00 ✓		657.62
5 July	CR	40012		45.90 ✓		
5 July	DR	Bank charges			5.23	
5 July	DD	English Telecom			94.00	
5 July	CHQ	100109			34.89 ✓	569.40

CHQ	Cheque	CT	Credit transfer	CR	Payment in
DR	Payment out	DD	Direct debit		

Step 2 A comparison of the items in the cash book with those in the bank statement reveals unticked items in both.

(a) We will first consider the items that are unticked on the bank statement;

- there is a credit transfer on 1 July of £123.90 – this must be checked to the related documentation and then entered into the cash receipts book;

- the bank charges of £5.23 must be entered into the cash payments book;

- the direct debit of £94.00 should be checked and then entered into the cash payments book.

(b) We will now consider the items that are unticked in the cash book. Remember that no adjustment is needed to these but we have to decide where they will appear in the bank reconciliation statement.

- the cheque paid in on 4 July has not yet appeared on the bank statement due to the time it takes for cheques to clear through the clearing system – an outstanding lodgement;
- cheque number 100108 has not yet cleared through the banking system – an unpresented cheque.

The cash receipts and cash payments book will now appear as follows after the adjustments in (a) above.

Cash receipts book

Date	Narrative	Total £	VAT £	SLCA £	Other £	Discount £
20X1						
2 July	Hill and French 40012	45.90 ✓		45.90		
3 July	Cash 40013	30.00 ✓			30.00	
4 July	Green and Holland 40014	245.89		245.89		3.68
1 July	Credit transfer	123.90 ✓		123.90		
		445.69	–	415.69	30.00	3.68

Cash payments book

Date	Details	Cheque	Code no	Total £	VAT £	PLCA £	Cash purchases £	Other £	Discounts received £
20X1									
2 July	Salary error	100107		56.89 ✓				56.89	
3 July	Preston Bros	100108		96.65		96.65			1.65
5 July	Petty cash	100109		34.89 ✓				34.89	
5 July	Bank charges			5.23 ✓				5.23	
5 July	English Telecom	DD		94.00 ✓		94.00			
				287.66	–	190.65	–	97.01	1.65

Note that the items we have entered in the cash book from the bank statement are ticked in both. There are no unticked items on the bank statement (not shown) and two unticked items in the cash book.

Step 3 Find the amended cash book balance.

	£
Balance at 28 June	560.61
Cash receipts in first week of July	445.69
Cash payments in first week of July	(287.66)
Balance at 5 July	718.64

Step 4 Reconcile the amended cash book balance to the bank statement balance.

Bank reconciliation as at 5 July 20X1

	£
Balance per bank statement	569.40
Less: unpresented cheque	(96.65)
Add: outstanding lodgement	245.89
Balance per cash book	718.64

This is the completed bank reconciliation.

Activity 2

The following are summaries of the cash receipts book, cash payments book and bank statement for the first two weeks of trading of Gambank, a firm specialising in selling cricket bats.

Cash receipts book

Date	Narrative	Total £	VAT £	SLCA £	Other £	Discount £
20X0						
01 Jan	Capital	2,000			2,000	
05 Jan	A Hunter	1,000		1,000		
09 Jan	Cancel cheque no 0009	90			90	
10 Jan	I M Dunn	4,800		4,800		

Bank reconciliations: Chapter 7

Cash payments book

Date	Details	Cheque no	Code	Total £	VAT £	PLCA £	Cash purchases £	Other £	Discount received £
20X0									
01 Jan	Wages	0001		50				50	
01 Jan	Fine	0002		12				12	
03 Jan	Dodgy Dealers	0003		1,500		1,500			
04 Jan	E L Pubo	0004		45			45		
05 Jan	Drawings	0005		200				200	
07 Jan	E L Wino	0007		30			30		
08 Jan	Toby	0008		1,400		1,400			
09 Jan	El Pubo	0009		70			70		
10 Jan	Marion's Emp	0010		200			200		
11 Jan	Speeding Fine	0011		99				99	

FINANCIAL BANK plc **CONFIDENTIAL**

YOU CAN BANK ON US

10 Yorkshire Street Account CURRENT Sheet no. 1
Headingley GAMBANK
Leeds LS1 1QT
Telephone: 0113 633061

Statement date 14 Jan 20X0   Account Number 40023986

Date	Details		Withdrawals (£)	Deposits (£)	Balance (£)
01 Jan	CR			2,000	2,000
02 Jan	0001		50		1,950
04 Jan	0003		1,500		450
05 Jan	0005		200		250
07 Jan	CR			1,000	
	0002		12		
	0004		45		
	0006		70		1,123
08 Jan	0007		30		1,093
10 Jan	0009		70		
	0009			70	
	0010		200		893
11 Jan	0012		20		
	Charges		53		820

| SO | Standing order | DD | Direct debit | CR | Credit |
| AC | Automated cash | OD | Overdrawn | TR | Transfer |

Prepare a bank reconciliation statement at 14 January 20X0.

2.5 Opening balances disagree

Usually the balances on the bank statement and in the cash book do not agree at the start of the period for the same reasons that they do not agree at the end, e.g. items in the cash book that were not on the bank statement. When producing the reconciliation statement it is important to take this opening difference into account.

Example

The bank statement and cash book of Jones for the month of December 20X8 start as follows.

Bank statement

		Debit £	Credit £	Balance £
1 Dec 20X8	Balance b/d (favourable)			8,570
2 Dec 20X8	0073	125		
2 Dec 20X8	0074	130		
3 Dec 20X8	Sundries		105	

Cash book

	£		£
1 Dec 20X8 b/d	8,420	Cheque 0075 Wages	200
Sales	320	Cheque 0076 Rent	500
	X		X
	X		X

Required:

Explain the difference between the opening balances.

Bank reconciliations: Chapter 7

> **Solution**
>
> The difference in the opening balance is as follows.
>
> £8,570 – £8,420 = £150
>
> This difference is due to the following.
>
> | | £ |
> |---|---|
> | Cheque 0073 | 125 |
> | Cheque 0074 | 130 |
> | | 255 |
> | Lodgement (sundries) | (105) |
> | | 150 |
>
> These cheques and lodgements were in the cash book in November, but only appear on the bank statement in December. They will therefore be matched and ticked against the entries in the November cash book. The December reconciliation will then proceed as normal.

3 Returned cheques

A customer C may send a cheque in payment of an invoice without having sufficient funds in his account with Bank A.

The seller S who receives the cheque will pay it into his account with Bank B and it will go into the clearing system. Bank B will credit S's account with the funds in anticipation of the cheque being honoured.

Bank A however will not pay funds into the S's account with Bank B and Bank B will then remove the funds from S's account.

The net effect of this is that on S's bank statement, the cheque will appear as having been paid in (a credit on the bank statement), and then later will appear as having been paid out (a debit on the bank statement).

The original credit on the bank statement will be in S's cash book as a debit in the normal way. But the debit on the bank statement (the dishonour of the cheque) will not be in S's cash book. This will have to be credited into the cash book as money paid out.

These cheques are technically referred to as 'returned cheques', but they are also called 'dishonoured cheques' or 'bounced cheques'.

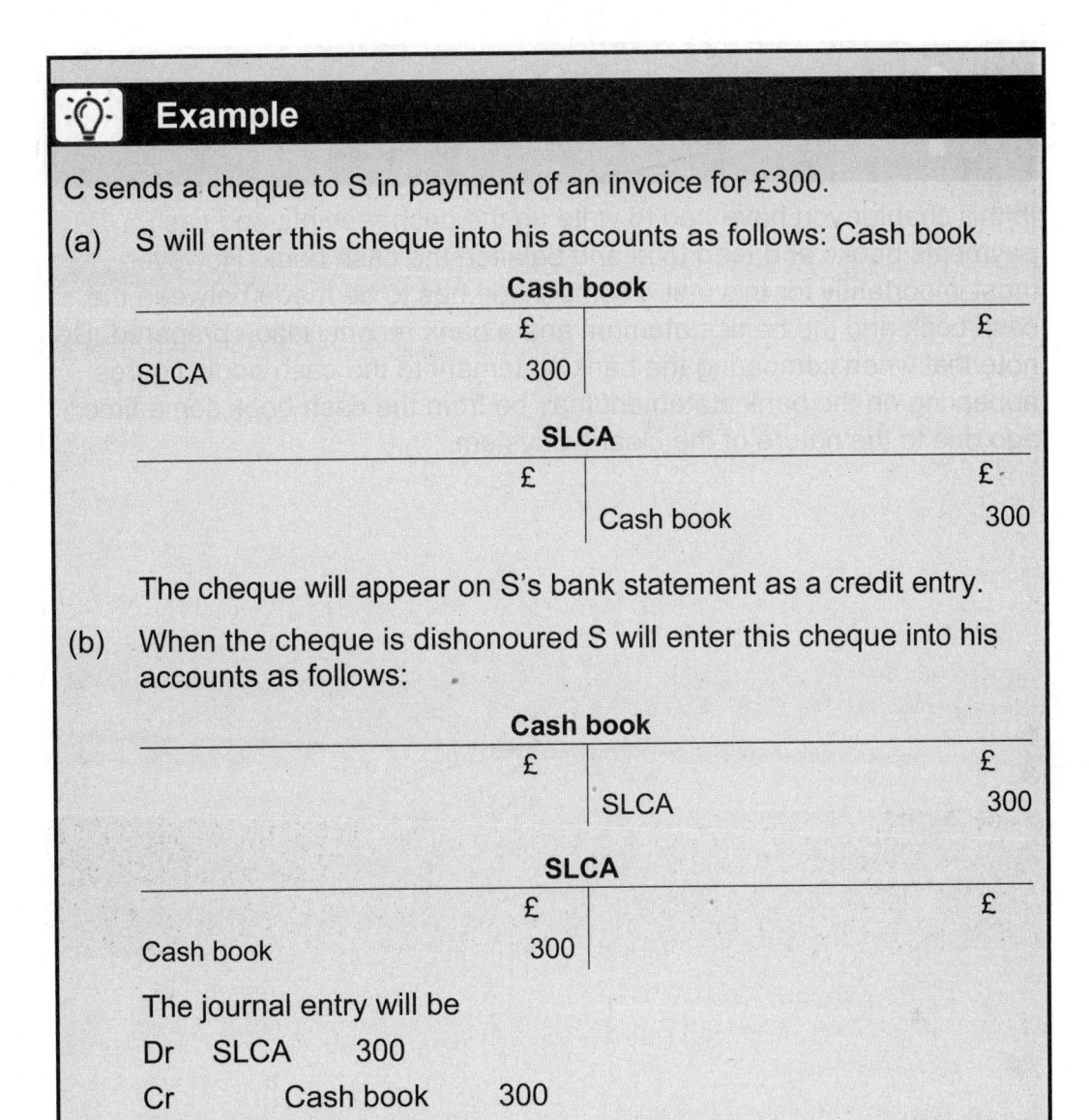

Example

C sends a cheque to S in payment of an invoice for £300.

(a) S will enter this cheque into his accounts as follows: Cash book

Cash book

	£		£
SLCA	300		

SLCA

	£		£
		Cash book	300

The cheque will appear on S's bank statement as a credit entry.

(b) When the cheque is dishonoured S will enter this cheque into his accounts as follows:

Cash book

	£		£
		SLCA	300

SLCA

	£		£
Cash book	300		

The journal entry will be

Dr   SLCA   300
Cr   Cash book   300

This reinstates the debtor.

The dishonoured cheque will appear on the bank statement as a debit entry.

Bank reconciliations: Chapter 7

4 Summary

In this chapter you have had to write up the cash receipts and cash payments books and then total and balance the cash book. However, most importantly for this unit a comparison has to be made between the cash book and the bank statement and a bank reconciliation prepared. Do note that when comparing the bank statement to the cash book, figures appearing on the bank statement may be from the cash book some time ago due to the nature of the clearing system.

Answers to chapter activities

Activity 1

	£
Opening balance	(673.42)
Payments	(6,419.37)
Receipts	6,488.20
Closing balance	(604.59)

The closing balance is £604.59 overdrawn.

Activity 2

Step 1 Tick the cash books and bank statement to indicate the matched items.

Cash receipts book

Date	Narrative	Total £	VAT £	Sales ledger £	Other £	Discount £
20X0						
01 Jan	Capital	2,000 ✓			2,000	
05 Jan	A Hunter	1,000 ✓		1,000		
09 Jan	Cancel cheque no 0009	90			90	
10 Jan	I M Dunn	4,800		4,800		
		7,890	–	5,800	2,090	–

Bank reconciliations: Chapter 7

Cash payments book

Date	Details	Cheque no	Code	Total £	VAT £	Purchases ledger £	Cash purchases £	Other £	Discounts received £
20X0									
01 Jan	Wages	0001		50	✓			50	
01 Jan	Fine	0002		12	✓			12	
03 Jan	Dodgy Dealers	0003		1,500	✓	1,500			
04 Jan	E L Pubo	0004		45	✓	45			
05 Jan	Drawings	0005		200	✓			200	
07 Jan	E L Wino	0007		30	✓	30			
08 Jan	Toby	0008		1,400		1,400			
09 Jan	El Pubo	0009		70	✓	70			
10 Jan	Marion's Emp	0010		200	✓	200			
11 Jan	Speeding Fine	0011		99				99	
				3,606	–	3,245	–	361	

ICB LEVEL II: MANUAL BOOKKEEPING

FINANCIAL BANK plc **fb** **CONFIDENTIAL**

YOU CAN BANK ON US

10 Yorkshire Street Account CURRENT Sheet no. 1
Headingley GAMBANK
Leeds LS1 1QT
Telephone: 0113 633061

Statement date 14 Jan 20X0   Account Number 40023986

Date	Details		Withdrawals (£)	Deposits (£)	Balance (£)
01 Jan	CR			2,000 ✓	2,000
02 Jan	0001		50 ✓		1,950
04 Jan	0003		1,500 ✓		450
05 Jan	0005		200 ✓		250
07 Jan	CR			1,000 ✓	
	0002		12 ✓		
	0004		45 ✓		
	0006		70		1,123
08 Jan	0007		30 ✓		1,093
10 Jan	0009		70 ✓		
	0009			70	
	0010		200 ✓		893
11 Jan	0012		20		
	Charges		53		820

| SO | Standing order | DD | Direct debit | CR | Credit |
| AC | Automated cash | OD | Overdrawn | TR | Transfer |

Step 2   Deal with each of the unticked items.

Cash receipts book — cheque number 0009 does appear to have been cancelled as it has appeared as a debit and a credit entry in the bank statement – however the bank statement shows that the cheque was for £70 and not the £90 entered into the cash receipts book – this must be amended in the cash book.

— the receipt from I M Dunn has not yet cleared through the banking system and is therefore not on the bank statement – it is an outstanding lodgement.

KAPLAN PUBLISHING   233

Cash payments book — cheque number 0008 to Toby and cheque number 0011 have not yet cleared through the clearing system – they are unpresented cheques.

Bank statement — cheque number 0006 has not been entered into the cash payments book but it has cleared the bank account – the cash book must be amended to show this payment.

— cheque number 0012 has not been entered into the cash payments book but it has cleared the bank account – the cash book must be amended to show this payment.

— the bank charges of £53 must be entered into the cash payments book.

Step 3 Amend the cash books and total them. Cash receipts book

Cash receipts book

Date	Narrative	Total	VAT	Sales ledger	Other	Discount
		£	£	£	£	£
20X0						
01 Jan	Capital	2,000 ✓			2,000	
05 Jan	A Hunter	1,000 ✓		1,000		
09 Jan	Cancel cheque no 0009	90			90	
10 Jan	I M Dunn	4,800		4,800		
10 Jan	Cancelled cheque adjustment 0009	(20) ✓			(20)	
		7,870	–	5,800	2,070	–

Cash payments book

Date	Details	Cheque no	Code	Total £	VAT £	Purchases ledger £	Cash purchases £	Other £	Discounts received £
20X0									
01 Jan	Wages	0001		50	✓			50	
01 Jan	Fine	0002		12	✓			12	
03 Jan	Dodgy Dealers	0003		1,500	✓	1,500			
04 Jan	E L Pubo	0004		45	✓	45			
05 Jan	Drawings	0005		200	✓			200	
07 Jan	E L Wino	0007		30	✓	30			
08 Jan	Toby	0008		1,400		1,400			
09 Jan	El Pubo	0009		70	✓	70			
10 Jan	Marion's Emp	0010		200	✓	200			
11 Jan	Speeding Fine	0011		99				99	
6 Jan		0006		70	✓	70			
10 Jan		0012		20	✓	20			
11 Jan	Bank charges			53	✓			53	
				3,749	–	3,335	–	414	

Step 4 Determine the amended cash book balance

	£
Opening balance	–
Cash receipts	7,870
Cash payments	(3,749)
Amended cash book balance	4,121

Step 5 Reconcile the amended cash book balance to the bank statement balance

	£	£
Balance per bank statement		820
Add: outstanding lodgement		4,800
Less: unpresented cheques 0008	1,400	
0011	99	
		(1,499)
Amended cash book balance		4,121

Bank reconciliations: Chapter 7

5 Test your knowledge

Workbook Activity 3

Given below are the cash receipts book, cash payments book and bank statement for a business for the week ending 11 March 20X1.

Required:

- Compare the bank statement to the cash book.
- Correct the cash receipts and payments books for any items which are unmatched on the bank statement.
- Total the cash receipts book and cash payments book and determine the final cash balance
- Using the reconciliation proforma reconcile the closing balance on the bank statement to the closing cash balance

Cash receipts book

Date 20X1	Narrative	Bank £	VAT £	Debtors £	Other £	Discount £
7/3	Balance b/f	860.40				
7/3	Paying in slip 0062	1,117.85	84.05	583.52	450.28	23.60
8/3	Paying in slip 0063	1,056.40	68.84	643.34	344.22	30.01
9/3	Paying in slip 0064	1,297.81	81.37	809.59	406.85	34.20
10/3	Paying in slip 0065	994.92	57.02	652.76	285.14	18.03
11/3	Paying in slip 0066	1,135.34	59.24	779.88	296.22	23.12

Cash payments book

Date	Details	Cheque no	Code	Bank £	VAT £	Creditors £	Cash purchases £	Other £	Discounts received £
20X1									
7/3	P Barn	012379	PL06	383.21		383.21			
	Purchases	012380	ML	274.04	45.67		228.37		
	R Trevor	012381	PL12	496.80		496.80			6.30
8/3	F Nunn	012382	PL07	218.32		218.32			
	F Taylor	012383	PL09	467.28		467.28			9.34
	C Cook	012384	PL10	301.40		301.40			
9/3	L White	012385	PL17	222.61		222.61			
	Purchases	012386	ML	275.13	45.85		229.28		
	T Finn	012387	PL02	148.60		148.60			
10/3	S Penn	012388	PL16	489.23		489.23			7.41
11/3	P Price	012389	PL20	299.99		299.99			
	Purchases	012390	ML	270.12	45.02		225.10		

Bank reconciliations: Chapter 7

FINANCIAL BANK plc   CONFIDENTIAL

YOU CAN BANK ON US

10 Yorkshire Street   Account   CURRENT   Sheet no. 00614
Headingley
Leeds LS1 1QT   Account name   T R FABER LTD
Telephone: 0113 633061

Statement date 11 March 20X1   Account Number 27943316

Date	Details	Withdrawals (£)	Deposits (£)	Balance (£)
7/3	Balance from sheet 00613			860.40
	Bank giro credit L Fernley		406.90	1,267.30
9/3	Cheque 012380	274.04		
	Cheque 012381	496.80		
	Credit 0062		1,117.85	1,614.31
10/3	Cheque 012383	467.28		
	Cheque 012384	301.40		
	Credit 0063		1,056.40	
	SO – Loan Finance	200.00		1,702.03
11/3	Cheque 012379	383.21		
	Cheque 012386	275.13		
	Cheque 012387	148.60		
	Credit 0064		1,297.81	
	Bank interest		6.83	2,199.73

DD	Standing order	DD	Direct debit	CP	Card purchase
AC	Automated cash	OD	Overdrawn	TR	Transfer

BANK RECONCILIATION STATEMENT AS AT 11 MARCH 20X1

                                                                          £

Balance per bank statement
Outstanding lodgements:

Unpresented cheques:

                                                              _____

Balance per cash book   £

Workbook Activity 4

Given below is the cash book of a business and the bank statement for the week ending 20 April 20X1.

Required:

Compare the cash book to the bank statement and note any differences that you find.

Cash Book

Date	Details	£	Date	Details	£
16/4	Donald & Co	225.47	16/4	Balance b/d	310.45
17/4	Harper Ltd	305.68	17/4	Cheque 03621	204.56
	Fisler Partners	104.67	18/4	Cheque 03622	150.46
18/4	Denver Ltd	279.57	19/4	Cheque 03623	100.80
19/4	Gerald Bros	310.45		Cheque 03624	158.67
20/4	Johnson & Co	97.68	20/4	Cheque 03625	224.67
			20/4	Balance c/d	173.91
		1,323.52			1,323.52

EXPRESS BANK   CONFIDENTIAL

High Street
Fenbury
TL4 6JY
Telephone: 0169 422130

Account   CURRENT   Sheet no. 0213
Account name   P L DERBY LTD

Statement date 20 April 20X1   Account Number 40429107

Date	Details	Withdrawals (£)	Deposits (£)	Balance (£)
16/4	Balance from sheet 0212			310.45 OD
17/4	DD – District Council	183.60		494.05 OD
18/4	Credit		225.47	
19/4	Credit		104.67	
	Cheque 03621	240.56		
	Bank interest	3.64		408.11 OD
20/4	Credit		305.68	
	Credit		279.57	
	Cheque 03622	150.46		
	Cheque 03624	158.67		131.99 OD

| DD | Standing order | DD | Direct debit | CP | Card purchase |
| AC | Automated cash | OD | Overdrawn | TR | Transfer |

Workbook Activity 5

Graham

The cash account of Graham showed a debit balance of £204 on 31 March 20X3. A comparison with the bank statements revealed the following:

		£
1	Cheques drawn but not presented	3,168
2	Amounts paid into the bank but not credited	723
3	Entries in the bank statements not recorded in the cash account	
	(i) Standing orders	35
	(ii) Interest on bank deposit account	18
	(iii) Bank charges	14
4	Balance on the bank statement at 31 March	2,618

Required:

(a) Show the appropriate adjustments required in the cash account of Graham bringing down the correct balance at 31 March 20X3.

(b) Prepare a bank reconciliation statement at that date.

Workbook Activity 6

The following are the cash book and bank statements of KT Ltd.

Receipts June 20X1

CASH BOOK – JUNE 20X1

Date	Details	Total	Sales ledger control	Other
1 June	Balance b/d	7,100.45		
8 June	Cash and cheques	3,200.25	3,200.25	–
15 June	Cash and cheques	4,100.75	4,100.75	–
23 June	Cash and cheques	2,900.30	2,900.30	–
30 June	Cash and cheques	6,910.25	6,910.25	–
		£24,212.00	£17,111.55	

Payments June 20X1

Date	Payee	Cheque no	Total £	Purchase ledger control £	Operating overhead £	Admin overhead £	Other £
1 June	Hawsker Chemical	116	6,212.00	6,212.00			
7 June	Wales Supplies	117	3,100.00	3,100.00			
15 June	Wages and salaries	118	2,500.00		1,250.00	1,250.00	
16 June	Drawings	119	1,500.00				1,500.00
18 June	Blyth Chemical	120	5,150.00	5,150.00			
25 June	Whitby Cleaning Machines	121	538.00	538.00			
28 June	York Chemicals	122	212.00	212.00			
			19,212.00	15,212.00	1,250.00	1,250.00	1,500.00

Bank Statement

Crescent Bank plc
High Street
Sheffield
Account: Alison Robb t/a KT Ltd
Account no: 57246661

Statement no: 721

Page 1

Date	Details	Payments £	Receipts £	Balance £
20X1				
1 June	Balance b/fwd			8,456.45
1 June	113	115.00		8,341.45
1 June	114	591.00		7,750.45
1 June	115	650.00		7,100.45
4 June	116	6,212.00		888.45
8 June	CC		3,200.25	4,088.70
11 June	117	3,100.00		988.70
15 June	CC		4,100.75	5,089.45
15 June	118	2,500.00		2,589.45
16 June	119	1,500.00		1,089.45
23 June	120	5,150.00		4,060.55 O/D
23 June	CC		2,900.30	1,160.25 O/D

Key:	S/O	Standing Order	DD	Direct Debit
	CC	Cash and cheques	CHGS	Charges
	BACS	Bankers automated clearing	O/D	Overdrawn

Bank reconciliations: Chapter 7

Required:

Examine the business cash book and the business bank statement shown in the data provided above. Prepare a bank reconciliation statement as at 30 June 20X1. Set out your reconciliation in the proforma below.

Proforma

BANK RECONCILIATION STATEMENT AS AT 30 JUNE 20X1

£

Balance per bank statement
Outstanding lodgements:

Unpresented cheques:

Balance per cash book   £

Accruals and prepayments

Introduction

In this chapter we start to deal with adjustments that are required to the trial balance figures in order to go from an initial trial balance to a final set of accounts.

In almost all cases these adjustments will include accruals and prepayments of expenses and possibly income.

CONTENTS

1 Recording income and expenditure
2 Accruals
3 Prepayments
4 Income accounts
5 Journal entries

Accruals and prepayments: **Chapter 8**

1 Recording income and expenditure

1.1 Introduction

One of the fundamental accounting concepts is the accruals concept. This states that the income and expenses recognised in the accounting period should be that which has been earned or incurred during the period rather than the amounts received or paid in cash in the period.

1.2 Recording sales and purchases on credit

Sales on credit are recorded in the ledger accounts from the sales day book. The double entry is to credit sales and debit the sales ledger control account (debtors account).

Therefore all sales made in the period are accounted for in the period whether the money has yet been received by the seller or not.

Purchases on credit are recorded in ledger accounts from the purchases day book and debited to purchases and credited to the purchases ledger control account (creditors account).

Again this means that the purchases are already recorded whether or not the creditor has yet been paid.

1.3 Recording expenses of the business

Most of the expenses of the business such as rent, rates, telephone, power costs etc will tend to be entered into the ledger accounts from the cash payments book. This means that the amount recorded in the ledger accounts is only the cash payment.

In order to accord with the accruals concept the amount of the expense to be recognised in the profit and loss account may be different to this cash payment made in the period.

Expenses should be charged to the profit and loss account as the amount that has been incurred in the accounting period rather than the amount of cash that has been paid during the period.

2 Accruals

2.1 Introduction

If an expense is to be adjusted to represent the amount incurred in a period rather than what has been paid, then the adjustment may be an accrual or a prepayment.

Definition

An accrual is an expense that has been incurred during the period but has not been paid for by the period end and has therefore not been entered in the ledger accounts.

Example

A business has a year end of 31 December. During the year 20X1 the following electricity bills were paid:

		£
15 May	4 months to 30 April	400
18 July	2 months to 30 June	180
14 Sept	2 months to 30 August	150
15 Nov	2 months to 31 October	210

It is estimated that the average monthly electricity bill is £100.

What is the total charge for the year 20X1 for electricity?

Solution

	£
Jan to April	400
May to June	180
July to August	150
Sept to Oct	210
Accrual for Nov/Dec (2 × 100)	200
Total charge	1,140

Accruals and prepayments: **Chapter 8**

Activity 1

Olwen commenced business on 1 May 20X0 and is charged rent at the rate of £6,000 per annum. During the period to 31 December 20X0, he actually paid £3,400.

What should his charge in the profit and loss account for the period to 31 December 20X0 be in respect of rent?

2.2 Accounting for accruals

The method of accounting for an accrual is to:

(a) **debit the expense account**

to increase the expense to reflect the fact that an expense has been incurred; and

(b) **credit an accruals account** (or the same expense account)

to reflect the fact that there is a creditor for the expense.

Note that the credit entry can be made in one of two ways:

(1) credit a separate accruals account; or
(2) carry down a credit balance on the expense account.

Example

Using the electricity example from above, the accounting entries will now be made in the ledger accounts.

Solution

Method 1 – Separate accruals account Electricity Account

Electricity account

	£		£
15 May CPB	400		
18 July CPB	180		
14 Sept CPB	150		
15 Nov CPB	210		
31 Dec Accrual	200	P&L Account	1,140
	———		———
	1,140		1,140
	———		———

246   **KAPLAN** PUBLISHING

Accruals account

	£		£
		Electricity account	200

Using this method the profit and loss account is charged with the full amount of electricity used in the period and there is an accrual or creditor to be shown in the balance sheet of £200 in the accruals account. Any other accruals such as telephone, rent, etc would also appear in the accruals account as a credit balance. The total of the accruals would appear in the balance sheet as a creditor.

Method 2 – Using the expense account Electricity Account

Electricity account

	£		£
15 May CPB	400		
18 July CPB	180		
14 Sept CPB	150		
15 Nov CPB	210		
31 Dec Accrual	200	P&L Account	1,140
	1,140		1,140
		Balance b/d	200

Again with this method the profit and loss account charge is the amount of electricity used in the period and the credit balance on the expense account is shown as an accrual or creditor in the balance sheet.

Activity 2

Olwen commenced business on 1 May 20X0 and is charged rent at the rate of £6,000 per annum. During the period to 31 December 20X0, he actually paid £3,400.

Write up the ledger account for rent for the period to 31 December 20X0. Clearly state whether the year-end adjustment is an accrual or prepayment.

Rent account

	£		£

2.3 Opening and closing balances

When the accrual is accounted for in the expense account then care has to be taken to ensure that the accrual brought down is included as the opening balance on the expense account at the start of the following year.

Example

Continuing with our earlier electricity expense example the closing accrual at the end of 20X0 was £200. During 20X1 £950 of electricity bills were paid and a further accrual of £220 was estimated at the end of 20X1.

Write up the ledger account for electricity for 20X1 clearly showing the charge to the profit and loss account and any accrual balance.

Solution

Electricity account

	£		£
Cash paid during the year	950	Balance b/d – opening accrual	200
Balance c/d – closing accrual	220	P&L account	970
	1,170		1,170
		Balance b/d	220

The opening accrual of £200 acts as a reduction against the increase to the expense account on the debit side of the cash paid of £950. The £200 opening accrual is part of this £950 payment but the accrued amount was recognised within the expense in the prior year- when the expense was incurred and hence we should not double count the expense.

Activity 3

The insurance account of a business has an opening accrual of £340 at 1 July X0. During the year insurance payments of £3,700 were made and it has been calculated that there is a closing accrual of £400.

Prepare the insurance expense account for the year ended 30th June X1 and close it off by showing the transfer to the profit and loss account

Insurance expenses

	£		£
	___		___
	___		___

3 Prepayments

3.1 Introduction

The other type of adjustment that might need to be made to an expense account is to adjust for a prepayment.

Definition

A prepayment is a payment made during the period (and therefore debited to the expense account) for an expense that relates to a period after the year end.

Accruals and prepayments: Chapter 8

💡 Example

The rent of a business is £3,000 per quarter payable in advance. During 20X0 the rent ledger account shows that £15,000 of rent has been paid during the year.

What is the correct charge to the profit and loss account for the year and what is the amount of any prepayment at 31 December 20X0?

Solution

The profit and loss account charge should be £12,000 for the year, four quarterly charges of £3,000 each. The prepayment is £3,000 (£15,000 – £12,000), rent paid in advance for next year.

📝 Activity 4

Julie paid £1,300 insurance during the year to 31 March 20X6. The charge in the profit and loss account for the year to 31 March 20X6 is £1,200.

What is the amount of the prepayment at 31 March 20X6?

3.2 Accounting for prepayments

The accounting for prepayments is the mirror image of accounting for accruals.

(a) **credit the expense account**

   to reduce the expense by the amount of the prepayment; and

(b) **debit a prepayment account**

   to show that the business has an asset (the prepayment) at the period end.

The debit entry can appear in one of two places:

(1) debit a separate prepayments account; or
(2) carry down a debit balance on the expense account.

Example

The rent of a business is £3,000 per quarter payable in advance. During 20X0 the rent ledger account shows that £15,000 of rent has been paid during the year.

Show how these entries would be made in the ledger accounts.

Solution

Method one – Separate prepayments account and rent account

Rent account

	£		£
Cash payments	15,000	Prepayments account	3,000
		P&L account	12,000
	15,000		15,000

Prepayments account

	£		£
Rent account	3,000		

The charge to the profit and loss account is now the correct figure of £12,000 and there is a debit balance on the prepayments account.

This balance on the prepayments account will appear as a debtor or prepayment in the balance sheet.

Method two – Balance shown on the expense account.

Rent account

	£		£
Cash payments	15,000	P&L account	12,000
		Balance c/d – prepayment	3,000
	15,000		15,000
Balance b/d – prepayment	3,000		

The expense to the profit and loss account is again £12,000 and the debit balance on the account would appear as the prepayment on the balance sheet.

3.3 Opening and closing balances

Again as with accounting for accruals, care must be taken with opening prepayment balances on the expense account. If there is a closing prepayment balance on an expense account then this must be included as an opening balance at the start of the following year. As we must recognise the expense of the prepayment in the year it relates to, despite is being paid in the prior year.

Example

Continuing with the previous rent example the prepayment at the end of 20X0 was £3,000. The payments for rent during the following year were £15,000 and the charge for the year was £14,000.

Write up the ledger account for rent clearly showing the charge to the profit and loss account and the closing prepayment at 31 December 20X1.

Solution

Rent account

	£		£
Balance b/d – opening prepayment	3,000	P&L account charge	14,000
Cash payments	15,000	Balance c/d – prepayment (bal fig)	4,000
	18,000		18,000
Balance b/d – prepayment	4,000		

Note that you were given the charge for the year in the question and therefore the prepayment figure is the balancing amount. The opening prepayment increases the current year expense as it is now being recognised due to it being the year the expense relates to. The closing prepayment reduces the expense as despite the £15,000 payment being partly related to this closing prepayment we shouldn't be recognising the expense of it until the next year.

Activity 5

The following information relates to a company's rent and rates account:

Balances as at:	1 April 20X0 £	31 March 20X1 £
Prepayment for rates expenses	20	30
Accrual for rent expense	100	120

The bank summary for the year shows payments for rent and rates of £840.

Prepare the rent and rates account for the year ended 31st March 20X1 and close it off by showing the transfer to the profit and loss account.

Rent and rates expense account

£ | £

3.4 Approach to accruals and prepayments

There are two approaches to writing up expenses accounts with accruals or prepayments. This will depend upon whether the charge to the profit and loss account is the balancing figure or whether the accrual or prepayment is the balancing figure.

Approach 1 – enter any opening accrual /prepayment

– enter the cash paid during the period

– enter the closing accrual/prepayment that has been given or calculated

– enter the charge to the profit and loss account as a balancing figure

Accruals and prepayments: Chapter 8

Approach 2 – enter any opening accrual/prepayment
– enter the cash paid during the period
– enter the profit and loss account charge for the period
– enter the closing accrual/prepayment as the balancing figure

4 Income accounts

4.1 Introduction

As well as having expenses some businesses will also have sundry forms of income. The cash received from this income may not always be the same as the income earned in the period and therefore similar adjustments to those for accruals and prepayments in the expense accounts will be required.

4.2 Accruals of income

If the amount of income received in cash is less than the income earned for the period then this additional income must be accrued for. This is done by:

(1) a credit entry in the income account;
(2) a debit entry/debtor in the balance sheet for the amount of cash due.

4.3 Income prepaid

If the amount of cash received is greater than the income earned in the period then this income has been prepaid by the payer. The accounting entries required here are:

(1) a debit entry to the income account;
(2) a credit entry/creditor shown in the balance sheet for the amount of income that has been prepaid.

Example

Minnie's business has two properties, A and B, that are rented out to other parties. The rental on property A for the year is £12,000 but only £10,000 has been received. The rental on property B is £15,000 and the client has paid £16,000 this year.

Write up separate rent accounts for properties A and B showing the income credited to the profit and loss account and any closing balances on the income accounts.

Explain what each balance means.

Solution

Rental income – A

	£		£
P&L account	12,000	Cash received	10,000
		Balance c/d – income accrued	2,000
	12,000		12,000
Balance b/d income accrued	2,000		

Accrued income would be a debtor balance in the balance sheet showing that £2,000 is owed for rental income on this property.

Rental income – B

	£		£
P&L account	15,000	Cash received	16,000
Balance c/d – income prepaid	1,000		
	16,000		16,000
		Balance b/d – income prepaid	1,000

Prepaid income would be a creditor balance in the balance sheet indicating that too much cash (cash in advance) has been received for this rental.

Accruals and prepayments: **Chapter 8**

Activity 6

Hyde, an acquaintance wishes to use your shop to display and sell framed photographs. He will pay £40 per month for this service in cash.

(a) How would you account for this transaction each month?

(b) If, at the end of the year, the acquaintance owed one month's rental, how would this be treated in the accounts?

(c) Which accounting concept is being applied?

5 Journal entries

5.1 Introduction

The accruals and prepayments are adjustments to the accounts which do not appear in the accounting records from the primary records. Therefore the adjustments for accruals and prepayments must be entered into the accounting records by means of a journal entry.

Example

An accrual for electricity is to be made at the year-end of £200. Show the journal entry required for this adjustment.

Solution

Journal entry			No:
Date			
Prepared by			
Authorised by			
Account	Code	Debit £	Credit £
Electricity account	0442	200	
Accruals	1155		200
Totals		200	200

256   **KAPLAN** PUBLISHING

Activity 7

A prepayment adjustment is to be made at the year end of £1,250 for insurance expense.

Record the journal entry required for this adjustment.

The following account codes and account names should be used.

0445 Insurance

1000 Prepayment

Journal entry			No:
Date			
Prepared by			
Authorised by			
Account	**Code**	**Debit £**	**Credit £**
Totals			

6 Summary

In order for the final accounts of an organisation to accord with the accruals concept, the cash receipts and payments for income and expenses must be adjusted to ensure that they include all of the income earned during the year and expenses incurred during the year.

The sales and purchases are automatically dealt with through the sales ledger and purchases ledger control account.

However the expenses and sundry income of the business are recorded in the ledger accounts on a cash paid and received basis and therefore adjustments for accruals and prepayments must be made by journal entries.

Accruals and prepayments: **Chapter 8**

Answers to chapter activities

Activity 1

$(\frac{8}{12} \times £6,000) = £4,000$

Activity 2

Rent account

	£		£
Cash payments	3,400	Profit and loss account $(6,000 \times \frac{8}{12})$	4,000
Balance c/d – accrual	600		
	4,000		4,000
		Balance b/d – accrual	600

Activity 3

Insurance expenses

	£		£
Cash payments	3,700	Balance b/d – opening accrual	340
Balance c/d – closing accrual	400	P & L account charge (bal fig)	3,760
	4,100		4,100
		Balance b/d – accrual	400

Activity 4

The prepayment is £1,300 − 1,200 = £100

Activity 5

Rent and rates expenses

	£		£
Balance b/d	20	Balance b/d	100
Cash	840	Profit and loss account	850
Balance c/d	120	(bal fig)	
		Balance c/d	30
	980		980
Balance b/d	30	Balance b/d	120

Activity 6

(a) DR Cash account £40

   CR Sundry Income a/c £40

(b) Accrued income – a sundry debtor

   (1) revenue in the Profit and Loss a/c

   (2) current asset in the Balance Sheet

(c) Accruals concept

Accruals and prepayments: **Chapter 8**

Activity 7

Journal entry			No:
Date			
Prepared by			
Authorised by			
Account	**Code**	**Debit £**	**Credit £**
Prepayment	1000	1,250	
Insurance	0445		1,250
Totals		1,250	1,250

7 Test your knowledge

Workbook Activity 8

Siobhan

Siobhan, the proprietor of a sweet shop, provides you with the following information in respect of sundry expenditure and income of her business for the year ended 31 December 20X4:

1 **Rent payable**

   £15,000 was paid during 20X4 to cover the 15 months ending 31 March 20X5.

2 **Gas**

   £840 was paid during 20X4 to cover gas charges from 1 January 20X4 to 31 July 20X4. Gas charges can be assumed to accrue evenly over the year. There was no outstanding balance at 1 January 20X4.

3 **Advertising**

   Included in the payments totalling £3,850 made during 20X4 is an amount of £500 payable in respect of a planned campaign for 20X5.

4 **Bank interest**

   The bank statements of the business show that the following interest has been charged to the account.

For period up to 31 May 20X4	Nil (no overdraft)
For 1 June – 31 August 20X4	£28
1 September – 30 November 20X4	£45

   The bank statements for 20X5 show that £69 was charged to the account on 28 February 20X5.

5 **Rates**

   Towards the end of 20X3 £4,800 was paid to cover the six months ended 31 March 20X4.

   In May 20X4 £5,600 was paid to cover the six months ended 30 September 20X4.

   In early 20X5 £6,600 was paid for the six months ending 31 March 20X5.

Accruals and prepayments: Chapter 8

6 Rent receivable

During 20X4, Siobhan received £250 rent from Joe Soap for the use of a lock-up garage attached to the shop, in respect of the six months ended 31 March 20X4.

She increased the rent to £600 pa from 1 April 20X4, and during 20X4 Joe Soap paid her rent for the full year ending 31 March 20X5.

Required:

Write up ledger accounts for each of the above items, showing:

(a) the opening balance at 1 January 20X4, if any;

(b) any cash paid or received;

(c) the closing balance at 31 December 20X4;

(d) the charge or credit for the year to the profit and loss account.

Workbook Activity 9

A Crew

The following is an extract from the trial balance of A Crew at 31 December 20X1:

	DR £
Stationery	560
Rent	900
Rates	380
Lighting and heating	590
Insurance	260
Wages and salaries	2,970

Stationery which had cost £15 was still in hand at 31 December 20X1.

Rent of £300 for the last three months of 20X1 had not been paid and no entry has been made in the books for it.

£280 of the rates was for the year ended 31 March 20X2. The remaining £100 was for the three months ended 31 March 20X1.

Fuel had been delivered on 18 December 20X1 at a cost of £15 and had been consumed before the end of 20X1. No invoice had been received for the £15 fuel in 20X1 and no entry has been made in the records of the business.

ICB LEVEL II: MANUAL BOOKKEEPING

£70 of the insurance paid was in respect of insurance cover for the year 20X2. Nothing was owing to employees for wages and salaries at the close of 20X1.

Required:

Record the above information in the relevant accounts, showing the transfers to the profit and loss account for the year ended 31 December 20X1.

Workbook Activity 10

A Metro

A Metro owns a number of antique shops and, in connection with this business, he runs a small fleet of motor vans. He prepares his accounts to 31 December in each year.

On 1 January 20X0 the amount prepaid for motor tax and insurance was £570.

On 1 April 20X0 he paid £420 which represented motor tax on six of the vans for the year ended 31 March 20X1.

On 1 May 20X0 he paid £1,770 insurance for all ten vans for the year ended 30 April 20X1.

On 1 July 20X0 he paid £280 which represented motor tax for the other four vans for the year ended 30 June 20X1.

Required:

Write up the account for 'motor tax and insurance' for the year ended 31 December 20X0.

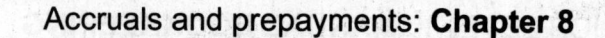

Depreciation

Introduction

You need to be able to understand the purpose of depreciation on fixed assets, calculate the annual depreciation charge using one of two standard methods, account correctly for the annual depreciation charge and treat the depreciation accounts in the trial balance correctly in a set of final accounts.

All of this will be covered in this chapter.

CONTENTS
1   The purpose of depreciation
2   Calculating depreciation
3   Accounting for depreciation
4   Assets acquired during an accounting period

Depreciation: Chapter 9

1 The purpose of depreciation

1.1 Introduction

Fixed assets are capitalised in the accounting records which means that they are treated as capital expenditure and their cost is initially recorded in the balance sheet and not charged to the profit and loss account. However this is not the end of the story and this cost figure must eventually go through the profit and loss account by means of the annual depreciation charge.

1.2 Accruals concept

The accruals concept states that the costs incurred in a period should be matched with the income produced in the same period. When a fixed asset is used it is contributing to the production of the income of the business. Therefore in accordance with the accruals concept some of the cost of the fixed asset should be charged to the profit and loss account each year that the asset is used.

1.3 What is depreciation?

> **Definition**
>
> Depreciation is the measure of the cost of the economic benefits of the tangible fixed assets that have been consumed during the period. Consumption includes the wearing out, using up or other reduction in the useful economic life of a tangible fixed asset whether arising from use, passage of time or obsolescence through either changes in technology or demand for the goods and services produced by the asset. (Taken from FRS 15 Tangible Fixed Assets.)

This makes it quite clear that the purpose of depreciation is to charge the profit and loss account with the amount of the cost of the fixed asset that has been used up during the accounting period.

1.4 How does depreciation work?

The basic principle of depreciation is that a proportion of the cost of the fixed asset is charged to the profit and loss account each period and deducted from the cost of the fixed asset in the balance sheet. Therefore as the fixed asset gets older its value in the balance sheet reduces and each year the profit and loss account is charged with this proportion of the initial cost.

> **Definition**
>
> Net book value is the cost of the fixed asset less the accumulated depreciation to date.

	£
Cost	X
Less: Accumulated depreciation	(X)
Net book value (NBV)	X

The aim of depreciation of fixed assets is to show the cost of the asset that has been consumed during the year. It is not to show the true or market value of the asset. So this net book value will probably have little relation to the actual market value of the asset at each balance sheet date. The important aspect of depreciation is that it is a charge to the profit and loss account of the amount of the fixed asset consumed during the year.

2 Calculating depreciation

2.1 Introduction

The calculation of depreciation can be done by a variety of methods (see later in the chapter) but the principles behind each method remain the same.

2.2 Factors affecting depreciation

There are three factors that affect the depreciation of a fixed asset:

- the cost of the asset
- the length of the useful economic life of the asset;
- the estimated residual value of the asset.

2.3 Useful economic life

> **Definition**
>
> The useful economic life of an asset is the estimated life of the asset for the current owner.

This is the estimated number of years that the business will be using this asset and therefore the number of years over which the cost of the asset must be spread via the depreciation charge.

One particular point to note here is that land is viewed as having an infinite life and therefore no depreciation charge is required for land. However, any buildings on the land should be depreciated.

2.4 Estimated residual value

Many assets will be sold for a form of scrap value at the end of their useful economic lives.

> **Definition**
>
> The estimated residual value of a fixed asset is the amount that it is estimated the asset will be sold for when it is no longer of use to the business.

The aim of depreciation is to write off the cost of the fixed asset less the estimated residual value over the useful economic life of the asset.

2.5 The straight line method of depreciation

> **Definition**
>
> The straight line method of depreciation is a method of charging depreciation so that the profit and loss account is charged with the same amount of depreciation each year.

The method of calculating depreciation under this method is:

$$\text{Annual depreciation charge} = \frac{\text{Cost} - \text{estimated residual value}}{\text{Useful economic life}}$$

ICB LEVEL II: MANUAL BOOKKEEPING

Example

An asset has been purchased by an organisation for £400,000 and is expected to be used in the organisation for 6 years. At the end of the six-year period it is currently estimated that the asset will be sold for £40,000.

What is the annual depreciation charge on the straight line basis?

Solution

$$\text{Annual depreciation charge} = \frac{400{,}000 - 40{,}000}{6}$$

$$= £60{,}000$$

Activity 1

The following task is about recording fixed asset information in the general ledger.

A new asset has been acquired. VAT can be reclaimed on this asset.

- The cost of the asset excluding VAT is £85,000 and this was paid for by cheque.
- The residual value is expected to be £5,000 excluding VAT
- The asset is to be depreciated using the straight line basis and the assets useful economic life is 5 years.

Make entries to account for:

(a) The purchase of the new asset
(b) The depreciation on the new asset

Asset at cost account

£	£
____	____
____	____

Accumulated depreciation

£	£
———	———
———	———

Depreciation charge

£	£
———	———
———	———

2.6 The reducing balance method

Definition

The reducing balance method of depreciation allows a higher amount of depreciation to be charged in the early years of an asset's life compared to the later years.

The depreciation is calculated using this method by multiplying the net book value of the asset at the start of the year by a fixed percentage.

Example

A fixed asset has a cost of £100,000.

It is to be depreciated using the reducing balance method at 30% over its useful economic life of four years, after which it will have an estimated residual value of approximately £24,000.

Show the amount of depreciation charged for each of the four years of the asset's life.

Solution

	£
Cost	100,000
Year 1 depreciation 30% × 100,000	(30,000)
Net book value at the end of year 1	70,000
Year 2 depreciation 30% × 70,000	(21,000)
Net book value at the end of year 2	49,000
Year 3 depreciation 30% × 49,000	(14,700)
Net book value at the end of year 3	34,300
Year 4 depreciation 30% × 34,300	(10,290)
Net book value at the end of year 4	24,010

Activity 2

A business buys a motor van for £20,000 and depreciates it at 10% per annum by the reducing balance method.

Calculate:

- The depreciation charge for the second year of the motor van's use.
- Calculate the net book value at the end of the second year.

Solution

	£
Cost	
Year 1 depreciation	
Net book value at the end of year 1	
Year 2 depreciation	
Net book value at the end of year 2	

2.7 Choice of method

Whether a business chooses the straight line method of depreciation or the reducing balance method (or indeed any of the other methods which are outside the scope of this syllabus) is the choice of management.

The straight line method is the simplest method to use. Often, however, the reducing balance method is chosen for assets which reduce in value more in the early years of their life than the later years. This is often the case with cars and computers and the reducing balance method is often used for these assets.

Once the method of depreciation has been chosen for a particular class of fixed assets then this same method should be used each year in order to satisfy the accounting objective of comparability. The management of a business can change the method of depreciation used for a class of fixed assets but this should only be done if the new method shows a truer picture of the consumption of the cost of the asset than the previous method.

Activity 3

Give one reason why a business might choose reducing balance as the method for depreciating its delivery vans?

(a) It is an easy method to apply.

(b) It is the method applied for fixed assets that lose more value in their early years.

(c) It is the method that is most consistent.

3 Accounting for depreciation

3.1 Introduction

Now we have seen how to calculate depreciation we must next learn how to account for it in the ledger accounts of the business.

3.2 Dual effect of depreciation

The two effects of the charge for depreciation each year are:

- there is an expense to the profit and loss account and therefore a debit entry to a depreciation expense account;

- therefore we create a provision for accumulated depreciation account and there is a credit entry to this account. Accumulated depreciation may also be referred to as 'provision for depreciation'.

> **Definition**
>
> The provision for accumulated depreciation account is used to reduce the value of the fixed asset in the balance sheet.

> **Example**
>
> An asset has been purchased by an organisation for £400,000 and is expected to be used in the organisation for six years.
>
> At the end of the six year period it is currently estimated that the residual value will be £40,000.
>
> The asset is to be depreciated on the straight line basis.
>
> Show the entries in the ledger accounts for the first two years of the asset's life and how this asset would appear in the balance sheet at the end of each of the first two years.
>
> **Solution**
>
> **Step 1**
>
> Record the purchase of the asset in the fixed asset account.
>
> **Fixed asset account**
>
> | | £ | | £ |
> |---|---|---|---|
> | Year 1 Bank | 400,000 | | |
>
> **Step 2**
>
> Record the depreciation expense for Year 1.
>
> Depreciation charge $= \dfrac{£400,000 - £40,000}{6}$
>
> $= £60,000$ per year
>
> DR Depreciation expense account
> CR Accumulated depreciation account

Depreciation: Chapter 9

Depreciation expense account

	£		£
Year 1 Accumulated depreciation	60,000		

Accumulated depreciation account

	£		£
		Expense account	60,000

Note the balance sheet will show the cost of the asset and the accumulated depreciation is then deducted to arrive at the net book value of the asset.

Step 3

Show the entries for the year 2 depreciation charge

Depreciation expense account

	£		£
Year 2 Accumulated depreciation	60,000		

Accumulated depreciation account

	£		£
		Balance b/d	60,000
		Expense account	60,000

Note that the expense account has no opening balance as this was cleared to the profit and loss account at the end of year 1.

However the accumulated depreciation account being a balance sheet account is a continuing account and does have an opening balance being the depreciation charged so far on this asset.

Step 4

Balance off the accumulated depreciation account and show how the fixed asset would appear in the balance sheet at the end of year 2.

Accumulated depreciation account

	£		£
		Balance b/d	60,000
Balance c/d	120,000	Expense account	60,000
	120,000		120,000
		Balance b/d	120,000

Balance Sheet extract

	Cost £	Accumulated depreciation £	Net book value £
Fixed asset	400,000	120,000	280,000

Activity 4

At 31 March 20X3, a business owned a motor vehicle which had a cost of £12,100 and accumulated depreciation of £9,075.

Complete the balance sheet extract below.

	Cost	Accumulated depreciation	NBV
Motor Vehicle			

3.3 Net book value

As you have seen from the balance sheet extract the fixed assets are shown at their net book value. The net book value is made up of the cost of the asset less the accumulated depreciation on that asset or class of assets.

The net book value is purely an accounting value for the fixed asset. It is not an attempt to place a market value or current value on the asset and it in fact often bears little relation to the actual value of the asset.

Depreciation: **Chapter 9**

3.4 Ledger entries with reducing balance depreciation

No matter what method of depreciation is used the ledger entries are always the same. So here is another example to work through.

Example

On 1 April 20X2 a machine was purchased for £12,000 with an estimated useful life of 4 years and estimated scrap value of £4,920. The machine is to be depreciated at 20% reducing balance.

The ledger accounts for the years ended 31 March 20X3, 31 March 20X4 and 31 March 20X5 are to be written up.

Show how the fixed asset would appear in the balance sheet at each of these dates.

Solution

Step 1

Calculate the depreciation charge.

			£
Cost			12,000
Year-end March 20X3 – depreciation	12,000 × 20%	=	2,400
			9,600
Year-end March 20X4 – depreciation	9,600 × 20%	=	1,920
			7,680
Year-end March 20X5 – depreciation	7,680 × 20%	=	1,536
			6,144

Step 2

Enter each year's figures in the ledger accounts bringing down a balance on the machinery account and accumulated depreciation account but clearing out the entry in the expense account to the profit and loss account.

Machinery account

	£		£
April 20X2 Bank	12,000	Mar 20X3 Balance c/d	12,000
April 20X3 Balance b/d	12,000	Mar 20X4 Balance c/d	12,000
April 20X5 Balance b/d	12,000	Mar 20X5 Balance c/d	12,000
April 20X5 Balance b/d	12,000		

Depreciation expense account

	£		£
Mar 20X3 Accumulated dep'n a/c	2,400	Mar 20X3 P&L a/c	2,400
Mar 20X4 Accumulated dep'n a/c	1,920	Mar 20X4 P&L a/c	1,920
Mar 20X5 Accumulated dep'n a/c	1,536	Mar 20X5 P&L a/c	1,536

Machinery: Accumulated depreciation account

	£		£
Mar 20X3 Balance c/d	2,400	Mar 20X3 Depreciation expense	2,400
		Apr 20X3 Balance b/d	2,400
Mar 20X4 Balance c/d	4,320	Mar 20X4 Depreciation expense	1,920
	4,320		4,320
		Apr 20X4 Balance b/d	4,320
Mar 20X5 Balance c/d	5,856	Mar 20X5 Depreciation expense	1,536
	5,856		5,856
		Apr 20X5 Balance b/d	5,856

Balance Sheet extract

Fixed assets		Cost £	Accumulated depreciation £	Net book value £
At 31 Mar 20X3	Machinery	12,000	2,400	9,600
At 31 Mar 20X4	Machinery	12,000	4,320	7,680
At 31 Mar 20X5	Machinery	12,000	5,856	6,144

Make sure that you remember to carry down the accumulated depreciation at the end of each period as the opening balance at the start of the next period.

Activity 5

ABC Co owns the following assets as at 31 December 20X6:

	£
Plant and machinery	5,000
Office furniture	800

Depreciation is to be provided as follows:

(a) plant and machinery, 20% reducing-balance method;

(b) office furniture, 25% on cost per year, straight-line method.

The plant and machinery was purchased on 1 January 20X4 and the office furniture on 1 January 20X5.

Required:

Show the ledger accounts for the year ended 31 December 20X6 necessary to record the transactions.

4 Assets acquired during an accounting period

4.1 Introduction

So far in our calculations of the depreciation charge for the year we have ignored precisely when in the year the fixed asset was purchased. This can sometimes be relevant to the calculations depending upon the policy that you are given for calculating depreciation. There are two main methods of expressing the depreciation policy and both of these will now be considered.

4.2 Calculations on a monthly basis

The policy may state that depreciation is to be charged on a monthly basis. This means that the annual charge will be calculated using the depreciation method given and then pro-rated for the number of months in the year that the asset has been owned.

Example

A piece of machinery is purchased on 1 June 20X1 for £20,000. It has a useful life of 5 years and zero scrap value. The organisation's accounting year ends on 31 December.

What is the depreciation charge for 20X1? Depreciation is charged on a monthly basis using the straight line method.

Solution

Annual charge = $\dfrac{£20,000}{5}$ = £4,000

Charge for 20X1: £4,000 × 7/12 (i.e. June to Dec) = £2,333

Activity 6

A business buys a machine for £40,000 on 1 January 20X3 and another one on 1 July 20X3 for £48,000.

Depreciation is charged at 10% per annum on cost, and calculated on a monthly basis.

What is the total depreciation charge for the two machines for the year ended 31 December 20X3?

Depreciation: **Chapter 9**

4.3 Acquisition and disposal policy

The second method of dealing with depreciation in the year of acquisition is to have a depreciation policy as follows:

'A full year's depreciation is charged in the year of acquisition and none in the year of disposal.'

Ensure that you read the instructions in any question carefully as in the exam you will always be given the depreciation policy of the business.

> **Activity 7**
>
> A business purchased a motor van on 7 August 20X3 at a cost of £12,640.
>
> It is depreciated on a straight-line basis using an expected useful economic life of five years and estimated residual value of zero.
>
> Depreciation is charged with a full year's depreciation in the year of purchase and none in the year of sale.
>
> The business has a year end of 30 November.
>
> What is the net book value of the motor van at 30 November 20X4?
>
> What does this amount represent?

5 Summary

This chapter considered the manner in which the cost of fixed assets is charged to the profit and loss account over the life of the fixed assets, known as depreciation.

Whatever the method of depreciation, the ledger entries are the same. The profit and loss account is charged with the depreciation expense and the accumulated depreciation account shows the accumulated depreciation over the life of the asset to date.

The accumulated balance is netted off against the cost of the fixed asset in the balance sheet in order to show the fixed asset at its net book value.

Answers to chapter activities

Activity 1

Annual depreciation charge $= \dfrac{85{,}000 - 5{,}000}{5}$

$= £16{,}000$

Asset at cost account

	£		£
Bank	85,000	Balance c/d	85,000
	85,000		**85,000**

Accumulated depreciation

	£		£
Balance c/d	16,000	Depreciation charge	16,000
	16,000		**16,000**

Depreciation charge

	£		£
Accumulated depreciation	16,000	Profit and loss account	16,000
	16,000		**16,000**

Depreciation: Chapter 9

Activity 2

	£
Cost	20,000
Year 1 depreciation	(2,000)
Net book value at the end of year 1	18,000
Year 2 depreciation	(1,800)
Net book value at the end of year 2	16,200

Activity 3

The answer is B.

The reducing balance method is used to equalise the combined costs of depreciation and maintenance over the vehicle's life (i.e. in early years, depreciation is high, maintenance low; in later years, depreciation is low, maintenance is high).

The reducing balance method is also used for fixed assets that are likely to lose more value in their early years than their later years such as cars or vans.

Activity 4

Balance sheet extract below.

	Cost	Accumulated depreciation	NBV
Motor Vehicle	12,100	9,075	3,025

Activity 5

Plant and machinery account

Date		£	Date		£
1.1.X6	Balance b/d	5,000	31.12.X6	Balance c/d	5,000
1.1.X7	Balance b/d	5,000			

Office furniture account

Date		£	Date		£
1.1.X6	Balance b/d	800	31.12.X6	Balance c/d	800
1.1.X7	Balance b/d	800			

Depreciation expense account

Date		£	Date		£
31.12.X6	Accumulated dep'n a/c – plant and machinery	640	31.12.X6	Trading and profit and loss account	840
31.12.X6	Accumulated dep'n a/c – office furniture	200			
		840			840

Accumulated depreciation account – Plant and machinery

Date		£	Date		£
31.12.X6	Balance c/d	2,440	1.1.X6	Balance b/d	1,800
			31.12.X6	Dep'n expense	640
		2,440			2,440
			1.1.X7	Balance b/d	2,440

Depreciation: **Chapter 9**

Accumulated depreciation account – Office furniture

Date		£	Date		£
31.12.X6	Balance c/d	400	1.1.X6	Balance b/d	200
			31.12.X6	Dep'n expense	200
		400			400
			1.1.X7	Balance b/d	400

The opening balance on the accumulated depreciation account is calculated as follows:

		Plant and machinery	Office furniture
		£	£
20X4	20% × £5,000	1,000	–
20X5	20% × £(5,000 – 1,000)	800	
	25% × £800		200
Opening balance 1.1.X6		1,800	200

The depreciation charge for the year 20X6 is calculated as follows:

	Plant and machinery	Office furniture	Total
	£	£	£
20% × (5,000 – 1,800)	640		
25% × £800		200	840

Activity 6

		£
Machine 1	£40,000 × 10%	4,000
Machine 2	£48,000 × 10% × 6/12	2,400
		6,400

Activity 7

Annual depreciation = $\dfrac{£12,640}{5}$ = £2,528

NBV = £12,640 − (2 × £2,528) = £7,584

This is the cost of the van less the accumulated depreciation to date. It is the amount remaining to be depreciated in the future. It is not a market value.

6 Test your knowledge

Workbook Activity 8

Mead is a sole trader with a 31 December year end. He purchased a car on 1 January 20X3 at a cost of £12,000. He estimates that its useful life is four years, after which he will trade it in for £2,400. The annual depreciation charge is to be calculated using the straight line method.

Required:

Write up the motor car cost and accumulated depreciation accounts and the depreciation expense account for the first three years, bringing down a balance on each account at the end of each year.

Workbook Activity 9

S Telford purchases a machine for £6,000. He estimates that the machine will last eight years and its scrap value then will be £1,000.

Required:

(1) Prepare the machine cost and accumulated depreciation accounts for the first three years of the machine's life, and show the balance sheet extract at the end of each of these years charging depreciation on the straight line method.

(2) What would be the net book value of the machine at the end of the third year if depreciation was charged at 20% on the reducing balance method?

Workbook Activity 10

Hillton

(a) Hillton started a veggie food manufacturing business on 1 January 20X6. During the first three years of trading he bought machinery as follows:

January	20X6	Chopper	Cost	£4,000
April	20X7	Mincer	Cost	£6,000
June	20X8	Stuffer	Cost	£8,000

Each machine was bought for cash.

Hillton's policy for machinery is to charge depreciation on the straight line basis at 25% per annum. A full year's depreciation is charged in the year of purchase, irrespective of the actual date of purchase.

Required:

For the three years from 1 January 20X6 to 31 December 20X8 prepare the following ledger accounts:

(i) Machinery account

(ii) Accumulated depreciation account (machinery)

(iii) Depreciation expense account (machinery)

Bring down the balance on each account at 31 December each year.

Tip: Use a table to calculate the depreciation charge for each year.

(b) Over the same three year period Hillton bought the following motor vehicles for his business:

January 20X6	Metro van	Cost £3,200
July 20X7	Transit van	Cost £6,000
October 20X8	Astra van	Cost £4,200

Each vehicle was bought for cash.

Hillton's policy for motor vehicles is to charge depreciation on the reducing balance basis at 40% per annum. A full year's depreciation is charged in the year of purchase, irrespective of the actual date of purchase.

Depreciation: Chapter 9

Required:

For the three years from 1 January 20X6 to 31 December 20X8 prepare the following ledger accounts:

(i) Motor vehicles account

(ii) Accumulated depreciation account (motor vehicles)

(iii) Depreciation expense account (motor vehicles)

Bring down the balance on each account at 31 December each year.

Tip: Use another depreciation table.

Workbook Activity 11

On 1 December 20X2 Infortec Computers owned motor vehicles costing £28,400. During the year ended 30 November 20X3 the following changes to the motor vehicles took place:

		£
1 March 20X3	Sold vehicle – original cost	18,000
1 June 20X3	Purchased new vehicle – cost	10,000
1 September 20X3	Purchased new vehicle – cost	12,000

Depreciation on motor vehicles is calculated on a monthly basis at 20% per annum on cost.

Complete the table below to calculate the total depreciation charge to profits for the year ended 30 November 20X3.

	£
Depreciation for vehicle sold 1 March 20X3	
Depreciation for vehicle purchased 1 June 20X3	
Depreciation for vehicle purchased 1 September 20X3	
Depreciation for other vehicles owned during the year	
Total depreciation for the year ended 30 November 20X3	

Preparation of final accounts for a sole trader

Introduction

You need to be able to prepare the final accounts; a profit and loss account and a balance sheet for a sole trader.

These final accounts may be prepared directly from a trial balance plus various adjustments or from an extended trial balance. The preparation of an extended trial balance is not part of the Level II syllabus and therefore we will just be considering the step by step approach to the final accounts preparation from an initial trial balance.

CONTENTS

1. The profit and loss account for a sole trader
2. The balance sheet for a sole trader
3. Preparing final accounts from the trial balance

Preparation of final accounts for a sole trader: **Chapter 10**

1 The profit and loss account for a sole trader

1.1 Introduction

> **Definition**
>
> The profit and loss account summarises transactions over a period and determines whether a profit or a loss has been made during that period.

Technically the profit and loss account is split into two elements:

- the trading account;
- the profit and loss account.

However, in general the whole statement is referred to as the profit and loss account.

1.2 Trading account

The trading account calculates the gross profit/loss that has been made from the trading activities of the sole trader; the buying and selling of goods.

> **Definition**
>
> The gross profit/loss is the profit/loss from the trading activities of the sole trader.

The trading account looks like this:

		£	£
	Sales		X
Less:	Sales returns		(X)
			X
Less:	Cost of sales		
	Opening stock	X	
	Purchases	X	
Less:	Purchases returns	(X)	
		X	
	Less: Closing stock	(X)	
			(X)
	Gross profit (loss)		X

KAPLAN PUBLISHING

290

Activity 1

Trading profit and loss account extract for the year ended 31 December 20X2.

Calculate the sales and cost of sales (complete the boxes).

	£	£
Sales		☐
Less: Cost of sales		
Opening stock	37,500	
Purchases	158,700	
	196,200	
Less: Closing stock	(15,000)	
		☐
Gross profit		111,300

1.3 Profit and loss account

The remaining content of the profit and loss account is a list of the expenses of the business. These are deducted from the gross profit to give the net profit or loss.

Definition

The net profit or loss is the profit or loss after deduction of all of the expenses of the business.

A proforma profit and loss account is shown on the following page.

Preparation of final accounts for a sole trader: Chapter 10

Profit and loss account for the year ended 31 December 20X2

	£	£
Sales		X
Less: Sales returns		(X)
		X
Less: Cost of sales		
Stock on 1 January (opening stock)	X	
Add: Purchases of goods for resale	X	
Less: Purchases returns	(X)	
	X	
Less: Stock on 31 December (closing stock)	(X)	
		(X)
Gross profit		X
Sundry income:		
Discounts received	X	
Commission received	X	
Rent received	X	
		X
		X
Less: Expenses:		
Rent	X	
Rates	X	
Lighting and heating	X	
Telephone	X	
Postage	X	
Insurance	X	
Stationery	X	
Payroll expenses	X	
Depreciation	X	
Accountancy and audit fees	X	
Bank charges and interest	X	
Bad debts	X	
Delivery costs	X	
Van running expenses	X	
Selling expenses	X	
Discounts allowed	X	
		(X)
Net profit/(Loss)		X/(X)

1.4 Preparation of the profit and loss account

The profit and loss account is prepared by listing all of the entries from the trial balance that are profit and loss account balances.

It is important to consider any adjustments that are required to the trial balance amounts prior to inserting the amounts into the profit and loss account.

Example

Given below is the trial balance for Lyttleton along with additional columns for some adjustments that are required.

Account name	Trial balance DR £	Trial balance CR £	Adjustments DR £	Adjustments CR £
Capital		7,830		
Cash	2,010			
Fixed assets	9,420			
Accumulated depreciation		3,470		942
SLCA	1,830			
Opening stock	1,680			
PLCA		390		
Sales		14,420		
Purchases	8,180			1,500
Rent	1,100		100	
Electricity	940		400	
Rates	950			200
Depreciation expense			942	
Bad debts expense			55	
Drawings			1,500	
Accruals				555
Prepayments			200	
Closing stock BS			1,140	
Closing stock P&L				1,140
	26,110	26,110	4,337	4,337

We will now show how the final profit and loss account for Lyttleton would look.

Solution

Trading and profit and loss account of Lyttleton for the year ended 31 December 20X5

		£	£
Sales			14,420
Less:	Cost of sales		
	Opening stock	1,680	
	Purchases	6,680	
		8,360	
Less:	Closing stock	(1,140)	
			(7,220)
Gross profit			7,200
Less: Expenses			
	Rent	1,200	
	Electricity	1,340	
	Rates	750	
	Depreciation	942	
	Bad debts expense	55	
Total expenses			(4,287)
Net profit			2,913

2 The balance sheet for a sole trader

2.1 Introduction

> **Definition**
>
> A balance sheet is a list of the assets and liabilities of the sole trader at the end of the accounting period.

The assets are split into fixed assets and current assets.

> **Definition**
>
> Fixed assets are assets for long-term use within the business e.g. buildings.

> **Definition**
>
> Current assets are assets that are either currently cash or are expected to soon be converted into cash e.g. stock.

The liabilities are split into current liabilities and long term liabilities.

> **Definition**
>
> Current liabilities are the short term creditors of the business. This generally means creditors who are due to be paid within twelve months of the balance sheet date e.g. trade creditors.

> **Definition**
>
> Long-term liabilities are creditors who are expected to be paid after more than 12 months e.g. long term loans. These are deducted to give the net assets.

Preparation of final accounts for a sole trader: **Chapter 10**

A proforma for a typical sole trader's balance sheet is given below:

Balance sheet at 31 December 20X2

	Cost £	Depreciation £	£
Fixed assets			
Freehold factory	X	X	X
Machinery	X	X	X
Motor vehicles	X	X	X
	X	X	X
Current assets			
Stocks		X	
Trade debtors		X	
Prepayments		X	
Cash at bank		X	
Cash in hand		X	
		X	
Current liabilities			
Trade creditors	X		
Accruals	X		
		(X)	
Net current assets			X
Total assets less current liabilities			X
Long-term liabilities			
Bank loan			(X)
Net assets			X
Capital at 1 January			X
Net profit for the year			X
			X
Less: Drawings			(X)
Proprietor's funds			X

2.2 Assets and liabilities

The assets and liabilities in a formal balance sheet are listed in a particular order:

- firstly the fixed assets less the accumulated depreciation (remember that this net total is known as the net book value);
- next the current assets in the following order – stock, debtors, prepayments then bank and cash balances;
- next the current liabilities – creditors and accruals that are payable within 12 months;
- finally the long-term creditors such as loan accounts;

The assets are all added together and the liabilities are then deducted. This gives the balance sheet total.

2.3 Capital balances

The total of the assets less liabilities of the sole trader should be equal to the capital of the sole trader.

The capital is shown in the balance sheet as follows:

	£
Opening capital at the start of the year	X
Add: Net profit/(loss) for the year	X
	X
Less: Drawings	(X)
Closing capital	X

This closing capital should be equal to the total of all of the assets less liabilities of the sole trader shown in the top part of the balance sheet.

Preparation of final accounts for a sole trader: **Chapter 10**

Example

Below is the trial balance along with adjustments for Lyttleton again. This time the balance sheet will be prepared.

Account name	Trial balance DR £	Trial balance CR £	Adjustments DR £	Adjustments CR £
Capital		7,830		
Cash	2,010			
Fixed assets	9,420			
Accumulated depreciation		3,470		942
SLCA	1,830			
Opening Stock	1,680			
PLCA		390		
Sales		14,420		
Purchases	8,180			1,500
Rent	1,100		100	
Electricity	940		400	
Rates	950			200
Depreciation expense			942	
Bad debt expense			55	
Drawings			1,500	
Accruals				555
Prepayments			200	
Closing stock – Profit and loss				1,140
Closing stock – Balance sheet			1,140	
	26,110	26,110	4,337	4,337

We now need to consider which ledger accounts will form part of the balance sheet.

Solution

Balance sheet of Lyttleton at 31 December 20X5

	Cost	Accumulated Dep'n	
	£	£	£
Fixed assets	9,420	4,412	5,008
Current assets			
Stocks		1,140	
Trade debtors		1,830	
Prepayments		200	
Cash		2,010	
		5,180	
Less:			
Current liabilities			
Creditors	390		
Accruals	555		
		(945)	
Net current assets			4,235
Net assets			9,243
Capital 1 January			7,830
Net profit for the year			2,913
			10,743
Less: Drawings			(1,500)
Proprietor's funds			9,243

Notes:

- the fixed assets are shown at their net book value;
- the current assets are sub-totalled as are the current liabilities – the current liabilities are then deducted from the current assets to give net current assets;
- the net current assets are added to the fixed asset net book value to reach the balance sheet total, net assets.

Preparation of final accounts for a sole trader: Chapter 10

The balance sheet total of net assets should be equal to the closing capital; the balance sheet is then said to balance. If your balance sheet does not balance then make some quick obvious checks such as the adding up and that all figures have been included at the correct amount but do not spend too much time searching for your error as the time can be better used on the rest of the examination. If you have time left over at the end then you can check further for the difference.

Activity 2

Place the following account names under the correct headings and correct order as they would appear in the balance sheet.

Debtors
Bank overdraft
VAT payable to HMRC
Motor van
Land

Stock
Creditors
Computers
Cash

Fixed Assets	Current Assets	Current Liabilities

Activity 3

Given below is a trial balance along with some adjustments that are required.

Trial balance at 31 December 20X6

Account name	Trial balance DR £	Trial balance CR £	Adjustments DR £	Adjustments CR £
Fittings	7,300			
Accumulated depreciation 1.1.X6		2,500		400
Leasehold	30,000			
Accumulated depreciation 1.1.X6		6,000		1,000
Stock 1 January 20X6	15,000			
Sales ledger control account	10,000			500
Cash in hand	50			
Cash at bank	1,250			
Purchases ledger control account		18,000		
Capital		19,850		
Drawings	4,750		1,200	
Purchases	80,000			1,200
Sales		120,000		
Wages	12,000			200
Advertising	4,000		200	
Rates	1,800			360
Bank charges	200			
Depreciation – Fittings			400	
Depreciation – Lease			1,000	
Bad debts			500	
Prepayments			360	
Closing stock BS			21,000	
Closing stock P&L				21,000
	166,350	166,350	24,660	24,660

Prepare the profit and loss account for the business.

For items in italics, select the appropriate account heading.

Profit and loss account for the year ended 31 December 20X6

	£	£

Sales
Less: **Cost of sales**
   Opening stock/ Closing stock/ Purchases
   Purchases/ Opening stock/ Closing stock
                  _____

Less: *Opening stock/ Closing stock/ Purchases*
                  _____
                      _____

Gross profit

Less: **Expenses**
   Trade debtors/Wages
   Advertising/ Prepayments
   Drawings/ Rates
   Bank charges/ Capital
   Depreciation/ Accumulated depreciation   – F&F
                       – lease

   Bad debts
                  _____

Total expenses
                       _____

Net profit
                       _____

Prepare the balance sheet for the business.

For items in italics, select the appropriate account heading.

Balance sheet as at 31 December 20X6

	£	£	£

Fixed assets:
Fittings/ Closing stock
Trade debtors/ Leasehold

Current assets:
Closing stock/ Opening stock
Trade creditors/ Trade debtors

Accruals/ Prepayments
Cash at bank/ Drawings
Capital/ Cash in hand

Current liabilities:
Trade debtors/ Trade creditors

Owner's capital
Capital at 1.1.X6
Drawings/ Net profit for the year
Less: Capital/ Drawings

3 Preparing final accounts from the trial balance

3.1 Introduction

Now that we have reviewed the preparation of the profit and loss account and the balance sheet from the trial balance, we will now work through a comprehensive example which will include the extraction of the initial trial balance, correction of errors and clearing a suspense account, accounting for year-end adjustments and finally the preparation of the final accounts.

Example

Given below are the balances taken from a sole trader's ledger accounts on 31 March 20X4

	£
Sales ledger control account	30,700
Telephone	1,440
Purchases ledger control account	25,680
Heat and light	2,480
Motor vehicles at cost	53,900
Computer equipment at cost	4,500
Carriage inwards	1,840
Carriage outwards	3,280
Wages	67,440
Loan interest	300
Capital	48,450
Drawings	26,000
Bank overdraft	2,880
Purchases	126,800
Petty cash	50
Sales	256,400
Insurance	3,360
Accumulated depreciation – motor vehicles	15,000
Accumulated depreciation – computer equipment	2,640
Stock at 1 April 20X3	13,200
Loan	8,000
Rent	23,760

The following information is also available:

(i) The value of stock at 31 March 20X4 was £14,400.

(ii) Motor vehicles are to be depreciated at 30% on reducing balance basis and computer equipment at 20% on cost.

(iii) A telephone bill for £180 for the three months to 31 March 20X4 did not arrive until after the trial balance had been drawn up.

(iv) Of the insurance payments, £640 is for the year ending 31 March 20X5.

(v) A bad debt of £700 is to be written off.

Solution

Step 1

The first stage is to draw up the initial trial balance. Remember that assets and expenses are debit balances and liabilities and income are credit balances.

	£	£
Sales ledger control account	30,700	
Telephone	1,440	
Purchases ledger control account		25,680
Heat and light	2,480	
Motor vehicles at cost	53,900	
Computer equipment at cost	4,500	
Carriage inwards	1,840	
Carriage outwards	3,280	
Wages	67,440	
Loan interest	300	
Capital		48,450
Drawings	26,000	
Bank overdraft		2,880
Purchases	126,800	
Petty cash	50	
Sales		256,400
Insurance	3,360	
Accumulated depreciation – motor vehicles		15,000
Accumulated depreciation – computer equipment		2,640
Stock at 1 April 20X3	13,200	
Loan		8,000
Rent	23,760	
	359,050	359,050

Step 2

Now to deal with the year-end adjustments:

(i) The value of stock at 31 March 20X4 was £14,400.

Closing stock – profit and loss

£		£
	Closing stock balance sheet	14,400

Closing stock – balance sheet

	£		£
Closing stock profit and loss	14,400		

We now have the closing stock for the profit and loss account and in the balance sheet.

(ii) The motor vehicles and computer equipment have yet to be depreciated for the year. Motor vehicles are depreciated at 30% on reducing balance basis and computer equipment at 20% on cost.

Motor vehicles depreciation (53,900 – 15,000) × 30% = £11,670

Computer equipment depreciation 4,500 × 20% = £900

Depreciation expense account – motor vehicles

	£		£
Accumulated depreciation	11,670		

Accumulated depreciation account – motor vehicles

	£		£
		Balance b/d	15,000
Balance c/d	26,670	Depreciation expense	11,670
	26,670		26,670
		Balance b/d	26,670

Depreciation expense account – computer equipment

	£		£
Accumulated depreciation	900		

Accumulated depreciation account – computer equipment

	£		£
		Balance b/d	2,640
Balance c/d	3,540	Depreciation expense	900
	3,540		3,540
		Balance b/d	3,540

(iii) A telephone bill for £180 for the three months to 31 March 20X4 did not arrive until after the trial balance had been drawn up.

This needs to be accrued for:

Debit Telephone £180
Credit Accruals £180

Telephone account

	£		£
Balance b/d	1,440		
Accrual	180	Balance c/d	1,620
	1,620		1,620
Balance b/d	1,620		

Accruals

	£		£
		Telephone	180

(iv) Of the insurance payments £640 is for the year ending 31 March 20X5.

This must be adjusted for as a prepayment:

Debit Prepayment £640
Credit Insurance account £640

Prepayments

	£		£
Insurance	640		

Insurance account

	£		£
Balance b/d	3,360	Prepayment	640
		Balance c/d	2,720
	3,360		3,360
Balance b/d	2,720		

(v) A bad debt of £700 is to be written off.

Debit	Bad debts expense	£700
Credit	Sales ledger control account	£700

Bad debts expense account

	£		£
Sales ledger control account	700		

Sales ledger control account

	£		£
Balance b/d	30,700	Bad debts expense	700
		Balance c/d	30,000
	30,700		30,700
Balance b/d	30,000		

Step 3

Now that all of the adjustments have been put through the ledger accounts, an amended trial balance can be drawn up as a check and as a starting point for preparing the final accounts. The amended and additional ledger accounts are all shown below.

Closing stock – profit and loss

	£		£
Balance c/d	14,400	Closing stock balance sheet	14,400
	14,400		14,400
		Balance b/d	14,400

Closing stock – balance sheet

	£		£
Closing stock profit and loss	14,400	Balance c/d	14,400
	14,400		14,400
Balance b/d	14,400		

Accumulated depreciation account – motor vehicles

	£		£
Balance c/d	26,670	Balance b/d	15,000
		Depreciation expense	11,670
	26,670		26,670
		Balance b/d	26,670

Depreciation expense account – motor vehicles

	£		£
Accumulated depreciation	11,670		

Depreciation expense account – computer equipment

	£		£
Accumulated depreciation	900		

Accumulated depreciation account – computer equipment

	£		£
Balance c/d	3,540	Balance b/d	2,640
		Depreciation expense	900
	3,540		3,540
		Balance b/d	3,540

Telephone account

	£		£
Balance b/d	1,440		
Accrual	180	Balance c/d	1,620
	1,620		1,620
Balance b/d	1,620		

Accruals

	£		£
		Telephone	180

Prepayments

	£		£
Insurance	640		

Insurance account

	£		£
Balance b/d	3,360	Prepayment	640
		Balance c/d	2,720
	3,360		3,360
Balance b/d	2,720		

Sales ledger control account

	£		£
Balance b/d	30,700	Irrecoverable debts expense	700
		Balance c/d	30,000
	30,700		30,700
Balance b/d	30,000		

Bad debts expense account

	£		£
Sales ledger control	700		
		Balance c/d	700
	700		700
Balance b/d	700		

Trial balance at 31 March 20X4

	£	£
Sales ledger control account	30,000	
Telephone	1,620	
Purchases ledger control account		25,680
Heat and light	2,480	
Motor vehicles at cost	53,900	
Computer equipment at cost	4,500	
Carriage inwards	1,840	
Carriage outwards	3,280	
Wages	67,440	
Loan interest	300	
Capital		48,450
Drawings	26,000	
Bank overdraft		2,880
Purchases	126,800	
Petty cash	50	
Sales		256,400
Insurance	2,720	
Accumulated depreciation – motor vehicles		26,670
Accumulated depreciation – computer equipment		3,540
Stock at 1 April 20X3	13,200	
Loan		8,000
Rent	23,760	
Stock at 31 March 20X4	14,400	14,400
Depreciation expense – motor vehicles	11,670	
Depreciation expense – computer equipment	900	
Accruals		180
Prepayments	640	
Bad debts expense	700	
	386,200	386,200

Step 4

We are now in a position to prepare the final accounts for the sole trader. Take care with the carriage inwards and carriage outwards. They are both expenses of the business but carriage inwards is treated as part of cost of sales, whereas carriage outwards is one of the list of expenses.

Profit and loss account for the year ended 31 March 20X4

	£	£
Sales		256,400
Less: Cost of sales		
Opening stock	13,200	
Carriage inwards	1,840	
Purchases	126,800	
	141,840	
Less: Closing stock	(14,400)	
		127,440
Gross profit		128,960
Less: Expenses		
Telephone	1,620	
Heat and light	2,480	
Carriage outwards	3,280	
Wages	67,440	
Loan interest	300	
Insurance	2,720	
Rent	23,760	
Depreciation expense – motor vehicles	11,670	
Depreciation expense – computer equipment	900	
Bad debts	700	
Total expenses		114,870
Net profit		14,090

Balance sheet as at 31 March 20X4

	Cost £	Accumulated depreciation £	Net book value £
Fixed assets			
Motor vehicles	53,900	26,670	27,230
Computer equipment	4,500	3,540	960
	58,400	30,210	28,190
Current assets			
Stock		14,400	
Trade debtors		30,000	
Prepayment		640	
Petty cash		50	
		45,090	
Current liabilities			
Bank overdraft	2,880		
Trade Creditors	25,680		
Accruals	180		
		28,740	
Net current assets			16,350
Total assets less current liabilities			44,540
Long term liability:			
Loan			(8,000)
Net assets			36,540
Capital			
Opening capital			48,450
Net profit for the year			14,090
			62,540
Less: Drawings			26,000
Proprietor's funds			36,540

Activity 4

Given below is the list of ledger balances for a sole trader at 30 June 20X4 after all of the year-end adjustments have been put through.

	£
Sales	165,400
Sales ledger control account	41,350
Wages	10,950
Bank	1,200
Rent	8,200
Capital	35,830
Purchases ledger control account	15,100
Purchases	88,900
Electricity	1,940
Telephone	980
Drawings	40,000
Stock at 1 July 20X3	9,800
Motor vehicles at cost	14,800
Accumulated depreciation – motor vehicles	7,800
Fixtures at cost	3,200
Accumulated depreciation – fittings	1,800
Accruals	100
Prepayments	210
Stock at 30 June 20X4 – balance sheet	8,300
Stock at 30 June 20X4 – profit and loss	8,300
Depreciation expense – motor vehicles	3,700
Depreciation expense – fittings	800

You are required to:

(i) Draw up a trial balance to check that it balances (you should find that the trial balance does balance).

(ii) Prepare the final accounts for the sole trader for the year ending 30 June 20X4.

(i) **Trial balance as at 30 June 20X4**

	£	£
Sales		
Sales ledger control account		
Wages		
Bank		
Rent		
Capital		
Purchases ledger control account		
Purchases		
Electricity		
Telephone		
Drawings		
Stock at 1 July 20X3		
Motor vehicles at cost		
Accumulated depreciation – motor vehicles		
Fixtures at cost		
Accumulated depreciation – fittings		
Accruals		
Prepayments		
Stock at 30 June 20X4 – profit and loss		
Stock at 30 June 20X4 – balance sheet		
Depreciation expense – motor vehicles		
Depreciation expense – fittings		
	234,330	234,330

(ii) **Profit and loss account for the year ending 30 June 20X4**

	£	£
Sales		
Less: Cost of sales		
Less:		
Gross profit		

Preparation of final accounts for a sole trader: Chapter 10

Less: Expenses

Total expenses

Net profit

Balance sheet as at 30 June 20X4

	Cost £	Depreciation £	NBV £
Fixed assets			
	———	———	———
	———	———	———
Current assets			
			———
Current liabilities			
		———	
Net current assets			
Net assets			44,260
			———
Capital			
Net profit for the year			
			———
Drawings			
			———
Proprietor's funds			44,260
			———

Activity 5

Tick as appropriate.

1. Opening stock is recorded in the profit and loss account as

    An expense ☐

    Cost of sales ☐

2. Indicate where the drawings should be shown in the final accounts

    Profit and loss expenses ☐

    Balance sheet as a deduction to capital ☐

3. Payroll expenses are recorded as

    A liability in the balance sheet ☐

    An expense in the profit and loss account ☐

4. Does the bad adjustment appear in the profit and loss account or balance sheet?

    Profit and loss account ☐

    Balance sheet ☐

5. Sales returns are deducted from purchases

    True ☐

    False ☐

Activity 6

Trial balance at 31 December 20X2

	Dr £	Cr £
Capital on 1 January 20X2		106,149
Freehold factory at cost	360,000	
Motor vehicles at cost	126,000	
Stocks at 1 January 20X2	37,500	
Debtors	15,600	
Cash in hand	225	
Bank overdraft		82,386
Creditors		78,900
Sales		307,500
Purchases	158,700	
Wages and salaries	39,060	
Rent and rates	35,400	
Postage	400	
Discounts allowed	6,600	
Insurance	2,850	
Motor expenses	5,500	
Loan from bank		240,000
Sundry expenses	1,000	
Drawings	26,100	
	814,935	814,935

Prepare a profit and loss account and balance sheet.

4 Summary

The profit and loss account (income statement) for the period summarises the transactions in the period and leads to a net profit or loss for the period.

The balance sheet (statement of financial position) lists the assets and liabilities of the business on the last day of the accounting period in a particular order.

When preparing the final accounts from a trial balance, you will have to recognise whether the balances should appear in the profit and loss account or in the balance sheet and also consider adjustments required.

Answers to chapter activities

Activity 1

Profit and loss account extract for the year ended 31 December 20X2

Calculate the sales and cost of sales.

	£	£
Sales		292,500
Less: Cost of sales		
Opening stock	37,500	
Purchases	158,700	
	196,200	
Less: Closing stock	(15,000)	
		(181,200)
Gross profit		111,300

Activity 2

Fixed Assets	Current Assets	Current Liabilities
Land	Stock	Bank overdraft
Motor Van	Debtors	VAT payable to HMRC
Computers	Cash	Creditors

Activity 3

Profit and loss account for the year ended 31 December 20X6

	£	£
Sales		120,000
Less: Cost of sales		
Opening stock	15,000	
Purchases	78,800	
	93,800	
Less: Closing stock	(21,000)	
		(72,800)
Gross profit		47,200
Less: **Expenses**		
Wages	11,800	
Advertising	4,200	
Rates	1,440	
Bank charges	200	
Depreciation – F&F	400	
– lease	1,000	
Bad debts	500	
Total expenses		(19,540)
Net profit		27,660

Balance sheet as at 31 December 20X6

	£	£	£
Fixed assets			
Fittings	7,300	2,900	4,400
Leasehold	30,000	7,000	23,000
	37,300	9,900	27,400
Current assets			
Stock		21,000	
Trade debtors		9,500	
Prepayments		360	
Cash at bank		1,250	
Cash in hand		50	
		32,160	
Current liabilities			
Trade creditors		(18,000)	

Net current assets		14,160
Net assets		41,560
Owner's capital		
Capital at 1.1.X6		19,850
Net profit for the year		27,660
Less: Drawings		(5,950)
Proprietor's funds		41,560

Activity 4

(i) Trial balance as at 30 June 20X4

	£	£
Sales		165,400
Sales ledger control account	41,350	
Wages	10,950	
Bank	1,200	
Rent	8,200	
Capital		35,830
Purchases ledger control account		15,100
Purchases	88,900	
Electricity	1,940	
Telephone	980	
Drawings	40,000	
Stock at 1 July 20X3	9,800	
Motor vehicles at cost	14,800	
Accumulated depreciation – motor vehicles		7,800
Fixtures at cost	3,200	
Accumulated depreciation – fittings		1,800
Accruals		100
Prepayments	210	
Stock at 30 June 20X4 – profit and loss		8,300
Stock at 30 June 20X4 – balance sheet	8,300	
Depreciation expense – motor vehicles	3,700	
Depreciation expense – fittings	800	
	234,330	234,330

(ii) **Profit and loss account for the year ending 30 June 20X4**

	£	£
Sales		165,400
Less: Cost of sales		
Opening stock	9,800	
Purchases	88,900	
	98,700	
Less: Closing stock	(8,300)	
		(90,400)
Gross profit		75,000
Less: Expenses		
Wages	10,950	
Rent	8,200	
Electricity	1,940	
Telephone	980	
Depreciation – motor vehicles	3,700	
Depreciation – fittings	800	
Total expenses		26,570
Net profit		48,430

Balance sheet as at 30 June 20X4

	Cost £	Depreciation £	NBV £
Fixed assets			
Motor vehicles	14,800	7,800	7,000
Fittings	3,200	1,800	1,400
	18,000	9,600	8,400

Current assets	
Stock	8,300
Trade debtors	41,350
Prepayments	210
Bank	1,200
	51,060

Current liabilities
Trade creditors	15,100	
Accruals	100	(15,200)

Net current assets	35,860
Net assets	44,260
Capital	35,830
Net profit for the year	48,430
	84,260
Drawings	(40,000)
Proprietor's funds	44,260

Activity 5

1. Opening stock is recorded in the profit and loss account as
   Cost of sales

2. Indicate where the drawings should be shown in the final accounts
   Balance sheet

3. Payroll expenses are recorded as
   An expense in the profit and loss account

4. Does the bad adjustment appear in the profit and loss account or balance sheet?
   Profit and loss

5. Sales returns are deducted from purchases
   False

Preparation of final accounts for a sole trader: Chapter 10

Activity 6

Profit and loss account for the year ended 31 December 20X2

	£	£
Sales		307,500
Less: Cost of sales		
Opening stock	37,500	
Purchases	158,700	
	196,200	
Less: Closing stock	0	
		(196,200)
Gross profit		111,300
Less: Expenses		
Rent and rates	35,400	
Insurance	2,850	
Motor expenses	5,500	
Wages and salaries	39,060	
Postage	400	
Sundry expenses	1,000	
Discounts allowed	6,600	
		(90,810)
Net profit		20,490

Balance sheet as at 31 December 20X2

	£	£	£
Fixed assets:			
Freehold factory	360,000	0	360,000
Motor vehicles	126,000	0	126,000
	486,000	0	486,000
Current assets:			
Stock		0	
Debtors		15,600	
Cash in hand		225	
		15,825	

Current liabilities:		
Creditors	78,900	
Bank overdraft	82,386	
	161,286	
Net current assets/ (liabilities)		(145,461)
Total assets less current liabilities		340,539
Loan from bank		(240,000)
Net assets		**100,539**
Owner's capital		
Capital at 1.1.X2		106,149
Net profit for the year		20,490
Less: drawings		(26,100)
Proprietors funds		**100,539**

5 Test your knowledge

Workbook Activity 7

David Pedley

The following information is available for David Pedley's business for the year ended 31 December 20X8. He started his business on 1 January 20X8.

	£
Creditors	6,400
Debtors	5,060
Purchases	16,100
Sales	28,400
Motor van	1,700
Drawings	5,100
Insurance	174
General expenses	1,596
Rent and rates	2,130
Salaries	4,162
Stock at 31 December 20X8	2,050
Sales returns	200
Cash at bank	2,628
Cash in hand	50
Capital introduced	4,100

Required:

Prepare a profit and loss account for the year ended 31 December 20X8 and a balance sheet at that date.

Workbook Activity 8

Karen Finch

On 1 April 20X7 Karen Finch started a business with capital of £10,000 which she paid into a business bank account.

The following is a summary of the cash transactions for the first year.

	£
Amounts received from customers	17,314
Salary of assistant	2,000
Cash paid to suppliers for purchases	10,350
Purchase of motor van on 31 March 20X8	4,000
Drawings during the year	2,400
Amounts paid for electricity	560
Rent and rates for one year	1,100
Postage and stationery	350

At the end of the year, Karen was owed £4,256 by her customers and owed £5,672 to her suppliers. She has promised her assistant a bonus for the year of £400. At 31 March 20X8 this had not been paid.

At 31 March 20X8 there were stocks of £4,257 and the business owed £170 for electricity for the last quarter of the year. A year's depreciation is to be charged on the motor van at 25% on cost.

Required:

Prepare a profit and loss account for the year ended 31 March 20X8 and a balance sheet at that date.

Workbook Activity 9

The trial balance of Elmdale at 31 December 20X8 is as follows

	DR £	CR £
Capital		8,602
Stock	2,700	
Sales		21,417
Purchases	9,856	
Rates	1,490	
Drawings	4,206	
Electricity	379	
Freehold shop	7,605	
Debtors	2,742	
Creditors		3,617
Cash at bank		1,212
Cash in hand	66	
Sundry expenses	2,100	
Wages and salaries	3,704	
	34,848	34,848

In addition, Elmdale provides the following information:

(a) Closing stock has been valued for accounts purposes at £3,060.

(b) An electricity bill amounting to £132 in respect of the quarter to 28 February 20X9 was paid on 7 March 20X9.

(c) Rates include a payment of £1,260 made on 10 April 20X8 in respect of the year to 31 March 20X9.

Required:

(a) Show the adjustments to the ledger accounts for the end-of-period adjustments (a) to (c).

(b) Prepare a trading and profit and loss account for the year ended 31 December 20X8.

Suspense accounts and errors

Introduction

We have already seen the use of suspense accounts and the correction of errors in Level I but we will revise it again for Level II. When preparing a trial balance it may be necessary to open a suspense account to deal with any errors or omissions. The suspense account cannot be allowed to remain permanently in the trial balance, and must be cleared by correcting each of the errors that have caused the trial balance not to balance.

CONTENTS

1. The trial balance
2. Opening a suspense account
3. Clearing the suspense account
4. Redrafting the trial balance

1 The trial balance

1.1 Introduction

We saw in Bookkeeping Level I that one of the purposes of the trial balance is to provide a check on the accuracy of the double entry bookkeeping. If the trial balance does not balance then an error or a number of errors have occurred and this must be investigated and the errors corrected.

1.2 Errors detected by the trial balance

The following types of error will cause a difference in the trial balance and therefore will be detected by the trial balance and can be investigated and corrected:

A single entry – if only one side of a double entry has been made then this means that the trial balance will not balance e.g. if only the debit entry for receipts from debtors has been made then the debit total on the trial balance will exceed the credit balance.

A casting error – if a ledger account has not been balanced correctly due to a casting error then this will mean that the trial balance will not balance.

A transposition error – if an amount in a ledger account or a balance on a ledger account has been transposed and incorrectly recorded then the trial balance will not balance e.g. a debit entry was recorded correctly as £5,276 but the related credit entry was entered as £5,726.

An extraction error – if a ledger account balance is incorrectly recorded on the trial balance either by recording the wrong figure or putting the balance on the wrong side of the trial balance then the trial balance will not balance.

An omission error – if a ledger account balance is inadvertently omitted from the trial balance then the trial balance will not balance.

Two entries on one side – instead of a debit and credit entry if a transaction is entered as a debit in two accounts or as a credit in two accounts then the trial balance will not balance.

1.3 Errors not detected by the trial balance

A number of types of errors however will not cause the trial balance not to balance and therefore cannot be detected by preparing a trial balance:

An error of original entry – this is where the wrong figure is entered as both the debit and credit entry e.g. a payment of the electricity expense was correctly recorded as a debit in the electricity account and a credit to the bank account but it was recorded as £300 instead of £330.

A compensating error – this is where two separate errors are made, one on the debit side of the accounts and the other on the credit side, and by coincidence the two errors are of the same amount and therefore cancel each other out.

An error of omission – this is where an entire double entry is omitted from the ledger accounts. As both the debit and credit have been omitted the trial balance will still balance.

An error of commission – with this type of error a debit entry and an equal credit entry have been made but one of the entries has been to the wrong account e.g. if the electricity expense was debited to the rent account but the credit entry was correctly made in the bank account – here both the electricity account and rent account will be incorrect but the trial balance will still balance.

An error of principle – this is similar to an error of commission but the entry has been made in the wrong type of account e.g. if the electricity expense was debited to a fixed asset account – again both the electricity account and the fixed asset account would be incorrect but the trial balance would still balance.

It is important that a trial balance is prepared on a regular basis in order to check on the accuracy of the double entry. However not all errors in the accounting system can be found by preparing a trial balance.

1.4 Correction of errors

Errors will normally be corrected by putting through a journal entry for the correction.

The procedure for correcting errors is as follows:

Step 1

Determine the precise nature of the incorrect double entry that has been made.

Step 2

Determine the correct entries that should have been made.

Suspense accounts and errors: Chapter 11

Step 3

Produce a journal entry that cancels the incorrect part and puts through the correct entries.

> ### Example
>
> The rent expense of £1,000 has been correctly credited to the bank account but has been debited to the entertainment expense account.
>
> **Step 1**
>
> The incorrect entry has been to debit the entertainment expense with £1,000
>
> **Step 2**
>
> The correct entry is to debit the rent account with £1,000
>
> **Step 3**
>
> The journal entry required is:
>
> DR   Rent account   £1,000
> CR   Entertainment expense account   £1,000
>
> Note that this removes the incorrect debit from the entertainment expense account and puts the correct debit into the rent account.

> ### Activity 1
>
> Jacob returned some goods to a supplier because they were faulty. The original purchase price of these goods was £900.
>
> The ledger clerk has correctly treated the double entry but used the figure £9,000.
>
> What is the correcting entry which needs to be made?

2 Opening a suspense account

2.1 Introduction

A suspense account is used as a temporary account to deal with errors and omissions. It means that it is possible to continue with the production of financial accounts whilst the reasons for any errors are investigated and then corrected.

2.2 Reasons for opening a suspense account

A suspense account will be opened in two main circumstances:

(a) the bookkeeper does not know how to deal with one side of a transaction;

or

(b) the trial balance does not balance.

2.3 Unknown entry

In some circumstances the bookkeeper may come across a transaction for which he is not certain of the correct double entry and therefore rather than making an error, one side of the entry will be put into a suspense account until the correct entry can be determined.

Example

A new bookkeeper is dealing with a cheque received from the writing of an article for a popular magazine for £250. He correctly debits the bank account with the amount of the cheque but does not know what to do with the credit entry.

Solution

He will enter it in the suspense account:

Suspense account

	£		£
		Bank account – receipt of article fee	250

2.4 Trial balance does not balance

If the total of the debits on the trial balance does not equal the total of the credits then an error or a number of errors have been made. These must be investigated, identified and eventually corrected. In the meantime the difference between the debit total and the credit total is inserted as a suspense account balance in order to make the two totals agree.

Example

The totals of the trial balance are as follows:

	Debits £	Credits £
Totals as initially extracted	234,987	209,876
Suspense account, to make the TB balance		25,111
	234,987	234,987

Suspense

£		£
	Opening balance	25,111

Activity 2

The credit balances on a trial balance exceed the debit balances by £3,333. Open up a suspense account to record this difference.

3 Clearing the suspense account

3.1 Introduction

Whatever the reason for the suspense account being opened it is only ever a temporary account. The reasons for the difference must be identified and then correcting entries should be put through the ledger accounts, via the journal, in order to correct the accounts and clear the suspense account balance to zero.

3.2 Procedure for clearing the suspense account

Step 1

Determine the incorrect entry that has been made or the omission from the ledger accounts.

Step 2

Determine the journal entry required to correct the error or omission – this will not always mean that an entry is required in the suspense account e.g. when the rent expense was debited to the entertainment expense account the journal entry did not require any entry to be made in the suspense account.

Step 3

If there is an entry to be made in the suspense account put this into the suspense account – when all the corrections have been made the suspense account should normally have no remaining balance on it.

Example

A trial balance has been extracted and did not balance. The debit column totalled £191,000 and the credit column totalled £190,000.

You discover the cash sales £1,000 have been correctly entered into the cash account but no entry has been made in the sales account.

Draft a journal entry to correct this error, and complete the suspense ledger account.

Solution

As the debit entries and credit entries do not match, we will be required to open up a suspense account to hold this difference until we can correct it.

Suspense

Detail	Amount £	Detail	Amount £
Journal 1 (below)	1,000	TB	1,000
	1,000		1,000

A credit entry is required in the sales account and the debit is to the suspense account.

		£	£
Dr	Suspense account	1,000	
Cr	Sales account		1,000

Being correction of double entry for cash sales.

Remember that normally a journal entry needs a narrative to explain what it is for – however in some assessments you are told not to provide the narratives so always read the requirements carefully.

Activity 3

On extracting a trial balance, the accountant of ERJ discovered a suspense account with a debit balance of £1,075 included therein; she also found that the debits exceeded the credits by £957. She posted this difference to the suspense account and then investigated the situation. She discovered:

(1) A debit balance of £75 on the postage account had been incorrectly extracted on the list of balances as £750 debit.

(2) A payment of £500 to a credit supplier, X, had been correctly entered in the cash book but no entry had been made in the supplier's account.

(3) When a motor vehicle had been purchased during the year the bookkeeper did not know what to do with the debit entry so he made the entry Dr Suspense, Cr Bank £1,575.

(4) A credit balance of £81 in the sundry income account had been incorrectly extracted on the list of balances as a debit balance.

(5) A receipt of £5 from a credit customer, Y, had been correctly posted to his account but had been entered in the cash book as £625.

(6) The bookkeeper was not able to deal with the receipt of £500 from the owner's own bank account, and he made the entry Dr Bank and Cr Suspense.

(7) No entry has been made for a cheque of £120 received from a credit customer M.

(8) A receipt of £50 from a credit customer, N, had been entered into his account as £5 and into the cash book as £5.

Required:

(a) Show the journal entries necessary to correct the above errors.

(b) Show the entries in the suspense account to eliminate the differences entered in the suspense account.

ICB LEVEL II: MANUAL BOOKKEEPING

4. Redrafting the trial balance

Once the suspense account has been cleared, it is important to redraft the trial balance to ensure that the debit column and credit column agree.

Example

On 30 July an initial trial balance was extracted which did not balance, and a suspense account was opened. On 1 July journal entries were prepared to correct the errors that had been found, and clear the suspense account. The list of balances and the journal entries are shown below.

Redraft the trial balance by placing the figures in the debit or credit column, after taking into account the journal entries which will clear suspense.

	Balances as at 30 June	Balances as at 1 July Debit £	Balances as at 1 July Credit £
Motor vehicles	19,000		
Stock	3,456		
Bank overdraft	190		
Petty cash	90		
Sales ledger control	5,678		
Purchases ledger control	3,421		
VAT owing to HMRC	1,321		
Capital	12,500		
Sales	52,678		
Purchases	23,982		
Purchase returns	1,251		
Wages	9,999		
Motor expenses	123		
Drawings	710		
Suspense (debit balance)	8,323		

Suspense accounts and errors: Chapter 11

Journals

Account	Debit £	Credit £
Sales ledger control	5,323	
Suspense		5,323
Being to correct allocation of credit sale as a debtor balance		

Account	Debit £	Credit £
Purchases	3,000	
Suspense		3,000
Being to correct allocation of purchase balance.		

Solution

	Balances as at 30 November	Balances as at 1 December Debit £	Balances as at 1 December Credit £
Motor vehicles	19,000	19,000	
Stock	3,456	3,456	
Bank overdraft	190		190
Petty cash	90	90	
Sales ledger control	5,678	**11,001**	
Purchases ledger control	3,421		3,421
VAT owing to HMRC	1,321		1,321
Capital	12,500		12,500
Sales	52,678		52,678
Purchases	23,982	**26,982**	
Purchase returns	1,251		1,251
Wages	9,999	9,999	
Motor expenses	123	123	
Drawings	710	710	
Suspense (debit balance)			
		71,361	71,361

The sales ledger control and the purchases figures have been amended for the journals and the trial balance columns agree without the need for a suspense account.

5 Summary

Preparation of the trial balance is an important element of control over the double entry system but it will not detect all errors. The trial balance will still balance if a number of types of error are made. If the trial balance does not balance then a suspense account will be opened temporarily to make the debits equal the credits in the trial balance. The errors or omissions that have caused the difference on the trial balance must be discovered and then corrected using journal entries. Not all errors will require an entry to the suspense account. However, any that do should be put through the suspense account in order to try to eliminate the balance on the account.

Suspense accounts and errors: Chapter 11

Answers to chapter activities

Activity 1

Step 1

The purchases ledger control account has been debited and the purchases returns account credited but with £9,000 rather than £900.

Step 2

Both of the entries need to be reduced by the difference between the amount used and the correct amount (9,000 – 900) = £8,100

Step 3

Journal entry:	£	£
Dr Purchases returns account	8,100	
Cr Purchases ledger control account		8,100

Being correction of misposting of purchases returns.

Activity 2

As the credit balances exceed the debit balances the balance needed is a debit balance to make the two totals equal.

Suspense account

	£		£
Opening balance	3,333		

Activity 3

		Dr £	Cr £
1	Debit Suspense account	675	
	Credit Postage		675
	being correction of extraction error of postage account		
2	Debit Creditors	500	
	Credit Suspense account		500
	being correction of omitted entry in creditors account		
3	Debit Motor Vehicles Cost	1,575	
	Credit Suspense account		1,575
	being correct recording of Motor Vehicle acquisition		
4	Debit Suspense account	162	
	Credit Sundry income		162
	Being correction of incorrect treatment of sundry income		
5	Debit Suspense account	620	
	Credit Cash		620
	Being correction of incorrect posting		
6	Debit Suspense account	500	
	Credit Capital		500
	Being correction treatment of capital		
7	Debit Bank	120	
	Credit Debtors		120
	Being correct treatment of debtor receipt		
8	Debit Cash	45	
	Credit Debtors		45
	Being incorrect amount posted for a debtor receipt		

Suspense account

	£		£
Balance b/f	1,075	Trial balance difference	957
Postage (1)	675	Creditor X (2)	500
Sundry income (4)	162	Motor Vehicle Cost (3)	1,575
Cash (5)	620		
Capital (6)	500		
	3,032		3,032

Suspense accounts and errors: Chapter 11

6 Test your knowledge

Workbook Activity 4

Which of the errors below are, or are not, disclosed by the trial balance? (Ignore VAT in all cases)

(a) Recording a discount allowed correctly in the general ledger but not recording it in the subsidiary ledger.

(b) Recording a cash sale as a debit to the receivables account and a credit to the sales account..

(c) Omitting a credit sale to a debtor completely from both the general and subsidiary ledgers.

(d) Recording purchase invoices on the debit side of the purchase ledger control account and the credit side of the purchases account for the correct amount.

(e) Recording a receipt from a receivable in the sales ledger control account only.

(f) Recording a payment of £300 to a credit supplier as: Dr PLCA £300, Cr Bank £30.

Workbook Activity 5

Mr Plum's trial balance was extracted and did not balance. The debit column of the trial balance totalled £109,798 and the credit column totalled £219,666.

What entry would be made in the suspense account to balance the trial balance?

ICB LEVEL II: MANUAL BOOKKEEPING

Workbook Activity 6

On 30 June Rick's Racers extracted an initial trial balance which did not balance, and a suspense account was opened. On 1 July journal entries were prepared to correct the errors that had been found, and clear the suspense account. The list of balances in the initial trial balance, and the journal entries to correct the errors, are shown below.

Redraft the trial balance by placing the figures in the debit or credit column. You should take into account the journal entries which will clear the suspense account.

	Balances extracted on 30 June £	Balances at 1 July Debit £	Balances at 1 July Credit £
Motor vehicles	24,200		
Plant and Equipment	22,350		
Stock	9,000		
Cash at Bank	11,217		
Cash	150		
Sales ledger control	131,275		
Purchases ledger control	75,336		
VAT owing to HMRC	15,127		
Capital	14,417		
Bank Loan	12,500		
Sales	276,132		
Purchases	152,476		
Wages	35,465		
Motor expenses	3,617		
Repairs and Renewals	2,103		
Rent and rates	3,283		
Light and Heat	4,012		
Insurance	4,874		
Sundry Expenses	1,230		
Suspense account (credit balance)	11,740		
Totals			

Journal entries

Account name	Debit £	Credit £
Capital		9,500
Suspense	9,500	
Capital		2,330
Suspense	2,330	

Account name	Debit £	Credit £
Suspense	1,230	
Sundry Expenses		1,230
Sundry Expenses	1,320	
Suspense		1,320

Workbook Activities Answers

1 Double entry bookkeeping

Workbook Activity 5

Assets		
	Fixed assets (5,000 + 6,000)	11,000
	Cash (15,000 – 6,000)	9,000
	Stock (4,000 – 1,500)	2,500
	Debtors	2,000
		24,500

Assets – Liabilities = Capital
£24,500 – £4,000 = £20,500

Capital (ownership interest) has increased by the profit made on the sale of stock.

Workbook Activity 6

The balance on the capital account represents the investment made in the business by the owner. It is a special liability of the business, showing the amount payable to the owner at the balance sheet date.

Workbook Activity 7

Tony

Cash

	£		£
Capital (a)	20,000	Purchases (b)	1,000
Sales (g)	1,500	Purchases (c)	3,000
Sales (i)	4,000	Insurance (d)	200
		Storage units (e)	700
		Advertising (f)	150
		Telephone (h)	120
		Stationery (j)	80
		Drawings (k)	500
		Balance c/d	19,750
	25,500		25,500
Balance b/d	19,750		

Capital

	£		£
Balance c/d	20,000	Cash (a)	20,000
	20,000		20,000
		Balance b/d	20,000

Purchases

	£		£
Cash ((b)	1,000	Balance c/d	4,000
Cash (c)	3,000		
	4,000		4,000
Balance b/d	4,000		

Insurance

	£		£
Cash (d)	200	Balance c/d	200
	200		200
Balance b/d	200		

Storage units – cost

	£		£
Cash (e)	700	Balance c/d	700
	700		700
Balance b/d	700		

Advertising

	£		£
Cash (f)	150	Balance c/d	150
	150		150
Balance b/d	150		

Telephone

	£		£
Cash (h)	120	Balance c/d	120
	120		120
Balance b/d	120		

Sales

	£		£
Balance c/d	5,500	Cash (g)	1,500
		Cash (i)	4,000
	5,500		5,500
		Balance b/d	5,500

Stationery

	£		£
Cash (j)	80	Balance c/d	80
	80		80
Balance b/d	80		

Drawings

	£		£
Cash (k)	500	Balance c/d	500
	500		500
Balance b/d	500		

Workbook Activity 8

Dave

Cash

	£		£
Capital	500	Rent	20
Sales	210	Electricity	50
		Car	100
		Drawings	30
		Balance c/d	510
	710		710
Balance b/d	510		

Capital

	£		£
Balance c/d	500	Cash	500
	500		500
		Balance b/d	500

Purchases

	£		£
Creditors (A Ltd)	200	Balance c/d	200
	200		200
Balance b/d	200		

Creditors (A Ltd)

	£		£
Balance c/d	200	Purchases	200
	200		200
		Balance b/d	200

Sales

	£		£
Balance c/d	385	Debtors (X Ltd)	175
		Cash	210
	385		385
		Balance b/d	385

Debtors (X Ltd)

	£		£
Sales	175	Balance c/d	175
	175		175
Balance b/d	175		

Electricity

	£		£
Cash	50	Balance c/d	50
	50		50
Balance b/d	50		

Rent

	£		£
Cash	20	Balance c/d	20
	20		20
Balance b/d	20		

Motor car

	£		£
Cash	100	Balance c/d	100
	100		100
Balance b/d	100		

Drawings

	£		£
Cash	30	Balance c/d	30
	30		30
Balance b/d	30		

Workbook Activity 9

Audrey Line

Bank

	£		£
Capital	6,000	Rent	500
Sales	3,700	Shop fittings	600
		Creditors	1,200
		Wages	600
		Electricity	250
		Telephone	110
		Drawings	1,600
		Balance c/d	4,840
	9,700		9,700
Balance b/d	4,840		

Capital

	£		£
		Cash	6,000

Sales

	£		£
		Cash	3,700

Shop fittings

	£		£
Cash	600		

Rent

	£		£
Cash	500		

Telephone

	£		£
Cash	110		

Drawings

	£		£
Cash	1,600		

Purchases

	£		£
Creditors	2,000		

Creditors

	£		£
Cash	1,200	Purchases	2,000
Balance c/d	800		
	2,000		2,000
		Balance b/d	800

Wages

	£		£
Cash	600		

Electricity

	£		£
Cash	250		

2 Accounting for sales – summary

Workbook Activity 8

(a) Cash receipts book

Narrative	SL Code	Discount £	Cash £	Bank £	VAT £	Cash sales £	SLCA £
G Heilbron	SL04			108.45			108.45
L Tessa	SL15	3.31		110.57			110.57
J Dent	SL17	6.32		210.98			210.98
F Trainer	SL21			97.60			97.60
A Winter	SL09	3.16		105.60			105.60
Cash sales			240.00		40.00	200.00	
		12.79	240.00	633.20	40.00	200.00	633.20

Workbook Activities Answers

(b) **General ledger accounts**

VAT account

£		£
	28/4 CRB	40.00

Sales ledger control account

£		£
	28/4 CRB	633.20
	CRB – discount	12.79

Sales account

£		£
	28/4 CRB	200.00

Discount allowed account

	£		£
28/4 CRB	12.79		

(Note that the total of the 'Discount' column is not included in the cross-cast total of £873.20. The discounts allowed are entered into the cash receipts book on a memorandum basis; the total at the end of each period is posted to the sales ledger control account and to an expense account.)

(c) **Subsidiary ledger**

H Heilbron   SL04

£		£
	28/4 CRB	108.45

L Tessa   SL15

£		£
	28/4 CRB	110.57
	CRB – discount	3.31

J Dent   SL17

£		£
	28/4 CRB	210.98
	CRB – discount	6.32

F Trainer			SL21
£			£
	28/4	CRB	97.60

A Winter			SL09
£			£
	28/4	CRB	105.60
		CRB – discount	3.16

Workbook Activity 9

Cash receipts book

Narrative	Discount £	Cash £	Bank £	VAT £	Cash Sales £	SLCA £
Irlam Transport		468.00		78.00	390.00	
Paulson Haulage		216.00		36.00	180.00	
Mault Motors		348.00		58.00	290.00	
James John Ltd	24.39		579.08			579.08
Exilm & Co	19.80		456.74			456.74
	44.19	1,032.00	1,035.82	172.00	860.00	1,035.82

Workbook Activities Answers

Workbook Activity 10

	True/False
Documents can be disposed of as soon as the year end accounts are prepared. *Explanation – Businesses must keep copies of business and financial documents as they can be inspected by HMRC and used as evidence in legal action.*	FALSE
Documents cannot be inspected by anyone outside the business. *Explanation – Documents can be inspected by HMRC in a tax or VAT inspection.*	FALSE
Documents can be used as legal evidence in any legal actions.	TRUE
Businesses must keep an aged debtor analysis as part of their financial documents. *Explanation – Many businesses do keep an aged debtors analysis but it is not necessary to do so.*	FALSE
Businesses do not need to keep copies of invoices *Explanation – Businesses do need to keep copies of invoices as they can be inspected by HMRC.*	FALSE
Businesses need to keep copies of their bank statements available for inspection.	TRUE

3 Accounting for purchases – summary

Workbook Activity 6

CASH PAYMENTS BOOK

Date	Details	Code	Discount £	Cash £	Bank £	VAT £	PLCA £	Cash purchases £	Other £
12/3/X1	Homer Ltd	PL12	5.06		168.70		168.70		
	Forker & Co	PL07	5.38		179.45		179.45		
	Purchases			342.00		57.00		285.00	
	Print Ass.	PL08			190.45		190.45		
	ABG Ltd	PL02	6.62		220.67		220.67		
	Purchases			200.40		33.40		167.00	
	G Greg	PL19			67.89		67.89		
			17.06	542.40	827.16	90.40	827.16	452.00	–

General ledger

Purchases ledger control account

			£			£
12/3	CPB		827.16	5/3	Balance b/d	4,136.24
12/3	CPB discount		17.06			

VAT account

		£			£
12/3	CPB	90.40	5/3	Balance b/d	1,372.56

Purchases account

		£		£
5/3	Balance b/d	20465.88		
12/3	CPB	452.00		

Discounts received account

		£			£
			5/3	Balance b/d	784.56
			12/3	CPB	17.06

Workbook Activities Answers

Purchases ledger

ABG Ltd — PL02

		£			£
12/3	CPB 03652	220.67	5/3	Balance b/d	486.90
12/3	CPB discount	6.62			

Forker & Co — PL07

		£			£
12/3	CPB 03649	179.45	5/3	Balance b/d	503.78
12/3	CPB discount	5.38			

Print Associates — PL08

		£			£
12/3	CPB 03651	190.45	5/3	Balance b/d	229.56

Homer Ltd — PL12

		£			£
12/3	CPB 03648	168.70	5/3	Balance b/d	734.90
12/3	CPB discount	5.06			

G Greg — PL19

		£			£
12/3	CPB 03654	67.89	5/3	Balance b/d	67.89

ICB LEVEL II: MANUAL BOOKKEEPING

Workbook Activity 7

Cash payments book

Narrative	Discount £	Cash £	Bank £	VAT £	Cash Purchases £	PLCA £	Expenses £
JD & Co		96.00		16.00	80.00		
LJ Ltd		240.00		40.00	200.00		
MK Plc		60.00		10.00	50.00		
TB Ltd	2.52		68.89			68.89	
CF Ltd	3.16		156.72			156.72	
Electricity			90.00				90.00
Stationery			84.00	14.00			70.00
	5.68	396.00	399.61	80.00	330.00	225.61	160.00

4 Ledger balances and control accounts

Workbook Activity 9

Account name	Amount £	Dr ✓	Cr ✓
Cash	2,350	✓	
Capital	20,360		✓
Motor Vehicles	6,500	✓	
Electricity	800	✓	
Office expenses	560	✓	
Loan from bank	15,000		✓
Cash at bank	6,400	✓	
Factory equipment	14,230	✓	
Rent	2,500	✓	
Insurance	1,000	✓	
Miscellaneous expenses	1,020	✓	

KAPLAN PUBLISHING

Workbook Activity 10

(a)

Purchases ledger control account

	£		£
Cash paid	47,028	Balance b/d	5,926
Purchases returns	202	Purchases (total from PDB)	47,713
Discounts received	867		
Sales ledger control account (contra)	75		
Balance c/d (bal fig)	5,467		
	53,639		53,639

(b)

Sales ledger control account

	£		£
Balance b/d	10,268	Bank account	69,872
Sales (total from SDB)	71,504	Bad debts account	96
		Sales returns account (total from SRDB)	358
		Discounts allowed (total from discount column in CB)	1,435
		Purchases ledger control account (contra)	75
		Balance c/d (bal fig)	9,936
	81,772		81,772

Workbook Activity 11

(a) **Sales ledger control account**

		£			£
30 Sep	Balance b/f	3,825	30 Sep	Bad debts account (2)	400
				Purchases ledger control account (4)	70
				Discount allowed (5)	140
				Balance c/d	3,215
		3,825			3,825
1 Oct	Balance b/d	3,215			

(b) **List of sales ledger balances**

	£
Original total	3,362
Add: Debit balances previously omitted (1)	103
	3,465
Less: Item posted twice to Sparrow's account (3)	(250)
Amended total agreeing with balance on sales ledger control account	3,215

Workbook Activities Answers

Workbook Activity 12

(a)

Account name	Amount £	Dr	Cr
Purchase ledger control account	1,000.00	✓	
Purchases	1,000.00		✓

(b)

Account name	Amount £	Dr	Cr
Purchase ledger control account	9.00	✓	
Discounts received	9.00		✓

(c)

Account name	Amount £	Dr	Cr
Purchase ledger control account	300.00	✓	
Sales ledger control account	300.00		✓

Workbook Activity 13

(a)

Details	Amount £	Dr	Cr
Balance of debtors at 1 July	60,580	✓	
Goods sold on credit	18,950	✓	
Payments received from credit customers	20,630		✓
Discounts allowed	850		✓
Bad debt written off	2,400		✓
Goods returned from credit customers	3,640		✓

(b)

	Amount £
Sales ledger control account balance as at 31 July	52,010
Total of sales ledger accounts as at 31 July	54,410
Difference	2,400

(c)

Goods returned may have been omitted from the sales ledger	
Bad debt written off may have been omitted from the sales ledger	✓
Goods returned may have been entered twice in the sales ledger	
Bad debt written off may have been entered twice in the sales ledger	

360   KAPLAN PUBLISHING

Workbook Activity 14

(a)

Details	Amount £	Dr ✓	Cr ✓
Balance of creditors at 1 July	58,420		✓
Goods bought on credit	17,650		✓
Payments made to credit suppliers	19,520	✓	
Discounts received	852	✓	
Contra entry with sales ledger control	600	✓	
Goods returned to credit suppliers	570	✓	

(b)

	Amount £
Purchases ledger control account balance as at 31 July	54,528
Total of purchase ledger accounts as at 31 July	52,999
Difference	1,529

(c)

	✓
Payments made to suppliers may have been understated in the purchase ledger	
Goods returned to suppliers may have been overstated in the purchase ledger	✓
Goods bought on credit may have been overstated in the purchase ledger	
Contra entry may have been omitted from the purchase ledger	

5 Accounting for VAT

Workbook Activity 7

VAT control account

	£		£
Bank	8,455	Opening balance	8,455
Input VAT 143,600 × 20%	28,720	Output VAT :	39,350
Balance carried down	10,630	236,100 × 20/120	
	47,805		47,805
		Balance brought down	10,630

The closing balance on the account represents the amount of VAT owing to HM Revenue and Customs.

Workbook Activity 8

1. True – it is only compulsory to issue VAT invoices to registered traders.
2. False – the £250 is VAT inclusive.
3. True – VAT invoices form the evidence for the reclaim of input tax.
4. True

Workbook Activity 9

VAT must be charged on the price payable after discount.

£176.40 (£1,000 – 10% of £1,000 = £900 – 2% of £900) × 20%

£380.00 (£2,000 – 5% of £2,000) × 20%

£138.00 (£750 – 8% of £750) × 20%

ICB LEVEL II: MANUAL BOOKKEEPING

Workbook Activity 10

A 1
B 2
C 3
D 1
E 3

Workbook Activity 11

A and C are false. A proforma invoice is NOT a valid tax invoice, nor is it evidence that allows the customer to reclaim input tax.

Workbook Activity 12

1 20 August. The invoice is raised within 14 days of the delivery date (the basic tax point) and hence a later tax point is created.

2 10 June. The issue of the proforma invoice is ignored so the receipt of payment is the tax point.

3 4 March. The invoice is raised more than 14 days after the delivery date so the tax point stays on the delivery date.

4 10 December. The goods are invoiced before delivery so this creates an earlier tax point.

Workbook Activities Answers

Workbook Activity 13

1. The correct answer is A.

   Receipt of cash on 19 October creates a tax point

2. The correct answer is B.

   £100 is VAT inclusive so the VAT element is £16.66 (£100 × 1/6)

3. The correct answer is C.

   The goods are invoiced within 14 days of delivery so a later tax point is created.

4. The correct answer is B.

   £350 is VAT inclusive so the VAT element is £58.33 (£350 × 1/6)

Workbook Activity 14

		£
VAT due in this period on **sales** and other outputs	Box 1	4,324.00
VAT due in this period on **acquisitions** from other EC Member States	Box 2	0.00
Total VAT due (**the sum of boxes 1 and 2**)	Box 3	4,324.00
VAT reclaimed in the period on **purchases** and other inputs, including acquisitions from the EC	Box 4	1,835.12
Net VAT to be paid to HM Revenue & Customs or reclaimed by you (**Difference between boxes 3 and 4**)	Box 5	2,488.88
Total value of **sales** and all other outputs excluding any VAT. **Include your box 8 figure**	Box 6	21,500
Total value of purchases and all other inputs excluding any VAT. **Include your box 9 figure**	Box 7	9,176

ICB LEVEL II: MANUAL BOOKKEEPING

Total value of all **supplies** of goods and related costs, excluding any VAT, to other **EC Member States**	Box 8	0
Total value of all **acquisitions** of goods and related costs, excluding any VAT, from other **EC Member States**	Box 9	0

Workings for VAT return

		£
Box 1:	From SDB	4,300.00
	Error on previous return	24.00
		4,324.00

		£
Box 4:	From PDB	1,820.00
	Petty cash	15.12
		1,835.12

		£
Box 7:	From PDB	9,100
	Petty cash (£75.60 rounded up)	76
		9,176

Workbook Activity 15

		£
VAT due in this period on **sales** and other outputs	Box 1	7,680.00
VAT due in this period on **acquisitions** from other EC Member States	Box 2	0.00
Total VAT due (**the sum of boxes 1 and 2**)	Box 3	7,680.00
VAT reclaimed in the period on **purchases** and other inputs, including acquisitions from the EC	Box 4	3,428.00

Workbook Activities Answers

Net VAT to be paid to HM Revenue & Customs or reclaimed by you (**Difference between boxes 3 and 4**)	Box 5	4,252.00
Total value of **sales** and all other outputs excluding any VAT. **Include your box 8 figure**	Box 6	38,400
Total value of purchases and all other inputs excluding any VAT. **Include your box 9 figure**	Box 7	16,740
Total value of all **supplies** of goods and related costs, excluding any VAT, to other **EC Member States**	Box 8	0
Total value of all **acquisitions** of goods and related costs, excluding any VAT, from other **EC Member States**	Box 9	0

Workings for VAT return

		£
Box 4:	From PDB	3,294.00
	Petty cash (W1)	54.00
	Bad debts (W2)	80.00
		3,428.00

		£
Box 7:	From PDB	16,470
	Petty cash (£324 – £54) (W1)	270
		16,740

(W1) Total petty cash expenditure = (£108 + £96 + £120) = £324

VAT on £324 = (20/120 × £324) = £54.00

(W2) Bad debts more than six months old = (£300 + £180) = £480

VAT on £480 = (20/120 × £480) = £80

6 Petty cash

Workbook Activity 5

The entries in the general ledger will be:

Account name	Amount £	Dr ✓	Cr ✓
Postage	26.25	✓	
Staff Welfare	31.40	✓	
Stationery	19.40	✓	
Travel Expenses	33.01	✓	
VAT	9.12	✓	

Workbook Activity 6

Postage

	£		£
Balance b/f	231.67		
PCB	20.01		

Staff welfare

	£		£
Balance b/f	334.78		
PCB	4.68		

Tea and coffee

	£		£
Balance b/f	53.36		
PCB	12.03		

Travel expenses

	£		£
Balance b/f	579.03		
PCB	20.17		

VAT account

	£		£
PCB	4.94	Balance b/f	967.44

7 Bank reconciliations

Workbook Activity 3

Cash receipts book

Date 20X1	Narrative	Bank £	VAT £	Debtors £	Other £	Discount £
7/3	Balance b/f	860.40✓				
7/3	Paying in slip 0062	1,117.85✓	84.05	583.52	450.28	23.60
8/3	Paying in slip 0063	1,056.40✓	68.84	643.34	344.22	30.01
9/3	Paying in slip 0064	1,297.81✓	81.37	809.59	406.85	34.20
10/3	Paying in slip 0065	994.92	57.02	652.76	285.14	18.03
11/3	Paying in slip 0066	1,135.34	59.24	779.88	296.22	23.12
	BGC – L Fernley	406.90✓		406.90		
	Bank interest	6.83✓			6.83	
		6,876.45	350.52	3,875.99	1,789.54	128.96

Cash payments book

Date 20X1	Details	Cheque no	Code	Bank £	VAT £	Creditors £	Cash purchases £	Other £	Discounts received £
7/3	P Barn	012379	PL06	383.21✓		383.21			
	Purchases	012380	GL	274.04✓	45.67		228.37		
	R Trevor	012381	PL12	496.80✓		496.80			6.30
8/3	F Nunn	012382	PL07	218.32		218.32			
	F Taylor	012383	PL09	467.28✓		467.28			9.34
	C Cook	012384	PL10	301.40✓		301.40			
9/3	L White	012385	PL17	222.61		222.61			
	Purchases	012386	GL	275.13✓	45.85		229.28		
	T Finn	012387	PL02	148.60✓		148.60			
10/3	S Penn	012388	PL16	489.23		489.23			7.41
11/3	P Price	012389	PL20	299.99		299.99			
	Purchases	012390	GL	270.12	45.02		225.10		
	Loan finance	SO	GL	200.00✓				200.00	
				4,046.73	136.54	3,027.44	682.75	200.00	23.05

368   KAPLAN PUBLISHING

FINANCIAL BANK plc

CONFIDENTIAL

YOU CAN BANK ON US

10 Yorkshire Street
Headingley
Leeds LS1 1QT
Telephone: 0113 633061

Account CURRENT
Account name T R FABER LTD

Sheet no. 00614

Statement date 11 March 20X1   Account Number 27943316

Date	Details	Withdrawals (£)	Deposits (£)	Balance (£)
7/3	Balance from sheet 00613			860.40 ✓
	Bank giro credit L Fernley		406.90 ✓	1,267.30
9/3	Cheque 012380	274.04 ✓		
	Cheque 012381	496.80 ✓		
	Credit 0062		1,117.85 ✓	1,614.31
10/3	Cheque 012383	467.28 ✓		
	Cheque 012384	301.40 ✓		
	Credit 0063		1,056.40 ✓	
	SO – Loan Finance	200.00 ✓		1,702.03
11/3	Cheque 012379	383.21 ✓		
	Cheque 012386	275.13 ✓		
	Cheque 012387	148.60 ✓		
	Credit 0064		1,297.81 ✓	
	Bank interest		6.83 ✓	2,199.73

DD	Standing order	DD	Direct debit	CP	Card purchase
AC	Automated cash	OD	Overdrawn	TR	Transfer

Workbook Activities Answers

BANK RECONCILIATION STATEMENT AS AT 11 MARCH 20X1

	£
Balance per bank statement	2,199.73
Add: Outstanding lodgements:	
Paying in slip 0065	994.92
Paying in slip 0066	1,135.34
Less: Unpresented cheques:	
Cheque 012382	(218.32)
Cheque 012385	(222.61)
Cheque 012388	(489.23)
Cheque 012389	(299.99)
Cheque 012390	(270.12)
Balance per cash book (Total of bank receipts – total of bank payments)	£2,829.72

Workbook Activity 4

Cash book

		£			£
16/4	Donald & Co	225.47✓	16/4	Balance b/d	310.45✓
17/4	Harper Ltd	305.68✓	17/4	Cheque 03621	204.56
	Fisler Partners	104.67✓	18/4	Cheque 03622	150.46✓
18/4	Denver Ltd	279.57✓	19/4	Cheque 03623	100.80
19/4	Gerald Bros	310.45		Cheque 03624	158.67✓
20/4	Johnson & Co	97.68	20/4	Cheque 03625	224.67
			20/4	Balance c/d	173.91
		1,323.52			1,323.52

There are three unticked items on the bank statement:

- direct debit £183.60 to the District Council;
- cheque number 03621 £240.56 – this has been entered into the cash book as £204.56;
- bank interest £3.64.

Cheques 03623 and 03625 are unticked items in the cash book but these are payments that have not yet cleared through the banking system.

EXPRESS BANK

CONFIDENTIAL

High Street
Fenbury
TL4 6JY
Telephone: 0169 422130

Account   CURRENT   Sheet no. 0213

Account name   P L DERBY LTD

Statement date 20 April 20X1   Account Number 40429107

Date	Details	Withdrawals (£)	Deposits (£)	Balance (£)
16/4	Balance from sheet 0212			310.45 OD
17/4	DD – District Council	183.60		494.05 OD
18/4	Credit		225.47 ✓	
19/4	Credit		104.67 ✓	
	Cheque 03621	240.56		
	Bank interest	3.64		408.11 OD
20/4	Credit		305.68 ✓	
	Credit		279.57 ✓	
	Cheque 03622	150.46 ✓		
	Cheque 03624	158.67 ✓		131.99 OD

DD	Standing order	DD	Direct debit	CP Card purchase
AC	Automated cash	OD	Overdrawn	TR Transfer

Workbook Activity 5

Graham

(a)

Cash account

	£		£
Balance b/f	204	Sundry accounts	
Interest on deposit account	18	Standing orders	35
		Bank charges	14
		Balance c/d	173
	222		222
Balance b/d	173		

(b)

BANK RECONCILIATION STATEMENT AT 31 MARCH 20X3

	£
Balance per bank statement	2,618
Add Uncleared lodgements	723
	3,341
Less Unpresented cheques	(3,168)
Balance per cash account	173

Workbook Activity 6

BANK RECONCILIATION STATEMENT AS AT 30 JUNE 20X1

	£	£
Balance per bank statement		(1,160.25) O/D
Outstanding lodgements: 30 June		6,910.25
		5,750.00
Unpresented cheques: 121	538.00	
122	212.00	
		(750.00)
Balance per cash book (7,100.45 + 17,111.55 – 19,212.00)		£5,000.00

8 Accruals and prepayments

Workbook Activity 8

Rent payable

	£		£
Cash paid	15,000	P&L account	12,000
		Balance c/d (prepayment)	3,000
	15,000		15,000
Balance b/d (prepayment)	3,000		

Gas

	£		£
Gas paid	840	P&L account	1,440
Balance c/d (840 × 5/7) (accrual)	600		
	1,440		1,440
		Balance b/d (accrual)	600

Advertising

	£		£
Cash	3,850	P&L account	3,350
		Balance c/d (prepayment)	500
	3,850		3,850
Balance b/d (prepayment)	500		

Bank interest

	£		£
Cash	28	P&L account	96
Cash	45		
Balance c/d ($1/3 \times 69$) (accrual)	23		
	96		96
		Balance b/d (accrual)	23

Workbook Activities Answers

Rates

	£		£
Balance b/d (prepayment $^3/_6$ × 4,800)	2,400	P&L account	11,300
Cash	5,600		
Balance c/d ($^3/_6$ × 6,600) (accrual)	3,300		
	11,300		11,300
		Balance b/d (accrual)	3,300

Rent receivable

	£		£
Balance b/d (250 × 3/6) (debtor = accrued income)	125	Cash	250
P&L account (W)	575	Cash	600
Balance c/d (3/12 × 600) (deferred income)	150		
	850		850
		Balance b/d (creditor = deferred income)	150

Working: Profit and loss account credit for rent receivable

	£
1 January 20X4 – 31 March 20X4 ($^3/_6$ × 250)	125
1 April 20X4 – 31 December 20X4 ($^9/_{12}$ × 600)	450
	575

Workbook Activity 9

A Crew

Stationery

	£		£
31 Dec Balance per trial balance	560	31 Dec P&L account	545
		31 Dec Balance c/d (prepayment)	15
	560		560
1 Jan Balance b/d (prepayment)	15		

Rent

	£		£
31 Dec Balance per trial balance	900	31 Dec P&L account	1,200
31 Dec Balance c/d (accrual)	300		
	1,200		1,200
		1 Jan Balance b/d (accrual)	300

Rates

	£		£
31 Dec Balance per trial balance	380	31 Dec P&L account	310
		31 Dec Balance c/d (prepayment (280 × 3/12)	70
	380		380
1 Jan Balance b/d (prepayment)	70		

Lighting and heating

	£		£
31 Dec Balance per trial balance	590	31 Dec P&L account	605
31 Dec Balance c/d (accrual)	15		
	605		605
		1 Jan Balance b/d (accrual)	15

Insurance

	£		£
31 Dec Balance per trial balance	260	31 Dec P&L account	190
		31 Dec Balance c/d (prepayment)	70
	260		260
1 Jan Balance b/d (prepayment)	70		

Wages and salaries

	£		£
31 Dec Balance per trial balance	2,970	31 Dec P&L account	2,970

Workbook Activities Answers

Workbook Activity 10

A Metro

Motor tax and insurance

	£		£
Balance b/d (prepayment)	570	P&L account (W2)	2,205
Cash		Balance c/d (W1) (prepayment)	835
1 April	420		
1 May	1,770		
1 July	280		
	3,040		3,040
Balance b/d (prepayment)	835		

Workings:

1 Prepayment at the end of the year

	£
Motor tax on six vans paid 1 April 20X0 ($\frac{3}{12} \times 420$)	105
Insurance on ten vans paid 1 May 20X0 ($\frac{4}{12} \times 1,770$)	590
Motor tax on four vans paid 1 July 20X0 ($\frac{6}{12} \times 280$)	140
Total prepayment	835

2 Profit and loss charge for the year

There is no need to calculate this as it is the balancing figure, but it could be calculated as follows.

	£
Prepayment b/d	570
Motor tax ($\frac{9}{12} \times 420$)	315
Insurance ($\frac{8}{12} \times 1,770$)	1,180
Motor tax ($\frac{6}{12} \times 280$)	140
Profit and loss charge	2,205

9 Depreciation

Workbook Activity 8

Motor car cost

	£		£
20X3		20X3	
1 Jan Purchase ledger control	12,000	31 Dec Balance c/d	12,000
20X4		20X4	
1 Jan Balance b/d	12,000	31 Dec Balance c/d	12,000
20X5		20X5	
1 Jan Balance b/d	12,000	31 Dec Balance c/d	12,000
20X6			
1 Jan Balance b/d	12,000		

Annual depreciation charge = $\dfrac{12,000 - 2,400}{4}$

= £2,400

Motor car – accumulated depreciation account

	£		£
20X3		20X3	
31 Dec Balance c/d	2,400	31 Dec Depreciation expense	2,400
20X4		20X4	
31 Dec Balance c/d	4,800	1 Jan Balance b/d	2,400
		31 Jan Depreciation expense	2,400
	4,800		4,800
20X5		20X5	
31 Dec Balance c/d	7,200	1 Jan Balance b/d	4,800
		31 Dec Depreciation expense	2,400
	7,200		7,200
		20X6	
		1 Jan Balance b/d	7,200

Depreciation expense account

	£		£
20X3		20X3	
31 Dec Motor car accumulated depreciation	2,400	31 Dec P&L a/c	2,400
20X4		20X4	
31 Dec Motor car accumulated depreciation	2,400	31 Dec P&L a/c	2,400
20X5		20X5	
31 Dec Motor car accumulated depreciation	2,400	31 Dec P&L a/c	2,400

Workbook Activity 9

(1) Straight line method

$$\text{Annual depreciation} = \frac{\text{Cost} - \text{Scrap value}}{\text{Estimated life}}$$

$$= \frac{£6,000 - £1,000}{8 \text{ years}}$$

$$= £625 \text{ p.a.}$$

Machine account

	£		£
Year 1:			
Cost	6,000		

Accumulated depreciation

	£		£
Year 1:		Year 1:	
Balance c/d	625	Depreciation expense	625
Year 2:		Year 2:	
Balance c/d	1,250	Balance b/d	625
		Depreciation expense	625
	1,250		1,250

Year 3:	Year 3:	
Balance c/d 1,875	Balance b/d	1,250
	Depreciation expense	625
─────		─────
1,875		1,875
─────		─────
	Year 4:	
	Balance b/d	1,875

Balance sheet extract:

		Cost	Accumulated depreciation	Net book value
		£	£	£
Fixed asset:				
Year 1	Machine	6,000	625	5,375
Year 2	Machine	6,000	1,250	4,750
Year 3	Machine	6,000	1,875	4,125

(2) Reducing balance method

		£
Cost		6,000
Year 1	Depreciation 20% × £6,000	1,200
		─────
		4,800
Year 2	Depreciation 20% × £4,800	960
		─────
		3,840
Year 3	Depreciation 20% × £3,840	768
		─────
Net book value		3,072
		─────

Workbook Activities Answers

Workbook Activity 10

Hillton

(a)

Workings:	Chopper £	Mincer £	Stuffer £	Total £
Cost	4,000	6,000	8,000	18,000
Depreciation 20X6 – 25%	(1,000)			(1,000)
Depreciation 20X7 – 25%	(1,000)	(1,500)		(2,500)
Depreciation 20X8 – 25%	(1,000)	(1,500)	(2,000)	(4,500)
Net book value at 31 Dec 20X8	1,000	3,000	6,000	10,000

Machinery

	£		£
20X6		**20X6**	
Cash – chopper	4,000	Balance c/d	4,000
20X7		**20X7**	
Balance b/d	4,000		
Cash – mincer	6,000	Balance c/d	10,000
	10,000		10,000
20X8		**20X8**	
Balance b/d	10,000		
Cash – stuffer	8,000	Balance c/d	18,000
	18,000		18,000
20X9			
Balance b/d	18,000		

Accumulated depreciation (machinery)

	£		£
20X6		**20X6**	
Balance c/d	1,000	Depreciation expense (25% × £4,000)	1,000
20X7		**20X7**	
Balance c/d	3,500	Balance b/d	1,000
		Depreciation expense (25% × £10,000)	2,500
	3,500		3,500

20X8 Balance c/d	8,000	20X8 Balance b/d	3,500
		Depreciation expense (25% × £18,000)	4,500
	8,000		8,000
		20X9 Balance b/d	8,000

Depreciation expense (machinery)

	£		£
20X6 Accumulated depreciation	1,000	20X6 Profit and loss account	1,000
20X7 Accumulated depreciation	2,500	20X7 Profit and loss account	2,500
20X8 Accumulated depreciation	4,500	20X8 Profit and loss account	4,500

(b)

Workings:

	Metro £	Transit £	Astra £	Total £
Cost	3,200	6,000	4,200	13,400
Depreciation 20X6 – 40%	(1,280)			(1,280)
NBV 31.12.X6	1,920			
Depreciation 20X7 – 40%	(768)	(2,400)		(3,168)
NBV 31.12.X7	1,152	3,600		
Depreciation 20X8 – 40%	(461)	(1,440)	(1,680)	(3,581)
Net book value at 31 Dec 20X8	691	2,160	2,520	5,371

Workbook Activities Answers

Motor vehicles

	£		£
20X6		20X6	
Cash – Metro	3,200	Balance c/d	3,200
20X7		20X7	
Balance b/d	3,200		
Cash – Transit	6,000	Balance c/d	9,200
	9,200		9,200
20X8		20X8	
Balance b/d	9,200		
Cash – Astra	4,200	Balance c/d	13,400
	13,400		13,400
20X9			
Balance b/d	13,400		

Accumulated depreciation (machinery)

	£		£
20X6		20X6	
Balance c/d	1,280	Depreciation charge	1,280
	1,280		1,280
20X7		20X7	
		Balance b/d	1,280
Balance c/d	4,448	Depreciation charge	3,168
	4,448		4,448
20X8		20X8	
		Balance b/d	4,448
Balance c/d	8,029	Depreciation charge	3,581
	8,029		8,029
		Balance b/d	8,029

Depreciation expense (motor vehicles)

	£		£
20X6 Accumulated depreciation	1,280	20X6 Profit and loss account	1,280
20X7 Accumulated depreciation	3,168	20X7 Profit and loss account	3,168
20X8 Accumulated depreciation	3,581	20X8 Profit and loss account	3,581

Workbook Activity 11

	£
Depreciation for vehicle sold 1 March 20X3 (18,000 × 20% × 3/12)	900
Depreciation for vehicle purchased 1 June 20X3 (10,000 × 20% × 6/12)	1,000
Depreciation for vehicle purchased 1 September 20X3 (12,000 × 20% × 3/12)	600
Depreciation for other vehicles owned during the year ((28,400 – 18,000) × 20%)	2,080
Total depreciation for the year ended 30 November 20X3	4,580

10 Preparation of final accounts for a sole trader

Workbook Activity 7

David Pedley

Profit and loss account for the year ended 31 December 20X8

	£	£
Sales		28,400
Less: Returns		(200)
		28,200
Opening stock		–
Purchases	16,100	
Less: Closing stock	(2,050)	
Cost of sales		(14,050)
Gross profit		14,150
Salaries	4,162	
Rent and rates	2,130	
Insurance	174	
General expenses	1,596	
Total expenses		(8,062)
Net profit		6,088

Balance sheet as at 31 December 20X8

	£	£
Fixed assets		
Motor van		1,700
Current assets		
Closing stock	2,050	
Trade Debtors	5,060	
Cash at bank	2,628	
Cash in hand	50	
	9,788	

Current Liabilities		
Trade creditors	(6,400)	
Net current assets		3,388
Net assets		5,088
Capital account		
Capital introduced		4,100
Profit for the year (per trading and profit and loss account)		6,088
Less: Drawings		(5,100)
Proprietors funds		5,088

Workbook Activity 8

Karen Finch

Profit and loss account for the year ended 31 March 20X8

	£	£
Sales (£17,314 + £4,256)		21,570
Purchases (£10,350 + £5,672)	16,022	
Closing stock	(4,257)	
		(11,765)
Gross profit		9,805
Assistant's salary plus bonus (£2,000 + £400)	2,400	
Electricity (£560 + £170)	730	
Rent and rates	1,100	
Postage and stationery	350	
Depreciation	1,000	
Total expenses		(5,580)
Net profit		4,225

Workbook Activities Answers

Balance sheet at 31 March 20X8

	£	£
Fixed assets		
Motor van at cost		4,000
Accumulated Depreciation		(1,000)
Net book value		3,000
Current assets		
Stocks	4,257	
Trade debtors	4,256	
Cash (W1)	6,554	
	15,067	
Current liabilities		
Trade creditors	5,672	
Accruals (400 + 170)	570	
	6,242	
Net current assets		8,825
Net assets		11,825
Capital		
Capital introduced at 1 April 20X7		10,000
Profit for the year		4,225
Less Drawings		2,400
Proprietors funds		11,825

Working:

1 **Cash balance at 31 March 20X8**

	£	£
Capital introduced at 1 April 20X7		10,000
Amounts received from customers		17,314
		27,314
Salary of assistant	2,000	
Cash paid to suppliers	10,350	
Purchase of motor van	4,000	
Drawings	2,400	
Electricity	560	
Rent and rates	1,100	
Postage and stationery	350	
		20,760
Cash balance at 31 March 20X8		6,554

Workbook Activity 9

(a) **Ledger accounts**

Closing stock (profit and loss)

	£		£
Balance to profit and loss account	3,060	Closing stock balance sheet	3,060

Closing stock (balance sheet)

	£		£
Closing stock profit and loss account	3,060	Balance c/d	3,060
	3,060		3,060
Balance b/d	3,060		

Rates

	£		£
Per trial balance	1,490	Profit and loss	1,175
		Balance c/d (1,260 × 3/12)	315
	1,490		1,490
Balance b/d	315		

Electricity

	£		£
Per trial balance	379	Profit and loss	423
Balance c/d (132/3)	44		
	423		423
		Balance b/d	44

Points to note:

- As regards electricity the accrual of £44 is shown on the balance sheet as a current liability, the effect of it being to increase the charge to profit and loss for electricity.

- With rates the prepayment of £315 is shown on the balance sheet as a current asset (being included between debtors and cash), the effect of it being to reduce the charge to profit and loss for rates.

- In the case of trading and profit and loss account items; income should be debited out of the relevant income account and credited to the trading and profit and loss account; expense should be credit out of the relevant expense account and debited to the trading and profit and loss account.

- Balance sheet items are carried down at the end of the year and included on the balance sheet and are consequently brought down in the ledger accounts as the opening balances at the beginning of the next period.

(b)

Elmdale
Trading and profit and loss account for the year ended 31 December 20X8

	£	£
Sales		21,417
Opening stock	2,700	
Purchases	9,856	
	12,556	
Closing stock	(3,060)	
Cost of sales		9,496
Gross profit		11,921
Rates	1,175	
Electricity	423	
Wages and salaries	3,704	
Sundry expenses	2,100	
Total expenses		7,402
Net profit		4,519

11 Suspense accounts and errors

Workbook Activity 4

(a) Error NOT disclosed by the trial balance
(b) Error NOT disclosed by the trial balance
(c) Error NOT disclosed by the trial balance
(d) Error NOT disclosed by the trial balance
(e) Error disclosed by the trial balance
(f) Error disclosed by the trial balance

Workbook Activity 5

Debit   Suspense   £109,868

Workbook Activity 6

	Balances at 1 July	
	Debit £	Credit £
Motor vehicles	24,200	
Plant and Equipment	22,350	
Inventory	9,000	
Cash at Bank	11,217	
Cash	150	
Sales ledger control	131,275	
Purchases ledger control		75,336
VAT owing to HMRC		15,127
Capital		26,247
Bank Loan		12,500
Sales		276,132
Purchases	152,476	
Wages	35,465	
Motor expenses	3,617	
Repairs and Renewals	2,103	
Rent and rates	3,283	
Light and Heat	4,012	
Insurance	4,874	
Sundry Expenses	1,320	
Suspense account (credit balance)		
Total	405,342	405,342

INDEX

A

Accrual(s), 245–249, 254, 256, 258, 266, 293, 296, 298, 299, 302, 307, 309, 311, 313–315, 321, 322

Accumulated depreciation, 273, 280, 293, 301–306, 309, 311, 313–315, 321

Allowance for doubtful debts increase, 294

Assets, 293, 295–299, 302, 305, 313, 315, 318, 320, 322

Authorisation stamp, 66

B

BACS, 218

Bad debt(s), 109, 116
    expense, 110
    relief, 170

Balance sheet, 300

Balancing a ledger account, 11

Bank, 4–10, 12, 15, 17, 18, 20, 21, 26–31
    reconciliation, 213, 217
        step by step procedure, 218
    statement, 218

Batch control, 97, 128

Book(s) of prime entry, 39, 43, 47, 81, 200

C

Cash, 1–7, 11, 13, 19, 109, 122
    book, 48, 65, 82, 85, 107, 213, 214, 218
    payments book, 88, 214
    receipts book, 49–51, 214
    sales, 51
    (settlement) discounts, 65, 84

Contra entry, 109, 110, 122

Credit, 1–3, 5–8, 10, 11, 13, 14, 18–22, 31
    note, 43, 44, 47, 74, 79, 81

Creditors, 97, 121

Current assets, 295, 296, 299, 302, 313, 315, 320, 322, 324

D

Debit, 19, 20, 21

Debtors, 97, 107

Deposits, 153

Depreciation, 265–277, 279–285, 292–294, 296, 298, 301, 302, 306, 309, 311, 312, 314, 315, 320–322

Direct debits, 218

Discount(s), 107
    allowed, 109
    received, 121, 122

Document retention, 56

Double entry, 1, 2, 4, 14, 15, 18–20, 22
    bookkeeping, 108

Drawings, 16, 293, 296–299, 301–305, 311, 313–315, 321, 322

Dual effect, 2

E

Errors, 118, 329, 339
    casting, 330
    compensating, 331
    correction of, 331, 332
    extraction, 330
    of commission, 331
    of omission, 331
    of principle, 331
    omission, 330

Estimated residual value, 268

Index

Exempt
  activities, 150
  supplies, 151

Expenses, 291, 292, 294, 302, 305, 312, 315, 317, 320, 322–324

F

Fixed assets, 295, 324

G

General ledger, 113

Gross profit, 290–292, 294, 302, 312, 315, 319, 322, 324

H

HM Revenue and Customs, 146, 149, 150, 172, 173

I

Imprest system – petty cash, 189

Income
  accruals, 243, 244, 254, 255, 257
  prepayments, 243, 254, 259
  statement, 291, 318

Invoice, 47

J

Journal, 100, 116, 256, 257, 260

L

Ledger(s), 2, 4, 8, 11, 13–15, 18, 19
  account(s), 1, 97
  general, 113
  main, 51, 121
    balancing of, 98
    opening balances, 99, 116

Liabilities, 295–297, 299, 303, 305, 313, 315, 318, 320, 322, 325

M

Main ledger, 51, 121

N

Net
  book value, 267, 271, 275, 282
  profit, 292, 294, 296, 297, 299, 302, 303, 312, 313, 315, 320, 322, 324

Non-imprest system – petty cash, 190

O

Omissions, 329

P

Petty cash, 187, 188, 207
  book, 191, 200, 207
  box, 188, 207
    reconciliation of, 203
  control account, 200
  voucher(s), 188, 189, 192, 203

Prepayment(s), 245, 247, 249–254, 257, 259, 293, 296, 298, 299, 301, 302, 307, 310, 314, 315, 320–322

Profit and loss, 290
  account, 289–291, 293, 301, 306, 317, 318, 323

Purchase(s), 6–10, 12, 15, 17, 18, 20, 23, 24, 26, 29, 30, 65, 77, 122
  credit, 121
  day book, 65, 66, 77, 82, 102, 121
  invoice(s), 66, 67, 121
  ledger, 65, 81, 121–123
    control account, 88, 97, 121, 122
    control account reconciliation, 122
  returns, 16, 17, 74
    day book, 75, 79, 102, 121, 122

R

Reducing balance, 270–272, 276, 282

Returned cheques, 228

Rounding, 158

S

Sales, 7, 9, 10, 12, 15, 16, 18, 20, 23–25, 27–30, 35, 39, 52, 109, 290, 291, 293, 294, 298, 301, 302, 304, 305, 308, 310–312, 314, 315, 319, 321, 322

cost of, 290–292, 294, 302, 312, 315, 317, 319, 322, 323
credit, 107
cycle, 57
day book, 35, 36, 39, 102, 107, 109
ledger, 35, 47, 107, 113, 116
    control account, 52, 97, 107, 109, 110, 113, 116
    control account reconciliation, 116, 118
returns, 16, 109
    day book, 35, 43–45, 107

Separate entity, 2

Settlement discount, 155

Single entry, 330

Sole trader, 289, 295–297, 312, 314

Standard rated, 147

Standing orders, 218

Stock, 292, 298, 301, 304, 305, 311, 313–315, 320–322

Straight line, 268, 272, 273

Subsidiary
ledger, 117
(purchases) ledger, 81
(sales) ledger, 47

Suspense account, 329, 333, 339
   clearing of, 334

T

Tax point, 152
   14-day rule, 153
   actual, 153
   basic, 152

Taxable
persons, 146
supplies, 147

Trade discount, 155

Trading, 294

Transposition error, 118, 330

Trial balance, 14, 18, 29, 30, 318, 329–331, 334, 339
errors detected by, 330
errors not detected by, 331
redrafting of, 337, 342

U

Useful economic life, 268

V

VAT, 39, 43, 51, 52, 65, 77, 82, 110, 146, 147, 149–151, 173, 174
account, 162
control account, 97, 129
exclusive, 148
inclusive, 148
input, 147
inspection, 57
invoices
    less detailed, 158
    modified, 159
output, 147
rates of, 147
registration and non-registration for, 146
return, paper, 161

Z

Zero-rated, 149
supplies, 151